WITHDRAWN

D1207435

The Literary Dream in French Romanticism

Laurence M. Porter
MICHIGAN STATE UNIVERSITY

The Literary Dream in French Romanticism

A Psychoanalytic Interpretation

WAYNE STATE UNIVERSITY PRESS
Detroit 1979

Copyright © 1979 by Wayne State University Press, Detroit, Michigan 48202. All rights are reserved. No part of this book may be reproduced without formal permission.

Library of Congress Cataloging in Publication Data

Porter, Laurence M   1936–
   The literary dream in French romanticism.

   Bibliography: p.
   Includes index.
   1. French literature—19th century—History and criticism.
2. Romanticism—France.   3. Dreams in literature.   4. Psychoanalysis and literature.
I. Title
PQ287.P64   843′.083   79–14035
ISBN 0–8143–1627–1

80--01576

For René Jasinski

CONTENTS

PART IV. The Aggrandizement of Self: Fantasies of Power

ACKNOWLEDGMENTS

Many people have helped this book take shape over the past eleven years. I am grateful to the professional staff of the Michigan State University Library, particularly to Ruth Adams, Walter Berlinski, Henry Koch, Doris Parks, and Henry Yaple, for tracking down reference materials and for providing a quiet place to work. The Michigan State University College of Arts and Letters has provided ongoing support for this research. Jean-Albert Bédé and Walter G. Langlois offered warm encouragement in the early stages. Grace Rutherford typed and styled the final manuscript. Richard Berchan, Frank Paul Bowman, Robert C. Carroll, Ross Chambers, Michael Koppisch, Colin Martindale, J. H. Matthews, and Morton D. Paley made helpful suggestions concerning individual chapters. For permission to reprint, in revised form, the discussion of literary versus real dreams in Chapter 1 and the description of the conventions of romantic dream literature at the end of Chapter 2, I am indebted to the *Journal of Altered States of Consciousness*; to *Nineteenth-Century French Studies* for Chapter 3; to *Symposium* for Chapter 6; and to *Studies in Romanticism* for the second portion of Chapter 9. Mrs. Jean Owen, of the Wayne State University Press, offered many constructive suggestions which improved nearly every page.

Among my friends and colleagues, I should especially like to thank Benjamin F. Bart, Cynthia Bart, Joseph Donohoe, Eugene F. Gray, Herbert Josephs, Marlies Kronegger, Bernard J. Paris, and Elizabeth Hart Porter for many years of support. My greatest debt of all, however, is to René Jasinski. It is an honor to have studied with such a scholar and such a man.

A Note on Translations

Statements by foreign psychologists and critics, and quotations from the non-fictional writing of the authors treated, have been provided in English translation only. The French texts of the fictional works analyzed are given, together with a translation, in the main body of the text whenever the original contains expressive nuances difficult to suggest in a translation. All translations are mine. I have respected the deliberately stilted quality of Ducasse's prose. I have also preserved the distinction between the elevated tone of philosophical musings and the more colloquial tone of dialogue and narration which characterizes all four of our authors.

INTRODUCTION

Before romanticism, many French writers like Montaigne, La Rochefoucauld, Marivaux, and Diderot had proven themselves keenly aware of the existence and activity of involuntary, unconscious mental forces. Indeed, the author of the earliest French literary monument, *La Chanson de Roland*, may well have been thinking of the psychopathology of everyday life when he had Roland ask, at the central *laisse* of the poem, whether his best friend Oliver had hit him with a sword on purpose.[1] But for a long time the portrayal of involuntary mental forces and their effects was limited to isolated incidents or to popular fantasy literature.

Then, during the course of the eighteenth century, Empiricism, Hume, and Kant cast doubt on whether man's five senses and his faculty of reason could guarantee an accurate perception either of the external world or of the self. In serious literature of the latter half of the eighteenth century, authors' intuitive understanding of the unconscious became the central subject of certain works. Diderot's *Rêve de D'Alembert* and *Le Neveu de Rameau*, and Cazotte's *Le Diable amoureux*, employed the dreamer, the madman, and the devil as major characters, thus challenging the Cartesian dichotomy of conscious self and unconscious world which had put all mental states other than waking rationality beyond the pale of humanness. But incidents in the plot remained linked by a logical continuity of temporal sequence and of cause and effect, or at least by a comprehensible pattern of free association. The latter, notably in Diderot and in his master, Sterne, shifted the metonymic chain of cause and effect from externality to the protagonist's mind, suggesting the relativity of knowledge deriving from its subjective source in our perceptions. Yet the persistence of the metonymic chain revealed the confident assumption that our psychological mechanisms can be traced and rationally explained, however irrational are their outward effects.

Finally, the revolutionary turmoil at the end of the eighteenth century called into question Europe's social, political, and religious institutions, together with the confident rationality which had created or justified them. Society seemed unable to improve itself; reason seemed unable to explain the world. Writers began to seek the basis for a new order in the supernatural realm, and they tried to apprehend this order with the non-rational faculties. The physical settings of late eighteenth-century literature provided a convenient way to hint at the existence of a subterranean mental life. The English Graveyard School of poetry and the descriptive "poetry of ruins" suggested the ghostly persistence of a vanished past amid present experience. Archeological investigation, rapidly expanding during the neoclassical revival of 1770 to 1820, had the same effect when described in literature.[2] Active volcanoes in Cazotte's *Le Diable amoureux* or Chateaubriand's *René* symbolized the repressed instinctual life. The secret compartments, basements, and passageways in the mansions, castles, and convents of the Gothic novel created a topographic image of a mind much of whose essential content is concealed. All these motifs occurred in French romanticism frequently from Chateaubriand and Lamartine onward, together with numerous other elements serving to represent a displacement of the normal conditions of perception: journeys, theaters, changes of lighting, metamorphosis, animism, and the intervention of supernatural beings.

Nodier, Nerval, Flaubert, and Lautréamont exploited all these devices in their fantasy literature—as did Balzac, Dumas, Gautier, and Mérimée—but they went further. In their literary dreams, the concept of a personal and of a collective unconscious began to affect narrative structure. Nodier's *Smarra*, *Trilby*, and *La Feé aux Miettes*, published from 1821 to 1832, were the first works of French prose fiction convincingly to simulate the apparent discontinuity of dream structure, and to anticipate the theories of Freud and Jung. Nodier's immediate precursors, most noteworthy of whom was Cazotte in *Le Diable amoureux*, treated the *états seconds*—mental states other than that of rational waking consciousness—with far less subtlety and penetration. Before Nodier, literary characters yielded passively to ecstasies which had no lasting effects upon their character and insight,[3] or they identified reality as the source of the perceptions of rational waking consciousness, and illusion or evil as the source of the perceptions in *états seconds*. But Nodier's most original *contes fantastiques* neither sink into nor condemn the unconscious. Like present-day Jungian critics, Nodier considers the unconscious as morally neutral, having potential for either good or ill; he attempts to reconcile it with the waking self. Narrative discontinuity, inspired by the model of the oriental tales popular in the eighteenth century, results from abrupt changes of subject, time, place, or identity, as the protagonist struggles to repress threatening thoughts from the unconscious (the three ceremonies of exorcism in *Trilby* represent the most primitive way of depicting such repression: they create discontinuity by banishing the disturbing influence—the fairy Trilby—from the scene). More subtly in later dream narratives, such shifts combined with the layering of narration (ABCBA) reflect our authors' intuitive understanding of the "layer cake" model of the psyche in which earlier mental states coexist with later ones. The adult psyche overlays the infantile psyche, which although lost to conscious awareness, remains dynamically active throughout life. The inner narrative layers correspond to archaic mental states of infantile regression, helpless dependency, or megalomania.

The greatest romantic dream literature treats mimetically the unconscious forces affecting human behavior, transforming fictional discourse through abrupt changes of subject, the layering of narration, the splitting and doubling of characters, and the archetype of Inversion (a peripety accompanied by a sudden reversal of values). These devices create dissociative effects similar to the influence on rational consciousness of the ego defense mechanisms of denial, regression, repression, psychic projection, and rationalization.

After Nodier, and thanks in large measure to his direct influence on Balzac, Dumas, Hugo, and Nerval, the dream narrative became one of the more common vehicles of French romantic prose fiction. It combined the romantic fascination with the irrational with the introspective stance of the confessional novel inherited from Rousseau, and with the prophetic voice of mystical lay philosophers like Bonnet, Saint-Martin, and Ballanche. The romantics did not clearly distinguish the dream per se from madness, fantasy, prophecy, or from the irrational in general. Each romantic dream by our four authors must be interpreted both rationalistically, as psychopathology, and mythically, as an anagogic progression toward the realization of a new spiritual order.[4] Often the romantics attempt to mediate between these two positions through the use of a sympathetic but relatively level-headed frame narrator, who witnesses, sanctions, and makes respectable the manifestations of the irrational in the inner layers of the story. In Lautréamont and Nerval, the frame narrator at times becomes the protagonist: he plays two separate roles. Flaubert can dispense with the frame narrator because his exhaustive historical documentation itself creates an adequate interface between subjective impressions and the external world.

A review of the explicit positions of Freud, Jung, and Erikson allows one to recognize those psychic phenomena which the romantics dramatized in their non-discursive literary dreams, in anticipation of modern psychoanalytic theory. Literary as well as real dreams can be said to have a "latent content," and certain psychoanalytic theories concerning real dreams may be appropriately applied to the analysis of literary dreams.[5] My admittedly controversial use of the term "psychoanalytic" to characterize literary criticism implies a belief that the effects of the protagonists' involuntary mental processes, and at times the persistent influence of their childhood experience as the author imagined it, are detectible in the texts and provide the best clues to their meaning.

In invoking psychoanalytic authorities, I am pluralistic, drawing upon what I hold to be the most enduring contributions of each of several figures. I rely upon Freud to explain the *mechanisms* of dream and fantasy production; on Jung to identify and describe the *symbolic vehicles* of dream narratives; and on Erikson to define the *dynamics of personality development* and its crises throughout the life cycle. I believe that dreams, although involuntary, are a creative mental process arising from the interplay of compulsions and strivings for self-realization. They provide an imaginary theater in which unacceptable or even disastrous potential responses to life's problems can be acted out without material risk. The archetype of Inversion characteristically resolves romantic dream narratives. What seemed bad (disgrace, insanity, or death) proves potentially good: even though the drama consumes the hero, it hints at a constructive reorientation in the personality of the eyewitness narrator.

My critical stance of "interpretation in the subjective mode" is governed by the hypothesis that all events, descriptions, transitions, and secondary characters in certain literary works may be interpreted as reflecting insights, trends, attitudes, and conflicts in the psyche of the protagonist. Such a heuristic principle works best for lyric poetry, fantasy, and the confessional novel. It is usually less effective for analyzing other forms of prose fiction, or theater. Interpretation in the subjective mode focuses on the personality of the protagonist rather than on the personality of the author. Thus it shifts psychoanalytic inquiry away from biographical speculation to the close reading of texts. Interpretation in the subjective mode helps the critic to avoid reductive rigidity, to respect the organic unity of an individual work of art, to illuminate details which might otherwise be neglected, and to reveal the anagogic dimension of the literary work. If one adopts this interpretive method, the narrative discontinuities which characterize major romantic fantasy can be made to provide clues to repressed emotions of the protagonist—particularly yearning, pride, anger, and fear—which, although frequently overlooked by readers, are the dramatic movers of the story.

From this viewpoint, the seven romantic works to be discussed in detail each correspond to one of the three major solutions to the problems of human development, as they are experienced by the irrational archaic psyche active in the deeper layers of dreams. Self-doubt stimulates either repression, regression, or self-glorification: "I am not," "I am less than," "I am more than" the undesirable self-image. In working out these inadequate solutions, the protagonist is overtaken by madness or death. But the more profound romantic dreams depict the apotheosis of the protagonist together with his failure. Such dreams are never simply an unfair fencing match between phalluses and prohibitions, nor are they mere theosophist tracts. The authors knowingly present two mutually exclusive but coexisting interpretations of experience, as they work toward an impossible reconciliation of id and superego.

I

The Dream in Psychology
and Literature

CHAPTER 1

Dreams Real and Literary

Why do we dream? Before romanticism, the dominant answers were either mechanistic or religious. Some believed that the gods spoke to them in dreams. Others, although they believed that dreams might afford moments of intuitive insight unavailable at other times, attributed such insights to the automatic functioning of a combinatorial, associative faculty in the brain. Still others dismissed the effects of dreams, if any, as inconsequential, and were content to identify their cause: physiological stimuli, the need to provide an outlet for the pointless activity of the sleeping mind, or a drive to work through fragmentary and suppressed waking thoughts.[1]

The romantics developed a richer, more nuanced, conception of the dream than had been found (with rare exceptions) earlier. Frequently they combined earlier ideas with anticipations of twentieth-century psychoanalytic theory regarding the function, materials, and structure of dreams. Most important of all, they considered dreaming to be a distinct, autonomous mental process—a notion corroborated in the 1950's by observations of REM brain waves. They believed that dream materials derived both from personal memory traces (Freud) and from a repository of the inherited collective wisdom of humanity (Jung). They knew that dreams had manifold and often simultaneous functions: to give vent to compulsions, to try to solve problems, and to communicate transcendent revelations. Beyond the ostensible discontinuity of dream imagery, they saw a concealed but explicable order.

Real dreams consist of a series of images. Their sources are the residue of thoughts from the previous day, earlier memories, "screen memories" (stylized, composite constructs unconsciously elaborated in childhood to represent the child's sense of relationships with the world, and his sense of self), and personal and universal symbolism. Words heard, read, or thought, and entire conversations, may be associated with these images. At times the series of dream images forms a dramatic whole as coherent as a story or a play. It then can be analyzed with the familiar, conventional techniques of literary criticism. At other times, however, the series of dream images appears discontinuous or disjointed. Then dream structure is diaphoric, to borrow Phillip Wheelwright's useful term. It juxtaposes events often widely separated in time or space, or both, "producing new meaning by juxtaposition alone."[2] Such discontinuity may result from repression, when a threatening thought risks becoming too obvious. On the other hand, it may result from the purgation of the dreamer's anxiety, moral scruples, fear, and disgust by a first, symbolically disguised reenactment of a troubling fantasy. This allows the fantasy to appear, in its second incarnation, in a more nearly recognizable form. Two discontinuous images may represent two features of a composite attitude presented separately (in dreams "either-or" means "both-and," Freud pointed out). The juxtaposition of images may represent the dreamer's perception of an analogy between two different situations. In any event, each image provides an implicit commentary on its neighbors.

Hidden or ostensible, the underlying pattern of dream images often follows what in rhetoric is called emphatic order: a progression from the unimportant to the important, from the emotionally neutral to the intense. Jung's analysis of thousands of dreams led him to comment:

> There are a great many "average" dreams in which a definite structure can be perceived, not unlike that of a drama. . . . The EXPOSITION . . . indicates the scene of action, the people involved, and often the initial situation of the dreamer. In the second

2

phase comes the DEVELOPMENT of the plot. . . . The situation is somehow becoming complicated, and a definite tension develops because one does not know what will happen. The third phase brings the CULMINATION or *peripeteia*. Here something decisive happens or something changes completely. . . . The fourth and last phase is the *lysis*, the SOLUTION or RESULT produced by the dream-work. . . . The last phase shows the final situation, which is at the same time the solution "sought" by the dreamer.[3]

The dream drama has a collective as well as an individual meaning. Both Freud and Jung considered myth to be a sort of collective dream, and Freud analyzed myth as such in *Moses and Monotheism* and in *Totem and Taboo*. Moreover, both Freud and Jung believed that the latent content of the dreams of an individual could contain collective as well as personal elements. Regarding the notion of a "collective unconscious," Freud declared: "I fully agree with Jung in recognizing the existence of this phylogenetic heritage."[4] Elsewhere he explained that the experiences of individual egos could be inherited if they recurred frequently, strongly, in many individuals, and in successive generations. He believed that such ego experiences were transformed into id experiences, which could then be transmitted by heredity. Thus the id preserves the residues of countless past egos, Freud claimed. He speculated that the ego might form its superego out of the id by resurrecting impressions derived from egos of former generations.[5]

So it is not the concept of a racial unconscious in the individual which distinguishes the theories of Freud from those of Jung. Freud simply claimed that Jung was too prompt to appeal to the collective unconscious in the course of psychotherapy—that he overlooked many explanations for elements of a patient's fantasy life which could be found in his personal experience. Unlike Freud, Jung and the romantics gave primacy to the manifestations of a collective unconscious in the dreams of individuals, as well as in ritual and myth. I believe that Freud's objection to Jung's interpretive method is valid in the domain of psychotherapy, but not in the domain of literary criticism. Books are more completely the products of tradition, of a collectivity, than are people. All the observable existence of books has to be mediated through language and literary genres, both of which are systems of conventions.

Today it has become widely recognized that dreams serve not only as catharses for repressed impulses but also as creative efforts and attempts at problem-solving. It has become a commonplace in psycho-therapy to interpret dreams as implicit comments on the progress of the therapy and on the patient's relationships with his present-day asso-ciates, and to assume that a cycle of dreams constitutes a repeated approach to the same conflict through trial and error.[6] The hypothesis that dreaming may involve creative thinking is borne out by physio-logical evidence that dreaming involves the higher cerebral centers: patients who have had lobotomies do not dream, except for occasional visions which consist in direct wish-fulfillment.[7]

To stress the problem-solving dimension of dreams is to reintegrate them into the total spectrum of mental activity rather than to consider them as aberrant and anomalous phenomena; "at all levels of cogni-tive [as distinguished from instinctual] activity we seem to operate by setting up and testing hypotheses, by problem-solving and selecting strategies."[8] Dreams attempt to find a suitable stance to adopt in the face of circumstances and of the facts of one's own personality. They result from the struggle between compulsions and regressive forces, on the one hand, and strivings for self-realization on the other—strivings to establish a mature identity appropriate for the phase of life the dreamer is presently in or is entering. Dreams seek *an avenue of approach* toward self-acceptance and social adjustment, whereas the problem-solving of waking life deals primarily with the *techniques* of such adjustment. In Erikson's terms, dreams help synthesize an ego identity and a self-identity from "abandoned and anticipated selves." He defines ego identity as our perceptions of our relationships to the outer world and society, and self-identity as the repertory of ideas, images, and configurations of the mind, and the perceived attributes of our physi-cal organism.[9]

Erikson, in a classic essay, effectively synthesized the wish fulfill-ment and the conflict-solving interpretations of dream function. He agrees with Freud that a "latent infantile wish . . . provides the energy for a renewed conflict, and thus for the dream," but he goes on to say that this wish "is embedded in a manifest dream structure which on every level reflects significant trends of the dreamer's total situation. Dreams, then, not only fulfill naked wishes [an infelicitous wording by Erikson, since the whole point of Freud's studies is to show how dreams *clothe* wishes] of sexual license, of unlimited dominance and of unrestricted destructiveness; where they work, they also lift the dreamer's isolation, appease his conscience, and preserve his identity each in specific and instructive ways."[10] Freud himself knew full well that dreams may deal with current problems in the life of the dreamer.[11]

Erikson's epigenetic description of human development clearly characterized the problems of maturation with which dreams are concerned.[12] Erikson refined the Jungian notion of individuation, setting it upon a detailed Freudian base. He divided the human life cycle into seven stages. The first four correspond approximately to Freud's oral, anal, phallic, and genital stages of child development, except that they are described in terms of self-concept and of relationships with others. Erikson's major specific contribution to developmental psychology—and to the study of literature—was to characterize three stages of personality growth in maturity. The first of these is inaugurated by an "identity crisis" at the time when one must define oneself as a working, sexual, social being outside the family. Failure results in "identity diffusion" and personal isolation. Success means choosing a satisfactory vocation, mate, and system of personal beliefs, and achieving the capacity for mature intimacy with persons outside the family.

During this period of crisis, which usually occurs sometime between the ages of sixteen and twenty-four, it is common to experience a temporary loss of sense of self. One may then desperately cling to authority figures serving as temporary replacements for the parents, regress into passive dependency, or at least postpone mature commitments as long as possible. The following stage, which occupies the period from young adulthood through middle age, involves a conflict between the temptation of self-absorption and the challenge of developing a capacity for generativity—caring for other people and things, and guiding the next generation.[13] The final stage, from late middle age to death, raises the issue of whether we shall sink into self-contempt and despair at the prospect of our limitations and our eventual annihilation, or whether we shall achieve a sense of integrity. Integrity means pride in one's achievements, however modest, and a sense of solidarity with other humans at all times and places, grounded in an awareness of our own life as a necessary and unique cycle which contributes to and then necessarily gives way to the next generation.[14] The physical limitations and circumstances of each stage of life impose their special tasks and identity crises upon us, but each successive task must be mastered in order that the next one may be successfully accomplished.[15]

Whether literary or real, another person's dream as we can know it is "a verbal report of a series of remembered images, mostly visual, which are usually endowed with affect." Both real and literary dreams employ defensive strategies of distortion and disguise. Primary elaboration conceals inadmissible thoughts beneath a symbolic disguise, and secondary elaboration transforms the bizarre, disconnected dream images into a coherent, rationally plausible sequence of verbal utterances. Literary and real dreams alike have a manifest and a latent content. The former is the dream as it is preserved in one's memory and then reported or recorded. The latter consists of the relevant material which emerges when the dreamer is asked for his free associations with the details of the manifest content, and for the emotional, historical, and mythic connotations both of the manifest content and of its associations.[16]

There are two major differences between literary and real dreams (leaving aside the question of whether any particular literary dream has a real dream as its ultimate source). According to Freud, the manifest content of the real dream is much more condensed than the thoughts for which it acts as a substitute.[17] In literary dreams, in contrast, secondary elaboration becomes not only the inevitable by-product, but also the conscious aim of the reporting of fantasies. Rather than abridging, it expands, to the point where Albert Sonnenfeld recently suggested the term "tertiary elaboration" to distinguish the linguistic encoding of literary dreams from that of real dreams.[18] For months, years, or decades—as Goethe did in his creation of *Faust*—an author may repeatedly overlay the subconscious sources of his fantasy with elaborate detail, carefully selected, lovingly expanded, and harmoniously patterned. Of course, the latent content of literary dreams is directly accessible only when the critic is personally acquainted with the author.

This second fact raises the central methodological question involved in psychoanalytic approaches to literature. Sophisticated literary critics like Gérard Genette warn that it is otiose to speculate on the hidden sentiments and motivations of literary characters. Their feelings are not real; they have only a fictional, linguistic existence; they are "exhausted by the totality of utterances by which the narration *signifies* them [italics in original]."[19] If one refers the acts of literary characters to a "deeper" reality, the argument goes, one is psychoanalyzing the author or the reader—in other words, one is examining the connotations of the text as it reverberates outside the domain of its own discourse. The same holds true, however, in the interpretation of any interpersonal communication: we seek the "deeper" meanings by appealing to our responses to the verbal and non-verbal gestures of others. Freud said that "interpretation means finding a hidden meaning in something." A further objection, however, remains valid: when we confront a text, it cannot respond to our questions as a person could respond, denying or confirming the relevance of the connotations which it evokes in us. Is it legitimate to claim to be doing a "psychoanalytic" interpretation of literary works if we do not know the authors' associations with the details of those works? Freud stressed "how impossible it is in general to understand a dream till the dreamer has given us his information about it."[20] Even Jung, who once boldly declared that "the 'manifest' dream picture is the dream itself and contains the whole meaning of the dream,"[21] elsewhere praised Freud for putting the art of dream interpretation "on the right track" by recognizing that "no interpretation can be undertaken without the dreamer" (*SDP*, pp. 284–85). What Jung means by these apparently contradictory statements is that we must indeed obtain the dreamer's associations to each detail of the manifest content: only the dreamer can reveal the subjective matrix in which the images of the manifest dream are embedded. But Jung rejects the practice of soliciting further associations *to the associations*, on the grounds that the resulting chain of associations will lead us even farther from the dream (*MAHS*, pp. 28–29).

Eventually, and largely owing to the influence of Wilhelm Stekel, Freud himself began to accept the notion of a general dream symbolism which could be understood without obtaining the associations of an individual dreamer. In 1907 he brilliantly analyzed Jensen's novel *Gradiva* without interviewing the author (who in fact vehemently protested against Freud's interpretation) or drawing upon Jensen's other writings. He devoted a special section to general dream symbolism in the fourth edition of *The Interpretation of Dreams*, published in 1914. In 1915, "Symbolism in Dreams," the tenth chapter of Freud's *Introductory Lectures on Psychoanalysis*, presented his most ambitious statement concerning universal symbolism. Ultimately, Freud came to believe that "dreams invented by writers will often yield to analysis in the same way as real ones" even without the help of the writers.[22]

When the available manifest content is sufficiently extensive, moreover, one can escape the necessity of exclusive reliance upon a universal dream symbolism. Given the wealth of material available, either in a series of real dreams or in the elaborate literary dream, one part of the record throws light upon the other parts because the same image or motif reappears in varying contexts. One can then learn an author's or dreamer's personal symbolism as a child learns a language or as a critic learns to read an obscure symbolist poet. In 1959 Walter J. Reis, a student of Calvin S. Hall, adduced from a limited amount of experimental evidence that the absence of a dreamer's associations with his or her dream series does not radically alter the conclusions arrived at by a psychologist's study of the manifest content alone. Reis collected dream series from twenty-four college students of both sexes, and recorded their associations with their dreams. Two psychologists rated twenty-five aspects of each dreamer's personality on a three-point scale. Each psychologist was shown associations with only twelve of the dream series—those not seen by the other psychologist. Thirty-four additional dream series had been rated in preliminary reliability studies while the personality rating system was being established. In the 1960's, Calvin Hall's studies of the dreams of Kafka, Freud, and Jung, and other studies by Leopold Caligor, Rollo May, and Carl Gustav Jung, offered additional examples of convincing dream interpretations accomplished without the aid of the dreamer's associations. [23] In another study of thirteen hundred dreams recorded by a living subject, concerning whom nothing was known except his age and sex, checked against a control group of five hundred dreams collected from one hundred young adult males, Hall concluded that as few as twenty-five dreams could provide sufficient evidence for a content analysis, although a comparison with the subject's clinical history showed that even thirteen hundred dreams failed to reveal the waking person's characteristic defenses, and that they dramatized much pathological behavior rarely or never acted out in real life. [24]

Finally, the unconscious life of both literary character and author may be revealed by linguistic features which make the text superdetermined (repetition, punning, conflation) or underdetermined (ellipsis, antithesis, preterition, litotes). Most psychoanalytic critics of literature have focused on its superdetermined elements. Thus Charles Mauron and Claude Lévi-Strauss have superimposed passages with constellations of similar features in order to isolate recurring elements which seem unrelated to the conscious, rational elaboration of the text, and which are claimed to betray obsessive, involuntary associations of ideas in the mind of the author (or of society as creator of myths). The *modus operandi* is to search for areas of the work of art in which the artist seems not to be in control. [25]

This method, valid so far as it goes, has three serious limitations in the eyes of a Jungian critic. First, it is reductive; it overlooks the fact that "motivated is not synonymous with determined," [26] that both the procedures and the products of sublimation—of individuation, rather—are infinitely varied, and that the solutions which each creative artist finds for the problems of his human heritage are unpredictable. Second, it runs the risk of tempting the critic to claim that he is a better human being than the artist, by virtue of his deeper insight, wider reading, and superior mental health. Unchecked, the critic can exalt himself far above the status of the psychoanalyst. The analyst may question his patient's statements; he may ask for elaboration; he may propose alternative or supplementary interpretations of a dream. However, if the patient does not eventually accept the analyst's interpretation of his behavior as being in harmony with his experiences, and if he does not, at last, voluntarily concur with the analyst's solutions and apply them to his life, then the analysis is a failure. The critic, on the other hand, lacks the salutory restraint of speaking with a living subject, who may accept, modify, or protest his ideas. Last, this method does not take account of the "third force" in the human psyche, the instinctual impulse toward personal development and the full realization of one's potential. It is anachronistically rooted in the deterministic hypotheses of nineteenth-century Positivism. A century ago, the most generally accepted myths were Enlightenment myths: in this century they are romantic. Jung and Maslow were neo-romantic. The educated person today is living through what the romantics imagined a century ago: the quest for an authentic self, in a supra-rational order.

The Jungian critic must take into account the underdetermined elements of a text as well as the superdetermined ones, identifying sudden changes of setting, time, identity, or subject as momentary refusals to confront the Shadow, momentary failures to understand the message of the archetype of spirit, or the collective nature of the *anima*. Gaps in the text provide clues to this latent content of the literary dream. Their motivation—an inadequate self-knowledge—usually is implied in the context immediately preceding them. In the belief that the artist is exceptionally lucid concerning the drama of personal development, the Jungian critic will tend to interpret textual discontinuities as intentional authorial solutions to the problem of implying, rather than stating overtly, the characters' strivings toward self-realization.

Jung characterized the "subjective" and "objective" modes as two equally valid methods for interpreting dreams:

> I call interpretations in which the dream symbols are treated as representations of the real objects *interpretation upon the objective plane*. The opposite interpretation is that which connects every fragment of the dream with the dreamer himself. This is *interpretation upon the subjective plane*. Objective interpretation is *analytical*,

because it dissects the dream contents into complexes of reminiscence, and finds their relation to real conditions. Subjective interpretation is *synthetic*, because it detaches the fundamental underlying complexes of reminiscence from their actual causes, regarding them as tendencies or parts of the subject, and reintegrating them with the subject.[27]

"If, therefore," Jung wrote elsewhere, "instead of reducing the dream symbols to circumstances, things, or persons which the analyst presumes to know in advance, we regard them as real symbols pointing to something unknown, then the whole character of analytical therapy is altered. The unconscious is then no longer reduced to known, conscious factors . . . but is recognized as in fact unconscious."[28] In short, interpretation in the subjective mode begins with the decision to consider events, settings, and characters other than the protagonist, as well as all doublings and discontinuities, as reflecting the protagonist's psychic state and evolution.

In real-life psychotherapy, the choice of interpretive method must emerge, for each dream, from the therapist's evaluation of conversations with his patient. Initially, observes Erikson, "one never knows whether to view the cast of puppets on the dreamer's stage as a microcosmic reflection of his present or past social reality or as a 'projection' of different identity fragments of the dreamer himself, of different roles played by him at different times or in different situations."[29] In literary criticism generally, both the subjective and the objective modes may be equally valid and mutually complementary, a fact dramatically illustrated by the diametrically opposed interpretations of Balzac by Barbéris and by Béguin. Roland Barthes has percipiently characterized these two modes of literary criticism, in *S/Z*:

> If one has a realistic view of the *character* . . . one will seek motives . . . (enthusiasm, unconscious refusal of the truth, etc.). If one has a realistic view of the *discourse* . . . one considers the story as a mechanism which must keep operating till the very end. . . . Now these two viewpoints, although they derive from different senses of reality and are in principle mutually independent (opposite, even), support each other. . . . The discourse generates its own accomplice in the character. . . . The characters are forms of discourse and inversely the discourse is a character like the others [italics in original].[30]

Where the romantic dream narratives discussed in this book are concerned, however, explicit statements by the authors have solved the problem of the choice of a method. These statements show that while some figures other than the dreamer have indeed been drawn from a recognizable objective past, or a present social reality, they have been summoned into the dream by the dreamer's desires and fears. Their presence reflects these emotions: the secondary characters are vehicles for the dreamer's fantasies. The main characters go farther than this: they interpret their "reality" as well as their dreams in the subjective mode. Nodier's Michel in *La Feé aux Miettes* admits that "the mental faculty of dreaming had been transformed in me. It seemed to me that it had shifted from my sleep to my waking life, where it thenceforth took refuge together with its illusions" (*C*, p. 246).

Elsewhere Nodier described the dreamer as an actor with a thousand faces and a thousand voices, who unwittingly creates and performs an extraordinary drama which surpasses the conceptions of genius.[31] Nerval's *Sylvie* identifies Adrienne and Sylvie as two aspects of the same love, i.e., as vehicles for two complementary aspirations of the hero. The narrator characterizes his perceptions in *Aurélia*, starting with chapter 3, as governed by "the overflowing of dreaming into real life."[32] Flaubert characterizes all Saint Anthony's experiences as hallucinations,[33] and elsewhere makes it clear that for him the source of hallucinations is entirely subjective.[34] And the beginning of Lautréamont's third *Chant de Maldoror* stresses the purely subjective origins of all the secondary characters. "Those imaginary beings, angelic in nature, that my pen, during the second canto, drew from a brain, shining with a radiance emanating from themselves. . . . I have let you fall back into chaos, like diving bells. . . . You must make way for other substances to be born of the stormy overflowing of a love which has resolved not to quench its thirst among human kind."[35] Neither the implied author nor the protagonist can determine which fantasies he will imagine, but the implied author decides which to record, and the organizing principle of his choice is the depiction of the protagonist's character. Psychological theory elucidates the gesture of character portrayal consciously effected by the writer.

What can psychoanalytic interpretation in the subjective mode contribute to an understanding of dream narratives and fantasies in general? First, it avoids the reductive rigidity which would attempt either to limit literary expression to the involuntary betrayal of an Oedipus complex, mother fixation, penis envy, and search for parental surrogates, or to confine it to a set of static symbols or "themes" in a way which neither Freud nor Jung ever intended. One need only reread

Freud's brilliant interpretation of Jensen's *Gradiva* or Jung's analysis of the Miss Miller fantasies in his *Symbols of Transformation* to see how overwhelmingly rich, varied, dramatic, and poignant was *their* psychological approach to literature. Second, it encourages the sensitive interpretation of isolated details, which otherwise would be neglected, as symbols of the condition of the self and the course of its development. A subjective interpretation can explain apparent discontinuities of plot, setting, time, and characters as generated by, and providing an implicit commentary upon, the inner conflicts of the protagonist. The presence of certain *dramatis personae* reflects the claims of his unconscious upon the protagonist's attention; their disappearance may betray his attempt to evade these claims. Above all, subjective interpretation throws light upon the anagogic dimension: the interplay of inner, psychic forces striving for a constructive resolution through personal development. Late in life, Freud himself wrote that his psychoanalysis—a psychology of the id and of its effect on the ego—should be complemented by a more fully developed psychology of the ego.[36] And however skeptical one may be about the ontological status of Jungian "archetypes of the collective unconscious"—I myself am an agnostic concerning them—one must admit that the concept is grounded in a vast erudition. Jung's prolonged, assiduous researches drew even from his arch-critic Edward Glover the grudging admission that Jung was "a good anthropologist."[37] Whether or not Jung's archetypes are inherited potentialities for embodying universal human experiences in images, they are indisputably literary and mythic *topoi* (timeless, recurring subjects in literature) reflecting the drama of personality development. Like Jung after them, our romantics are optimists. Their literature aims toward transcendence.

CHAPTER 2

The Romantic Dream

Romanticism represents a revival rather than the beginning of literary interest in the unconscious. The earliest known literature—and the behavior of preliterate societies—at times reveals considerable psychological sophistication. And the widespread folk traditions of incubation (methodical ceremonies of preparation and self-purification in the attempt to elicit a desired dream vision) reveal a clear, pragmatic sense of the connections between dream thoughts and waking thoughts.

Before about 1780, however, the motifs exploited by the literary dream were surprisingly limited: erotic fantasies, a visit by a god or dead person, visions of heaven or hell. As early as the ninth century, authors used dream narrations to put their enemies in Hell (cf. Dante and Quevedo). Later, demonic imagery was widely used for political satire. A garden of paradise was converted to a frame for dream visions of secular love (Andreas Cappelanus, Lorris, Boccaccio, Chaucer), and from the fifteenth century on this setting was used frequently for presenting alchemical and Neoplatonic love subjects.

Such secularization of religious motifs in art robbed them of much of their force. From 1650 on, they were generally rejected in France, notably in Boileau's *Art poétique* (bk. 3, vv. 199–204, 235–36).[1] In French classical tragedy (e.g., Racine's *Athalie*) dreams served occasionally to introduce a prophetic anticipation of the future into a flow of action occurring on stage in a perpetual present. Thus they were a counterpart to the *récits* which embodied the past. But such dreams functioned as they had in Scripture: they presented an intimation of the divine will, rather than creating a realistic semblance of the inner life of the mind.

Like pleasurable dreams, seventeenth- and eighteenth-century utopias offered imaginary compensations for the shortcomings of daily life. But they differed from dream narratives in recommending or implying a program of social action. They were organized around suggestions for modifying and improving social institutions, although the hypothetical ideal society itself—like Plato's *Republic*—was admittedly unobtainable. By changing from the depiction of a highly organized social structure to the evocation of an idealized, simpler past, some of the later utopias moved closer to dream-like wish fulfillment. Fénelon's *Télémaque* already reveals this tendency, more fully expressed in Montesquieu's fable of the Troglodytes in his *De l'Esprit des lois* (the caves these creatures inhabit suggest the subconscious) and in the hypothetical, ideal primitive society of Rousseau's *Discours sur les origines de l'inégalité*. But the emphasis remains collective, not individual: the daring speculations made possible by the utopian frame are intended to have social utility.

From the eighteenth century on, however, there was an increasing insistence on personal inspiration in all the arts and more frequent attempts to put dreams and fantasies into words.[2] Generally speaking, the sense of an unpredictable realm lying beyond the purview of man's rational waking consciousness was reflected in the non-linear structure of many eighteenth-century French and English novels: "Digressions, syntactical discontinuity, shifts from one level to another, contrasts of tone, interweaving of several narratives: all the characteristics of the sinuous line."[3] Aside from Sterne's *Tristram Shandy*, the best-known models of such discontinuous narrative were provided by the *conte oriental* popularized by Galland's translation of the *Arabian Nights* in 1704. The literary current of fantasy and mysterious fatality in these tales was swelled by a revival of interest in the fairy tale in late seventeenth- and early eighteenth-century France.[4]

Antoine Hamilton combined the two forms, *conte oriental* and fairy tale.[5] He has the sultana Dinarzède relate the fairy tale *Fleur d'Epine* within which is embedded *Les Quatre Facardins*. Puzzling adventures accumulate disconnectedly in an aleatory world, but at length the reader realizes that this systematic disruption of narrative continuity conceals a single story beneath the multiple viewpoints and the uncertainties concerning causes and motivations.[6] Hamilton also uses the technique of the layering of narration in *Zeneyda*. He parodies the oriental tale by creating, as it does, a *monde gigogne* of nesting stories. A first narrator relates a tale in which he encounters a second narrator, who relates a tale in which he encounters a third narrator, and so forth; eventually one rises back through the successive layers to the starting point: the structure could be schematically represented as ABCBA.

This resembles an expanded chiasmus, and like chiasmus it creates an inner world or worlds isolated from the outer world, and therefore implicitly subject to different, idiosyncratic laws. The popularity of this narrative technique made it available to later, romantic writers, and it was perfectly suited to suggest their intuitive awareness of the layer cake model of the psyche (the adult psyche overlays an infantile psyche which remains dynamically active throughout life) and of a world of dreams embedded within our waking experience but none the less real for all that.

Diderot consolidated the theoretical basis for the layer cake model of the psyche by providing a striking example of the phenomenon of involuntary memory in the section "Mémoire" of his *Eléments de physiologie*. He claimed that all impressions received by the senses are preserved within our minds without our knowing it.[7] To be sure, the *Encyclopédie* article "Rêve" echoes the superficially similar Aristotelian opinion that the day residue is the main source of dreams: "the things which have made the strongest impression on us during the day, appear to our soul when it is at rest." Voltaire more than once concurred.[8] But Diderot went further by formulating a concept which broke down the wall between dream thought and waking thought; which proposed that a slight recent impression, as well as a strong one, could initiate the associative processes of either involuntary memory or dream; and which suggested that, through the associative process, a seemingly unimportant present impression could revive great constellations of past impressions within us.

Diderot further believed that the synthetic processes of dream thought, analogous to those of involuntary memory, might lead to inspiration and insights unobtainable otherwise. The intuitive combination of impressions effected by Mangogul's dream in *Les Bijoux indiscrets*, and by the geometrician D'Alembert's feverish, delirious dream in *Le Rêve de D'Alembert*, circumvents an impasse reached by waking reason. Thus the philosophical dream according to Aram Vartanian "has a basic affinity with the function of the genuine dream." It makes the " 'unthinkable' somehow thinkable" and gives form to "ideas which would otherwise be imperfectly grasped precisely because they would remain, for the lucid consciousness, merely theoretical, that is, abstractions divorced from a corresponding affective experience." But "Diderot and his contemporaries had as yet no notion that dreams could be understood as symbolically meaningful expressions, on a different level of consciousness, of the personal experiences of waking reality. They attempted above all to explain dream phenomena *physiologically* as partial and confused versions of the normal thought-processes of the mind [italics in original]." For them the dream exemplified "the subjective illusion of freedom within the objective reality of a deterministic universe."[9] This dichotomy is perfectly illustrated by the concluding paragraph of Voltaire's article "Somnambules, et songes" in his *Dictionnaire philosophique*:

> So, while dreaming [Voltaire has just given several examples of literary inspiration occurring in dreams], I have said things that I scarcely would have said awake; so I've had lucid thoughts despite myself, and without taking the least [voluntary] part in them. I had neither will, nor freedom; and yet I combined ideas shrewdly, even with a certain genius. What am I then if not a machine?

The final sentence is startling to a modern reader, led by the preceding language to expect the invocation of some mystical force.

Rousseau described the phenomenon of involuntary memory in several passages of the *Confessions*, and depicted a state of mindless ecstasy in the *Rêveries*, but his influence in this regard was diffuse: so far as I can determine, he exerted no precise, concrete influence on the elaboration of the romantic dream per se. During the nineteenth century, the *Rêveries* "contribute to imposing an orientation on that introspective romanticism, which constitutes as it were an introduction to a metaphysics of the dream." For the description of dreams as such, Rousseau employs "a strictly *evasive* language [italics in original]. With each clause, the sentence seems to break off, it seems to reach a point of suspension, where it could either stop or fade away, completely absorbed by the vaguest daydream. Thus Rousseau indicates diffusion [of the personality], apathy, perfect tranquility, a beatific indifference." This state is ultimately inexpressible; language yields to silence. The all-encompassing personal sensibility engulfs all possibilities of dramatic development or interaction between characters.[10]

In short, few preromantic writers saw the dream as a potentially constructive and relatively autonomous function of the sleeping mind. They thought dreams resulted from a rapid association of ideas analogous to the mental processes of madness and hallucination, or to Kant's, Schelling's, and Coleridge's "fancy" as contrasted with the creative imagination. Many of the leading visionary romantics, however—Blake, Novalis, Nodier, Nerval, Lautréamont, and Flaubert—anticipated Freud in believing that dreaming was a motivated, purposeful symbolic activity. They dramatized this belief in their fiction. Like most modern psychoanalysts and psychiatrists, they considered that human mental activity involves both conscious ratiocination and unconscious, involuntary processes. They thought that subliminal past impressions, which we cannot summon up consciously, are preserved in the mind and influence it. As Freud was to do, they assumed that dreams offer the most direct access to the unconscious. [11]

The next and the decisive step in providing a conceptual basis for dream literature was for the romantics to distinguish the domain of objective, material, rational perceptions from the domain of intuitively associated ideas; to consider the dream an expression of these ideas; and to assert that the latter refer to a common center of spiritual truth which it is the purpose of their writing to reveal. Thus they arrived at a concept of the mission of art analogous to what Joseph Campbell defined as one of the four functions of myth: "formulating and rendering an image of the universe . . . of such kind that . . . all things should be recognized as parts of a single great holy picture . . . all opening back to mystery."[12] The image of this great picture was preserved, thought the romantics, in the collective unconscious. They did not call it by that name, nor by any single name, but in fiction, the French romantics (including some skeptics among them) suggested the existence of a collective unconscious in various ways. They evoked the presence of collective past memories haunting the present (e.g., the opening pages of Mme de Staël's *De l'Allemagne*, or Nodier's travel journals); they created parallels between the Christian story and the myths of other religions (e.g., in *Atala*); they exhibited a propensity for the sort of exoticism which tacitly assumes that man may come to know himself better by studying other times and cultures (e.g., the January 1829 preface to Hugo's *Orientales* in which he speaks of himself in the third person: "his [Hugo's] daydreams and his thoughts found themselves each in turn, and almost unintentionally, Hebrew, Turkish, Greek, Persian, or Arab"); and they associated their protagonists with archeology in, for example, Mérimée's *La Vénus d'Ille* and several of Gautier's tales.

Like Jung after them, the visionary romantics generally believed that dreams provided revelation by putting man in contact with the wisdom of the collective unconscious, the supernatural order, or both.

Nodier declared that "certainly sleep is the most powerful as well as the most lucid mode of thought. . . . Take the visions of the marvellous away from genius, and you take away its wings. The map of the imaginable universe is traced only in dreams." Nerval claimed that "dreams are a second life . . . [in which] the spirit world is revealed to us . . . a new life begins, freed from the limitations of time and space, similar, no doubt, to the life that awaits us after death. Who knows whether there is not a bond between these two forms of existence [waking and sleeping] and whether it is not possible for the soul to make the connection between them at this very moment [before death]?"[13]

There remained the need for developing a literary character type who could somehow communicate the impressions of a vast world of sensations which surpass human reason in range and complexity, but whose meanings could be intuitively grasped. Indirectly and informally, Diderot had suggested two possibilities for such a character:

> Insanity, dreams, the disconnectedness of a conversation consist in passing from one object to another through the mediation of a shared attribute.
> The madman is not aware that he is changing the subject. He holds a shining yellow straw in his hand, and shouts that he has captured a sunbeam. How many people are like that madman without suspecting it.[14]

So the visionary character could be either a madman or a dreamer. Diderot created literary models for both: the dreamer in *Le Rêve de D'Alembert*, and the madman in *Le Neveu de Rameau*. With Rameau's Nephew, the literary madman became a social individual in conversation with a "normal" person, for the first time since the great confinement of the insane in the mid-seventeenth century.[15] In the late eighteenth century, proselytizing mystics and occultists offered non-literary models of the visionary active in society: Swedenborg, Saint-Martin, and Cazotte. Saint-Martin admitted that he must seem mad to his contemporaries, but claimed he was the sort of lunatic that should be loosed, rather than one fit to be tied. The example of these visionaries greatly influenced Nodier, Nerval, and Balzac. Nodier commemorated Cazotte in his *Contes*; Nerval treated Cazotte and several similar figures in *Les Illuminés*; Balzac depicted visionaries in *Séraphîtâ* and *Louis Lambert*.[16]

From the classical period onward, madness was frequently associated with the dream. Kant called the madman a waking dreamer. The 1812 journal of the cure of Alexandre Hébert speculated: "Lunatics, madmen, maniacs and convulsives—might they not be nothing more than disturbed sleepwalkers?"[17] Nodier agreed that "most mental obsessions . . . are probably only the continuing perception of an impression acquired from that fantastic existence which makes up half our lives, the existence of the sleeper."[18] He frequently insisted that our impressions during sleep may be as "real" and significant as those of our waking life. He decisively integrated insight with madness and fiction by creating a series of mad protagonists whose supposed ravings were presented as the accounts of dreams or visions granting access to the supernatural in *Une Heure ou la vision*, *Jean-François les bas-bleus*, *Lydie ou la résurrection*, and elsewhere. Heavily influenced by Nodier, Nerval took up these themes in his turn, notably in *Aurélia*. As the elder statesman of romanticism in his salon at the Arsénal from 1824 to 1830, Nodier inspired Hugo, Balzac, and Dumas with the fantastic anecdotes which he loved to relate, and he served as the main avenue by which the influence of Diderot and the English Gothic novel reached French literary circles.[19]

The years 1820 and 1821 were critical for the development of French dream literature, and consequently for the flowering of romanticism. Most manuals of literary history find either lyric poetry or theater to be the cutting edge of innovation within this literary movement. They consider Lamartine's *Méditations* of 1820 and Hugo's *Hernani* of 1830 to be the major literary monuments of romanticism, considered as a reaction against classicism.[20] But Lamartine, Vigny, and Hugo remained within well-established generic traditions in poetry during the 1820's. French romantic theater was mainly a dramatization of the historical novel or an offshoot of melodrama, or both. In contrast, during the 1820's Nodier was devising a new genre, the *conte fantastique*, which was to be exploited for more than a century by Balzac, Dumas, Gautier, Mérimée, Maupassant, Villiers de L'Isle-Adam, Supervielle, Aymé, and many others.

Nodier was stimulated by an unusually abundant influx of masterpieces of the English Gothic and fantastic novel into France during the early 1820's. Although these works did not characterize themselves as dreams, they contributed many motifs to the French romantic dream narrative. Scott's *The Monastery*, published in 1820, was immediately translated into French for a public which already held his works in great esteem. Its White Lady of Avenel provided the best example of the mysterious supernatural in Scott's novels.[21] Her apparition returns several times to terrify or protect the human characters. She appears to have helped to inspire Nodier's *Trilby* (1822). Like him she belongs to a race of elemental spirits; she is neither saved nor damned; her destiny is mysteriously bound to the family of Avenel as Trilby's is to Jeannie.

Furthermore, the rigid intolerance of the monk Ronald in *Trilby* has a probable source in Scott's portrait of the monk Eustace (*The Monastery*, vol. 1, ch. 8). Finally, Nodier claimed that the preface or a note to an unnamed novel by Scott gave him the idea for *Trilby*, and Scott's preface to *The Monastery* discusses popular superstitions at length. Polidori's *Vampire* (attributed to Byron) and Maturin's *Melmoth* also were published in 1820, Thomas de Quincey's *Confessions of an English Opium-Eater* in 1821 (translated by Musset in 1828). De Quincey described the interpenetration of waking and sleeping vision, and of past and present.[22] Nodier immediately associated himself with efforts to translate and dramatize Mathurin's *Bertram* (published in 1816 in English) and Polidori's *Vampire*, and in 1821 he edited a collection of fantastic tales under the title *Infernalia*. His masterpiece, *Smarra*, was completed the same year, inaugurating the true dream narrative in France.[23]

Nodier was prepared to respond to this English influence: he knew the language well, he had long admired Shakespeare (a collection of whose thoughts he published in 1804), and earlier he had been influenced by the Gothic novel. In fact, he was one of the first Frenchmen so affected. His "Rendez-vous de la Trépassée" in *Essais d'un jeune barde* (1804) imitates the famous ballad "Alonzo and Imogene" in Lewis' *Monk*. Young and Ann Radcliffe probably influenced Nodier's *Méditations du cloître* (1803) and *Une Heure ou la vision* (1806). The first chapter of Radcliffe's *The Mysteries of Udolpho* (the main source of Lewis' *Monk*) provided the decor for Nodier's *Jean Sbogar* in 1818, and probably for *Inès de las Sierras* in 1837.[24]

The English Gothic settings and characters showed the French romantics how to suggest the existence and influence of unconscious and of involuntary mental activity. The underground chambers, hidden passageways, and intricate spirals of rooms in the Gothic mansion or castle superseded the caves of Hell as a physical representation of an unconscious from which frightening, unpredictable apparitions can emerge, lying beneath the threshhold of our awareness. Among literary characters, the devil as tempter and the monk with criminal impulses— in Lewis' *The Monk*, Hoffmann's *The Devil's Elixirs*, Hugo's *Notre-Dame de Paris*, Flaubert's *Tentation de saint Antoine*, or Goethe's *Faust*—clearly suggest a repressed "second self." Generally speaking, the early English Gothic appears to be "the first modern prose form disposed to [a] fairly intensive concern with the various phenomena of the divided self," and as such an eminently suitable model for French romantic literary reactions to a national identity crisis.[25]

The Conventions of French Romantic Dream Literature

Fiction is a verbal semblance of human experience. Fantasy literature is a subclass of fiction. Its essential characteristic is a sense of estrangement resulting from the interpenetration of two normally distinct categories of experience—human/non-human, natural/supernatural, dream/waking, love/death—in such a way as to make protagonist and reader feel a loss of control and an inability to comprehend the new world in which they find themselves. The boundaries of the fantastic are culturally determined. The visions of the Book of Revelation are true portents to some, fantasy to others. What may be diverting to one age (for instance the notion of reincarnation in Crébillon fils' *Le Sophâ*) becomes a doctrine in the next (Hugo's *Contemplations*), and later reverts to the status of diversion.

In other words, the fantastic is an effect. For the reader, it occurs at the mid-point of a line running from the absurd to the plausible. The protagonist in fantasy realizes that he is surrounded and affected by natural, social, economic, and historical forces which he cannot understand, predict, or control. His emotional reaction to this situation lies at the mid-point between psychosis—whose pure forms preclude communication and art—and "adjustment."

I would propose that fantasy assumes five dominant forms, singly or combined. It may alienate the characters from the setting by placing humans in a non-human environment. Anthropomorphism may endow subhuman entities with human characteristics. The intervention of supernatural characters may create a sense of estrangement in the human characters who confront them. Magical wish fulfillment, erotic or otherwise, alienates characters by detaching them from the restraints of the real world. Finally, the narrative structure may disorient the characters and the reader by confronting them with disruptions of their ordinary mental categories: spatial, temporal, and logical continuity.

Humans in a Non-Human Environment

Jules Verne's and H. G. Wells' sagas of journeys to the moon, under the sea, or to the center of the earth are classic examples. The progress of technology steadily shrinks this domain by making more and more formerly alien environments accessible to man. At the same time the anthropomorphic domain increases as we learn more about other forms of life.

Anthropomorphism

Latent in the common rhetorical figures of apostrophe, prosopopoeia, and personification, this mode comes into being when adult human attributes—speech, planning, volition—are ascribed to children (*If; The Bad Seed*) or to non-human concepts or entities who then become actors in a drama (*Flatland; 2001: A Space Odyssey; Star Wars;* Fabre's insects). The benign epitome of such fantasy is the familiar cartoon of a large, complicated computer cut away to reveal a little man in an undershirt, a glass of beer beside him, doing the computations for the machine with pencil and scratch pad. This mode should be distinguished from conventional allegories in which human beings are represented as animals (La Fontaine's *Fables*) or abstractions as human beings (*Le Roman de la Rose; Pilgrim's Progress*). In such allegories the human protagonist, if any, is neither amazed nor horrified by the beings he encounters. The effect of the alienation which characterizes serious fantasy literature, and which is generally absent from the erotic wish fulfillment type, can enter into the anthropomorphic type when the ultimate destiny of a human character is involved (most frequently, he is threatened with death), and when the threat comes from a role reversal which transforms the powerless into the powerful, the servant into the master. The child who dominates the adult, the hunted who becomes the hunter, the malevolent machine, the guardian who betrays, all illustrate this pattern. Without such a threat, role reversal amounts to no more than an episodic, anodyne saturnalia.

Naive Erotic Wish Fulfillment

Théophile Gautier frequently exploited this genre. In his stories a ghost, corpse, tapestry figure, or even a coffee pot transforms itself into a voluptuous woman infatuated with the hero. When such tales are expanded to novel length, as in Villiers' *L'Eve future* or Charles Williams' *Descent into Hell*, they characteristically add a cautionary moral regarding the soullessness of pure gratification. When the sexual object acquires the additional attribute of a source of artistic inspiration, it becomes a muse figure, as in Gautier's *Spirite*, shifting the tale in the direction of conventional allegory.[26] Tales of non-erotic gratification through magic (Balzac's *La Peau de chagrin*) are uncommon in French romanticism.

Intervention of Supernatural Beings

All hostile superior beings may be interpreted as an unavowed aspect of the self in revolt against repression. This vast category of the fantastic includes all tales of devils, monsters, vampires, apparitions, and so forth, morally inferior to man and yet superior in power. As for benevolent supernatural intervention, the notion is an old one. The obvious gulf between the powers of men and gods has induced writers to people the intervening void with spirits ever since Hesiod asserted that the souls of persons from the Golden Age remained on earth to guide their descendants. Around A.D. 500, the pseudo-Dionysus had Christianized this idea by proposing a hierarchy of angels ranked according to their respective degrees of illumination. Gregory the Great later revised these categories to form the nine orders of angels familiar in Catholic literature.[27] This scheme has inspired writers as recent as Anatole France in his *Révolte des anges* (1914). The romantics imagined many ranks between men and angels on the Great Chain of Being (in French: "l'échelle des êtres"), which could be peopled by poetic beings such as gnomes, sylphs, and fairies.[28] In general, A. O. Lovejoy speculates, our abiding fascination with "the missing link," "ape-men," the Abominable Snowman, and kindred legends derives from the subconscious idea of a continuous hierarchy of beings.[29] In any event, Nodier explicitly identifies his character "La Fée aux Miettes" with a species superior to man in the Great Chain of Being, and calls Michel, the hero of the same story, a superior soul placed by mistake in a human body.[30]

Since the authors of French romantic dream narratives feel ambivalent toward their fantasies, however, their supernatural characters usually do not have such a clear-cut rank and moral status as does Nodier's Fée. It is difficult to tell whether they are saved, damned, or neither. The narrator of *Aurélia* prays for her salvation and sees her being dragged down into an abyss, yet she also functions as a reigning goddess and a Beatrice figure. Nodier's Trilby belongs to "a mysterious race whose destiny is not yet irrevocably fixed" in the mind of God (*C*, p. 107). Lautréamont's Maldoror falls altogether outside the categories of Christian thought: "nobody knows where he comes from nor what is his ultimate purpose" (*OC*, Chant VI, stanza 8, p. 241). Nerval once speculated that Lucifer may not be damned, that he may be like Pan or Demogorgon.[31] Generally speaking, many writers and philosophers believed that the elemental spirits—gnomes, sylphs, salamanders, and undines—did not take part in the struggle between God and Satan. Until the coming of Christ, they had a certain power over men and the elements. The legend of the giant Arthur in Nodier's *Trilby* exemplifies this belief. Such moral ambiguity is equally reflected in the status of the fairies in medieval folklore, and in that of the White Lady of Avenel in Scott's *The Monastery*. In such supernatural tales, apparitions and spirits are associated, sometimes directly and sometimes by implication, with the unconscious. Orthodox Christianity of the period asserted that all inexplicable phenomena were delusions and snares devised by Satan. In contrast, the visionary romantics like Jung after them believed that the contents of the unconscious as such are morally neutral—as is Nature itself—because they are dissociated from the structures of what we would today call the superego (see Jung, *MAHS*, p. 103).

When supernatural intervention occurs merely episodically within a work, it constitutes what the French call the *merveilleux*, as opposed to the fantastic in the strict sense. In the *merveilleux*, the intervening being is usually benevolent. Therefore his superior powers do not create a sense of estrangement by calling into question the widely accepted hierarchy of the Great Chain of Being, in which the superior is always morally better. If he is malevolent, the sense of estrangment is usually neutralized because the superior being is allegorical or is part of a familiar literary convention (e.g., the Goddess Discord). Examples of the *merveilleux* are the angels, gods, or spirits of the dead who appear to advise and encourage the heroes of epics, or the wish-fulfilling fairy godmothers of folktale.

Disruption of Normal Mental Categories

The fantastic narrative may violate our normal expectations of spatial, temporal, or logical continuity, or a combination of these. We may perceive the effects of the imaginative thought of either narrator or protagonist without being shown its causes. These causes may be located in the verbal medium rather than in the story—in the mechanisms of word play and in free-associative concatenations of sound and meaning, as in the work of Sterne and Rabelais, in Nodier's *Histoire du roi de Bohème*, or in the surrealists.

Romantic dream literature per se combines two modes of fantasy: the disruption of normal mental categories, and the intervention of a supernatural being, who functions as the dramatic mover. These are the two modes of fantasy which can suggest that a revelation of some transcendent order may be granted to the protagonist. Disruption usually results from a narrative structure of nesting layers (suggesting regression to earlier stages of psychic development) or from an involuntary defensive repression and redirection of attention on the part of the protagonist. The climax of such works is informed by the archetype of Inversion—a peripety accompanied by a sudden reversal of values.[32] In the optimistic form typical of the romantic dream, this reversal means that what seemed bad, proves good: the Beatitudes; Christ's Passion; Dante's descent beneath Lucifer's feet to discover that down is up.

Dream narratives by Balzac, Mérimée, and Gautier employ supernatural intervention and inversion but lack discontinuity. In contrast, the structure of the more authentic dream narratives by Nodier, Nerval, Lautréamont and Flaubert is "diaphoric": it juxtaposes apparently unrelated events and characters, often separated widely in time and space. Thus it imitates the dream work—dislocation and distortion as a defensive disguise. But our authors insist upon the hidden, underlying coherence of their narratives. As the narrator of Nerval's *Aurélia* declares:

> I resolved to hold the dream fast and to learn its secret . . . Isn't it possible to tame this alluring, fearsome illusion, to impose discipline on those nocturnal spirits who make sport of our reason? . . . I thought I understood that there was a link between the outer and the inner world; that only inattentiveness or mental disorder conceal their obvious relationships—this explains why some images are strange, like those distorted appearances of real objects reflected upon the surface of troubled waters.[33]

Nodier's preface to *Smarra*, the beginning of Lautréamont's fifth *Chant de Maldoror*, and Flaubert's manuscript notes and correspondence regarding *La Tentation de saint Antoine*[34] all concur with Nerval. So the apparent discontinuities in the romantic dream narrative invite us to participate through the imaginative act of interpretation.

Our authors believe that such participation will lead us to religious revelation. This is evident in Flaubert and Lautréamont, whose heroes encounter Satan and God, respectively. Even these authors, like their more optimistic precursors, are largely concerned with depicting the contemplation of the sacred. At the outset of *Aurélia*, Nerval calls his dream life a *vita nuova*. And Nodier insists that "the Bible, which is the only book that we are obligated to consider true, bases its most valuable traditions on the revelations of sleep."[35] Nodier's *Lydie ou la résurrection* is little more than a lightly dramatized theosophist tract.

So if one takes the claims of the romantic dream at face value, it is anagogic: it represents inner psychic forces striving for a constructive resolution in the maturation of the hero. From a Freudian viewpoint, however, it seems regressive, for it characteristically associates love with death—an association which, as Todorov has rightly observed, characterizes the fantastic in general. The union of Nodier's Trilby and of the hero of *Aurélia* with the women they love can be consummated, if at all, only in death. In Nodier's *Smarra*, Polémon goes to bed with Méroé, only to be tortured by her and her paramour, until finally she rips out his heart and devours it raw. Nodier's Michel in *La Fée aux Miettes* feels a "nearly fatal ecstasy" with his Belkiss, and can rejoin her only by leaving the world of men in two ways: first by being shut up in an asylum, then by ascending into the upper air. Maldoror's sexual acts are immediately followed by or replaced with cruelty and murder. Flaubert's Saint Anthony has lustful fantasies of a naked woman being beaten, fearful fantasies of his old mother's body being devoured by jackals (animals which Flaubert, a few pages later, associates explicitly with lust), and finally identifies the twin phantoms of Lust and Death, both women, as "the devil in his double aspect."

A Freudian interpreting the love-death relationship would say that our preconscious preserves childhood memories of having been left alone by the beloved parent. This parent's later death is experienced as a similar abandonment: it reactivates subliminal fantasies of child-like helplessness. So we construct compensatory visions of reunion in the Beyond, "the mysterious land of boundless possibilities." Since to the child death merely means departure, in our unconscious, which is ruled by archaic, infantile emotions, death "can then come to signify simply setting forth with the beloved [parent] away from the disturbing influence of the hated [rival parent]."[36] The child-like unconscious secretly wishes to die so as to possess the loved one forever. Moreover, all liberties may be taken with a dead person's unresisting body. Such erotic fantasies finally degenerate into sadism as the dream regresses to ever deeper psychic·layers. The most primitive form of such sadism is devouring the corpse's decaying flesh, an episode which occurs at the central climax of

Smarra as well as—overtly incestuous—in the visions of Maldoror and Saint Anthony.

According to Freudian theory, nightmares express mental conflict over incestuous desires. The dream work disguises these desires by transforming the dead relatives who have aroused sexual feelings into supernatural beings. A secondary ego defense of psychic projection then attributes to the dead the dreamer's desire for reunion with them. Hence the flirtations of La Fée aux Miettes and the legends of vampires such as those who plague Maldoror and Nodier's Polémon in *Smarra*.

I would agree that in the love/death fantasy the undertones of a childhood attraction to the parents—an attraction which becomes retrospectively guilt-producing under the stress of adult sexuality and its taboos—may arouse in the dreamer's psyche images of his injury, death, or imprisonment as punishment for such forbidden feelings. Desire and its punishment may be represented simultaneously. Thus Nodier's heroes who are led to the guillotine in *Smarra* and in *La Fée aux Miettes* are observed, respectively, by young men with female companions whom Nodier describes as "their lovers or their mothers," and by girls with male companions whom Nodier describes as "their fathers or their lovers," and who caress them. "Either-or" means "both-and" in dreams: these paternal figures are *also* lovers. Decapitation is punishment for being sexually aroused by them.

Romantic authors of fantasy were not more emotionally immature and mentally unbalanced than writers of other periods. Their fiction gives this impression because it brings to light the infantile strata of the mind and their continuing influence on our fantasy lives. So one must modify the Freudian insights concerning the nightmare as they apply to the romantic literary dreams by distinguishing the insightful authors from their troubled creations. Moreover, the association of love with death has a collective meaning as well as an individual one. Because the dead are people whom the living dreamers have known only in the past, to encounter dead loved ones in a dream is to return to a past reexperienced and transformed. In an age shaken by political turmoil, the Industrial Revolution, and the decline of religious institutions, works like *Sylvie* or *Trilby* employ the love-death equation to express nostalgia for a simpler, bygone age: rural, Catholic, and monarchical. A love which endures after death is one which transcends the emotional and physical vicissitudes of the material order. An age which has lost its religious faith, as had the early nineteenth century, seeks a semblance of divine love from idealized creatures. Finally, our authors may explicitly depict the supernatural loved person as a psychopomp, or guide for spiritual development. This figure, the "third force" in the psyche, represents the impulse toward constructive personality change. Goethe refers to this notion at the end of *Faust* by saying that the Eternal Feminine leads us on. Since sexual and aggressive impulses are only intermittent in human beings, and since parents and parent figures spend more time playing the roles of teachers, trainers, and guides than they do those of potential sexual objects—both in real life and in fantasy—it is natural for superior beings in the romantic dream to represent sources of unexpected or forgotten wisdom.

The anagogic dimension of the romantic dream is obscured because dreams dramatize problems more than solutions. Much of their energy and content is usually devoted to depicting the obstacles to personal development: anxiety, primordial lust and agression, regressive dependency needs. Since dreams provide a theater for the harmless acting out of unsatisfactory solutions, their material outcome often seems disastrous and their emotional climate infantile. The central problem of dreams, both real and literary, is that they confront us with ugly, debased, threatening visions of ourselves—the repressed id impulses. We risk feeling too defeated and discredited to hope for further development. The double in Nerval's *Aurélia* and the devil in Flaubert's *Tentation de saint Antoine* dramatize this situation. If we shrink from the confrontation with the repressed "unworthy" traits of our unconscious—the Jungian Shadow—they become our enemy and rival the ego for control of the personality. But if we acknowledge the Shadow and attempt communication, it becomes our helper and brother. Then an intuition may reveal the fantastic—a projection of the protagonist's unconscious—as no longer alien. He accedes to a superior stage of maturation. The narrator of *Aurélia* ascends with the lover-mother-goddess into heaven; Nodier's Michel sees his grotesque, dwarfish wife transformed into the lovely Queen of Sheba; Saint Anthony overcomes demonic temptations and perceives Christ's face in the rising sun.

The resolution of the fantastic tale by revelation is usually overlooked by theoreticians of the genre. At best, they consider it as merely an episode tacked onto the story, rather than as a decisive reconciliation of conscious and unconscious. Todorov, for example, in his *Introduction à la littérature fantastique*, defines the fantastic as an event which the familiar laws of our world cannot explain. He claims that there are four possible ways of dealing with such an event in fiction: the mystery may remain unresolved; the event may be integrated into a system of religious belief; a rational, material causality may be revealed; or the fantastic event may be dismissed as a trivial illusion of the senses. But our romantic dream narratives fit none of these categories. They may not be explained away: the authors claim their visions to be as real and true as waking life. They may not be integrated into a system of religious belief: they are concerned with an individual rather than a collective destiny. In fact the romantic dream is doing what Todorov claims was not done until the advent of psychoanalysis: the fantastic, serving the social function of providing an acceptable way of expressing the inadmissible, is superseded by a myth of the unconscious.

So each romantic dream must be read in at least two ways: rationalistically, as psychopathology, and mythically, as a striving for the realization of a new spiritual order. In the words of Edward Glover, a Freudian of unimpeachable orthodoxy, the romantic dream narrative, like other art, illustrates "the processes of *compromise-formation* whereby repressed and repressing forces can obtain expression in one and the same product. [The work of art must] not only represent the kernel fantasies giving rise to conflict in the mind of the artist, but also the expiation or negation of these same fantasies."[37] I agree, except that for the words "expiation or negation" I would substitute "sublimation or integration." For this integration, the Jungian archetypes are the essential vehicles.

The romantic dream narrative, like many a fairy tale, begins with an implicit but imperative call to self-definition. The hero finds himself isolated. One or both parents are absent or unmentioned. If the hero has friends (as in *Sylvie, Aurélia, La Fée aux Miettes*), they do not understand him. The absence of a suitable role model and of a tradition to inherit impels the hero to leave home and seek his mature identity elsewhere.

The archetype of the Quest usually informs the romantic dream narrative. The building, room, city, hut, cave, or theater in which the protagonist finds himself at the outset represents his undeveloped personality, his initial mode of being, as a *given*. Mentally or physically, the hero soon departs from his initial location and wanders from place to place. At first his search leads only to the "wrong" place symbolizing blocked psychic development: prison, madhouse, ordeal, or servitude. Ultimately he recognizes another room, building, or city as his goal, and he attempts to enter (compare Kafka's *Castle*, the fortress in *Le Roman de la Rose*, etc.). Caught up in the strenuous labyrinth of maturation, he may never reach his promised land. The heroes of *Smarra* are struck down outside the city they are besieging; Maldoror, immobilized, fails to storm the gates of heaven; both Maldoror-Lautréamont and Lorenzo-Lucius finally awake to find themselves back in their own bedrooms, defeated.

The narrator of *Sylvie* enters several rooms, but in none of them is union with the loved woman possible. Even when heroes "succeed" in the romantic dream, the locus of their triumph is at best ambivalent. In *Trilby*, Jeannie falls into an open grave and receives her supreme illumination as she dies; Nodier's Michel and the narrator of *Aurélia* achieve apotheosis in a madhouse; Saint Anthony's final divine vision follows a series of demonic visions in the desert.[38]

With such ambiguous outcomes, the romantic dream implies that self-actualization is impossible in ordinary human society. Balzac's *Louis Lambert* for instance, drives this point home. But there is also a profounder, personal reason for the equivocal denouements. The heroes of the romantic dream are not the whole self, but only part of it. They embody the desire and drive for maturation, "the symbolic means by which the ego separates itself from the archetypes evoked by the parental images in early childhood."[39] Therefore they become expendable once maturity is attained. They may assume the role of the father, but they may also die or disappear. This does not mean that their quest was a failure: it simply means that in the work of art—unlike life—the strife is over, the battle won, and the energy provided by the hero no longer is needed to foment change.

From a rationalistic viewpoint, which would interpret the narrative and judge its resolution as if it were a sample of waking reality, the heroes' adventures end in dismal failure. If taken literally, the return to more primitive states of thinking in the course of the dream experience, and the fragmentary revival of earlier, more helpless stages of personality development, suggest a failure of maturation and a crippling regression in the face of stress. In this perspective, dream and fantasy represent, on the face of it, a failure to encounter and to cope with reality. They can depict three basic destinies for the dreamer who seeks self-definition. He may deny his shameful personality traits through repression or projection, leading to the obdurate return of the repressed through the very instruments of the repression, or to an explosion of horrifying visions embodying the repressed in disguised form. He may try to simplify his existence by retreating to an earlier stage of it—a protected childhood, or an infancy in which the mature self is absorbed by a parental self, an overwhelming punitive Father or a devouring Terrible Mother. Finally, he may indulge in self-glorifying, wish-fulfilling fantasies of limitless power and influence, corresponding to the oceanic feelings of infantile omnipotence remembered from earliest childhood. In sum, says Adelson, "dreaming on the whole is a regression to the dreamer's earliest condition, a revival of his childhood, of the instinctual forces which dominated it and of the methods of expression which were then available to him," except, I would add, that this childhood is complicated by the admixture of the dreamer's adult lust and rage.[40] All three of the regressive, disastrous outcomes of the dream reflect a retreat from menacing sexual and aggressive impulses, which the dreamer manages successfully to disguise.

On the mythic level, however, the dream makes the mysteries of human experience comprehensible by communicating them in a narrative form. The central thrust of romantic dreams and fantasies, interpreted mythically, is the quest for individuation, the reconciliation of the unconscious with the conscious parts of the personality.[41] Through symbolic disguise and displacement of identity, dreams grant indirect expression to the unconscious elements of the supraordinate personality—the whole self, including what is repressed from consciousness as well as what the ego consciousness retains in its sphere of awareness.[42] The supernatural beings who confront the dreamer embody some aspects of his unconscious: their appearance makes possible a union, through acknowledgment or recognition, of hitherto neglected areas of the personality. Thus apparitions may serve—particularly in nineteenth-century as opposed to classical and modern literature—as the catalyst for potentially constructive personality change.[43] Then the dominant romantic myth of paradise lost and paradise regained operates retrospectively to transform the nightmare confusion of the protagonist into a series of redemptive ordeals.

The literary dream, formerly subordinated to the visions of a Christian supernatural which it was charged to convey, acquired autonomy in romanticism: the medium became a message of imaginative freedom and the quest for self-definition.[44] The romantics annexed the logical anarchy of the unconscious to narrative structure through the doubling and splitting of characters, discontinuity, the archetype of Inversion, and the layering of narration, as Freud's study of wit and dreams was later to annex unconscious mental processes to the domain of science. Combining the mythic with the psychoanalytic view, the romantics arrived at the modern conclusion that the dream is an involuntary creative process, arising from the interplay of compulsions with strivings for self-realization.[45]

The romantic writer tried to play the same role toward his public as his supernatural apparitions played toward his protagonists. Nodier, Nerval, Hugo, Lamartine, and Ballanche believed that the creative artist's mission was to mediate between the spiritual order and ordinary men. They found an inspiring model in statements by Chateaubriand and Madame de Staël which identified poetry and religion, writer and priest. "At the end of an era of atheism and social dissolution, romantic literature has been the interpreter of all man's moral needs," claimed Nodier. Ballanche had stated even more explicitly that "the poet simply translates into human language what was revealed to him on the spiritual level. . . . It is always a religious truth that the poet is charged with communicating. Religion and poetry are one and the same. . . . The poet is a priest."[46] The torments and injustice of present-day society were explained by such thinkers as a series of redemptive, purifying trials. Aware, thanks to the poet's revelations, of the value of suffering and of his ultimate goal, man would make more rapid progress toward spiritual perfection and ultimate reunification with God.

II

The Denial of Self:
Repression and Psychic Projection

CHAPTER 3

Temptation and Repression in Nodier's *Trilby*

> *By ties mysterious link'd, our fated race*
> *Holds strange connexion with the sons of men.*
> —*Scott*, The Monastery

Nodier's preface to *Trilby*, although it mentions several literary sources, locates the tale's essential origins in folklore: "Like all popular traditions, this one has traveled around the world and can be found everywhere." This tradition, "the prettiest fancy devised by the modern imagination," relates the love of a superior being for a human, a love based on spiritual and emotional affinity as well as on sexual attraction (*C*, p. 96). This situation expresses man's desire for a love more perfect than that of which ordinary people are capable. Such love seeks a compromise between the sexual love of creatures and the spiritual love of God by choosing a love object intermediate between the two. It remains precariously balanced between seduction and suicide. The combination of these two extremes at the climax of romantic works produces a characteristic vignette: Chateaubriand's Atala, imagining herself in her lover's arms, while rolling through the debris of a shattered cosmos; Lautréamont's Maldoror, clasping a huge female shark in a chaste and hideous embrace, as they spiral down toward the bottom of the sea; Jeannie, achieving spiritual union with Trilby only when she falls into an open grave and dies.

The romance of the Scottish fairy Trilby and the beautiful fisher-man's wife Jeannie follows the same course as love in most of Nodier's other stories. Dissatisfied with an oppressive material order, two beings of superior sensitivity fall in love; obstacles intensify their passion; the suffering of separation purifies their souls; they find deliverance from frustration, at first in dreams, then in the permanent dream of madness, and finally in death. Nodier, like Nerval, associated dreams with death and madness as a threefold form of religious revelation.[1] But *Trilby*, unlike Nodier's other stories, employs three formal ceremonies of exorcism to dramatize the conflicts between a love ideal and reality. Both for society as a whole and for the individual, Nodier's exorcisms illus-trate the psychic mechanism of repression and its pyrrhic victory over the subject's libido.

By initially describing the fairies as having all the good and bad qualities of a spoiled child, Nodier suggests that they represent the spontaneous child in each of us, half-buried beneath the accretions of adult restraints (p.102). The most charming of them, Trilby, dwells in Jeannie's hearth and watches over her house and farmyard while she sleeps. He embodies Jeannie's *animus* or soul-image, a constellation of "masculine" personality traits repressed from a woman's consciousness. As Jung explains, the repressed *animus*-figure is unconsciously projected outward onto a person or image in the outside world. There results an unconditional, almost magical attraction between the female subject and the male figure selected as the vehicle for her fantasies.[2]

More precisely, Trilby represents a projection of "a particular form of the *animus* that lures women away from all human relationships and especially from all contact with real men. He personifies a cocoon of dreamy thoughts . . . which cut a woman off from the reality of life."[3] Jeannie loves Trilby in her daydreams, "cet espace indécis entre le repos et le réveil, où le coeur se rappelle malgré lui les impressions qu'il s'est efforcé d'éviter pendant le jour" ("that vague area between sleeping and waking, where the heart recollects despite itself the impressions it has struggled to avoid during the day"), but her sense of obligation toward her husband Dougal prevents her from summoning Trilby except during "l'erreur involontaire des songes" ("the involuntary error of dreams" [*C*, pp. 105, and 111]). Nodier's use of the words "despite itself" and "involuntary" shows that he is aware of a conflict between the moral imperatives of rational consciousness and the impulses of instinctive desire (libido), whose objects can reveal themselves only when the vigilance of the public self has relaxed.

"The relation between conscious and unconscious is compensatory," according to Jung. "This is one of the best-proven rules of dream interpretation. When we set out to interpret a dream, it is always helpful to ask: What conscious attitude does it compensate?"[4] Here Jeannie is unconsciously discontented with her childless marriage to Dougal, who is loyal, but harsh, insensitive, and inarticulate. "Il est vrai," she says, toward the end of the story, "que Dougal a quelquefois une humeur difficile et rigoureuse, mais je suis assurée qu'il m'aime. Il est vrai aussi qu'il ne sait pas exprimer les sentiments qu'il éprouve" ("It's true that Dougal can be harsh and difficult to get along with sometimes, but I'm sure he loves me. It's also true that he doesn't know how to express his feelings" [*C*, p. 141]). Her need to offer maternal and wifely affection, and to have it returned, finds an outlet in Trilby's timid flirtations with her as she dozes over her spinning wheel and in "the innocently voluptuous dreams" of a loving child which Trilby sends her.

Jeannie's wish-fulfilling fantasies will gradually invade her waking life and acquire hallucinatory force. At first she does not confide her fantasies to Dougal: at length, however, she does complain of Trilby's attentions. She feels vaguely guilty because she has become absorbed with thoughts of a male being other than her husband. She has found Trilby's courtship pleasurable: by describing it to Dougal as if it were a nuisance, she attempts to dissociate herself from her secret desires so as to absolve herself in her own eyes. Ronald, a hundred-year-old monk, arrives at this moment and, at Dougal's request, expels Trilby from the cottage by reciting the Litanies of the Virgin.[5] The plot provides no reason for Ronald's appearance here; it seems fortuitous. In this way Nodier implies that Jeannie's thoughts have summoned him: he functions as if he were an instrument of her superego. His great age associates him with previous generations, whose values and demands become introjected to form the superego during the course of personality development.[6]

This ceremony of exorcism is only the first of three in the story. They have a collective as well as an individual meaning. As Jung explains, the primitive mind uses the notion of spirits to explain the manifestations of the personal and collective unconscious. Some of these spirits take upon themselves the individual's guilt and responsibility for suppressed thoughts. A ceremony of exorcism gives social sanction to a "possessed" person's projections of inadmissible fantasies onto the outside world, where they assume the shape of spirits. These spirits become scapegoats, punished in place of the person who had imagined them.[7]

Ronald will return unexpectedly and conduct another exorcism the next time that Jeannie's conflict between love and marital duty becomes unendurable. But the outcome of events will demonstrate that Nodier does not consider repression an adequate solution to Jeannie's problem. To banish Trilby does not make her dissatisfaction disappear. It simply deprives that dissatisfaction of an outlet, so that it turns against her and becomes destructive.[8] The first exorcism results only in making Jeannie *consciously* unhappy in her marriage; the second one will drive her insane; and after the third, she dies.

After the first exorcism, Trilby soon reappears in Jeannie's dreams, but as a handsome young Scottish chieftain rather than a child. His sexual maturity and greater size reveal the increasing strength of Jeannie's fantasy and its now patently erotic character. Seeing him in his new form, she realizes that it is no longer possible to take an innocent interest in him. Fearing Trilby's return, she still longs for him and jealously imagines that he has found new shelter with women more aristocratic, wealthy, and beautiful than she.

Jeannie's complaints of Trilby's attentions amount to a tacit appeal for Dougal to treat her more affectionately, to demonstrate for her the solicitude she ascribed to Trilby. This implicit, unfavorable comparison between the phantom and himself hurts Dougal's feelings and causes him to withdraw further rather than inspiring him to act with greater tenderness toward his wife. In effect, his request for the exorcism means that he unconsciously refuses to acknowledge Jeannie's dissatisfaction. Consciously, however, Dougal's primitive mentality attributes Jeannie's unhappiness to a curse placed on her by evil spirits. He finds it embarrassing to acknowledge, even to himself, his jealousy of Trilby—that part of Jeannie's thoughts from which he is excluded. So he will again resort to religious intervention, in a more radical form (pp. 112–13); he undertakes a pilgrimage to Ronald's monastery of Balva.

Nodier's account of this pilgrimage attempts to enhance our estimation of Jeannie's love for Trilby by associating it with her unspoiled Christian faith and by contrasting her faith with the materialistic concerns of her fellow villagers. All Dougal's village makes this journey for the feast of Saint Columba. Like the crumbling monastery to which they go, their naive faith is falling into ruins at the time of the story, and when the building collapses, says the narrator, Satan shall rule for a time in Scotland. The pilgrims' self-centered petitions reflect this deterioration. Dougal prays that he will net a box of treasure. He seems to have been corrupted by an ambitious discontent with his life as a simple fisherman. Jeannie's female neighbors pray for fine clothes so as to outshine her at the next holiday. They envy her because Trilby's attachment proves her to be the loveliest woman in the village.

Ronald himself represents official Christianity corrupted by pride and intolerance. His very asceticism, since he advertises it to inspire respect, serves as the instrument of self-aggrandizement. He receives the pilgrims in the refectory, and attempts to incite them to enmity against the fairies. These beings have always treated Jeannie's village with benevolence, but to Ronald they represent a rival for the love and loyalty of his flock. He wishes to destroy all rivals. He urges the pilgrims to join in a collective curse, which, aided by his spiritual power, can be strong enough to expel all the fairies from Scotland, leaving Christianity to rule unchallenged. As she listens, Jeannie must decide whether to obey his religious authority at the cost of renouncing her love for Trilby.

Along the wall hangs a gallery of MacFarlane family portraits, a detail familiar to readers of the Gothic novel, in which the physical setting expresses the author's intuitive understanding of depth psychology. The portrait gallery suggests the total contents of the mind, childhood memories and present impressions alike, passed in review during a mental crisis. Jeannie's conflicting impulses are indirectly suggested by Nodier's description of two groups of MacFarlanes, servants of God and rebels. The earlier generations had paid tribute to the monastery out of gratitude to its founder, who drove the storm-giant Arthur from the land. More recent generations had forgotten their obligations to the monastery and oppressed it. There are empty spaces on the wall, from which the oppressors' portraits have been mysteriously hurled down. An isolated, veiled portrait seems to belong to neither group: its moral status is uncertain. This portrait can be explained in Jungian terms: the picture gallery or projection apparatus results from the *animus* mediating between the conscious and the unconscious. The *animus* transmits images from the unconscious, which become manifest in dreams and fantasies, particularly in a woman's imagined relations with fictional heroes and spirits who love or persecute her.[9] An intense, mysterious curiosity draws Jeannie away from Ronald's audience and toward the veiled portrait. Lifting the veil, she recognizes at a glance all the beloved features of her dreams. Her libido, projected upon the painted image, makes her perceive it as Trilby's face.

Ronald, meanwhile, in his harangue to the pilgrims, unwittingly admits to spiritual weakness by saying that the monks are forced to use the most uncompromising means to dissociate themselves from the "sinful" parts of their personality. Unlike Jeannie, who nourishes her dream, they combat it:

La haire sacrée et le cilice rigoureux des saintes épreuves ne nous défendent pas eux-mêmes contre les prestiges du mauvais esprit. . . . Oh! que de rêves délicieux ont assailli notre jeunesse! que d'ambitions criminelles ont tourmenté notre âge mur! que de regrets amers ont hâté la blancheur de nos cheveux, et de combien de remords nous arriverions chargés sous les yeux de notre Maître, si nous avions hésité à nous armer de malédictions et de vengeances contre l'esprit du péché! [*C*, p. 119]

[Even the blessed, rigorous hair shirt of religious ordeals does not protect us from the illusions created by the Evil One. . . . Oh! how many delightful dreams have assailed our youth! How many criminal ambitions have tortured our maturity! How many bitter regrets have turned our hair prematurely white, and how remorsefully would we come before our Master's sight, should we hesitate to arm ourselves with avenging maledictions against the spirit of sin!]

What really torments the monks is not an evil spirit but their unacknowledged thoughts. The more strongly the unconscious is repressed, Jung claims, the more destructive it becomes. When long denied an outlet, it may eventually erupt, as it does here, in spectacular apparitions of temptations and devils. Such terrors then create a vicious circle by inciting a redoubled effort at repression.[10]

The most recent persecution of the monks by the fairies, according to Ronald, occurred during a burial in the crypt, when the torches suddenly went out, leaving each monk to confront his own fears and desires alone.

La nuit si humide, si obscure, si redoubtable partout: effrayante, horrible sous le dôme de nos basiliques où est promis le jour éternel: . . . Nos moines éperdus s'égaraient . . . trompés par la confusion de leurs voix plaintives qui se heurtaient dans les échos et qui rapportaient à leurs oreilles des bruits de menace et de terreur, ils fuyaient épouvantés, prêtant des clameurs et des gémissements aux tristes images du tombeau qu'ils croyaient entendre pleurer. [*C*, p. 121]

[The night, so damp, so dark, so fearsome everywhere: terrifying, horrible beneath the dome of our basilicas where eternal light is promised! . . . Our frantic monks wandered helplessly . . . deceived by the confusion of their plaintive voices, which blended with the echoes and carried back threatening, terrifying noises to their ears, they fled in dismay, ascribing shouts and groans to the mournful tomb sculptures which they thought they heard weeping.]

What has happened, one may surmise, is that one monk's burial has reminded his fellows of their own death. Their resulting sense of the transience of life and its opportunities for pleasure temporarily weakens their religious faith, and reactivates their desires for the world they thought they had renounced. Ashamed to admit to these desires in themselves, the monks project them onto the outside world, which thus becomes menacing. Their own voices, disavowed by them, are then perceived as the voices of evil spirits.

Two monks die in this darkness and confusion. The hand of a saint's statue seems to seize one, who dies of fright. The other is crushed when the statue of the recently canonized Virgin of Lothian falls on him. She died of grief because she had been separated from her betrothed (*C*, p.122). This Virgin's odd credentials for sainthood suggest a heterodox morality whose highest values are idealized passion and *sensibilité*. Nodier insinuates this morality behind and around that of Ronald. These deaths, which the old monk ascribes to the persecution of spirits, Nodier implicitly presents as a liberation from the cruel frustrations of material existence and as the doorway to reunion with loved persons in the afterlife. The narrative implies that the young monk crushed by the girl's statue was her former fiancé. And later in the story, the revelation that Saint Columba is Trilby's brother as well as the patron saint of unhappy lovers further glorifies human passion by associating it with the disinterested *caritas* of a saint. But Ronald, by choosing Columba's feast day to execute his project of vengeance against the fairies, proves himself insensitive to the spiritual order. Urging the pilgrims to damn the fairies without hesitation, he says: "Savez-vous que la charité peut être un grand péché?" ("Do you know that Christian love can be a great sin?" [*C*, p. 119]).

When Ronald thus denies love, Jeannie overcomes her fear of him, inwardly rejects his authority, and rushes to the statue of Saint Columba to pray for Trilby's salvation. Her *animus*-image having erupted into her consciousness, the world becomes a replica of this inner face, permanently distorting her perception of reality. "C'en était fait pour elle," comments Nodier. "Rien ne pouvait plus la distraire de ses souvenirs" ("It was all up with her. From then on nothing could distract her from her memories" [p. 126]). Jeannie will henceforth consider the hallucinatory manifestations of her own unconscious to be a real lover. With the collective ceremony of exorcism, everyone else in her society has embraced the contrary delusion that such manifestations are the assaults of an external enemy.[11] Jeannie now has no way to reconcile her private self with social reality.

The story resumes several months later. Early the next spring, Jeannie is drifting with the tide in her boat on the Clyde River basin, musing. The landscape suggests spiritual transcendence. The extraordinarily clear upper air allows distant mountain peaks to be seen, and "tout se confondait dans une nuance indéfinissable et sans nom qui étonnait l'esprit d'une sensation si nouvelle qu'on aurait pu s'imaginer qu'on venait d'acquérir un sens" ("everything blended into a nameless, indefinable hue which astonished the mind with a sensation so novel that one could have imagined having acquired an extra sense" [*C*, p. 127]). Jeannie recalls the legend of the giant Arthur, separated from the nymph he loved by the walls of Edinburgh, and then driven by the prayers of Saint Oran from his refuge among the peaks that she now contemplates. Officially, this legend represents the triumph of a benevolent Christianity over destructive paganism. Having loved Trilby and lost him through the intolerance of institutional Christianity, Jeannie now understands Arthur's fate differently (p. 128). She no longer identifies herself with the society that expelled Arthur, for she has come emotionally to belong to the world of the giant and the vanishing heritage of folk traditions which had offered her the consoling image of Trilby.

As night falls, a frail voice calls from across the river. Jeannie rows there to find an aged dwarf, Trilby in disguise. Here, as frequently elsewhere, the dwarf symbolizes the unconscious, and his age implies spiritual wisdom.[12] The phallic overtones of a small male being evoke the reawakening of Jeannie's frustrated sexual feelings, as the beginning of the ensuing—and logically unmotivated—conversation reveals. It has to do with hibernating snakes and with catching fish in baskets.[13] Both the spiritual and the sexual implications of Jeannie's visions are sustained till the end of the story. Her ensuing behavior cannot be exclusively interpreted by a diagnosis of hallucinatory madness brought about by an erotic obsession, nor by a claim that she enjoys a superior sensitivity to the spiritual order. For Nodier seeks to create in his reader's mind an equilibrium of material and spiritual, of sentiment and reason.[14]

Without preparation, an implausible assortment of fantastic lights now floods the scene: the aurora borealis, falling stars, and phosphorescence (p. 132). Jeannie has either become deranged or is experiencing a visionary insight. Her memories of past love become stronger. Trilby doffs his disguise, and begins a passionate entreaty. His language, in keeping with the rest of Nodier's morally ambiguous narration, combines exalted spirituality with immoderate non-Christian passion: "Ah! le néant, l'enfer même n'aurait que des tourments imparfaits pour l'heureux damné dont les lèvres auraient effleuré tes lèvres" ("Ah! the void, even hell could not utterly torment the fortunate damned soul whose lips had brushed yours" [p. 138]). When Dougal approaches in his boat, Trilby dives into the water, to be fished up again in the form of the precious casket which Dougal had prayed for on his pilgrimage. Jeannie is told to carry it to their cottage.

The casket, like the dwarf, has an ambivalent meaning. In spiritual terms, the treasure inside is supernatural wisdom: it could be revealed by opening the casket and reestablishing contact with the secrets of the unconscious. In physical terms, to open the box would suggest Jeannie's sexual submission. In psychological terms, the closed box contains repressed memories. Trilby speaks from within the box, telling Jeannie he will be freed if she says she loves him. Then they can share a pure spiritual love: "L'amour que j'ai pour toi, ma Jeannie, n'est pas une affection de la terre. . . . Tes organes trop faibles encore n'ont pas compris l'amour ineffable d'une âme dégagée de tous les devoirs, et qui peut sans infidélité embrasser toutes les créatures de son choix d'une affection sans limites" ("The love I bear for you, my Jeannie, is not a terrestrial one. . . . Your senses are as yet too weak to comprehend the ineffable love of a soul freed from all duties, who can embrace without faithlessness all the creatures of his choice in a boundless affection" [p. 140]).

As in *Atala* or *Le Lys dans la vallée*, heaven would appear to mean the reconciliation of one's moral sense with one's instinctive desire. Until now, despite the author's obvious sympathy for him, Trilby might have proved either benevolent, or as wayward as any human lover of someone else's wife. In Jung's words, "our actual knowledge of the unconscious shows that it is a natural phenomenon and that, like Nature itself, it is at least *neutral*. It contains all aspects of human nature—light and dark, beautiful and ugly, good and evil, profound and silly."[15] The ambiguous nature of the *animus*-figure as it first appears is illustrated by Ronald's admission that Trilby belongs to a mysterious race whose destiny is still hidden in the mind of God (p. 107). But from this point on in the story, Trilby as *animus*-figure appears unequivocally in his positive aspect of spiritual guide.[16] Jeannie, however, still hears his words as an invitation to adultery. " 'Non, non,' dit Jeannie, en s'échappant avec effroi de la chambre. . . .'je ne trahirai jamais les serments que j'ai faits à Dougal. . . . qui sait si . . . ce n'est pas [le démon] qui me séduit dans les discours artificieux du lutin?' " (" 'No, no,' said Jeannie, fleeing from the room in terror. . . . 'I never shall break my vows to Dougal. . . . who knows whether . . . this is not [the Devil] seducing me with the fairy's artful talk?' " [p. 104]). Repeating her marriage vows, she runs from her cottage:

symbolically, the conflict between libido and superego drives her "out of her mind."

Fortuitously in terms of plot, inevitably in terms of Jeannie's psychology, Dougal and Ronald return, and the superego reasserts its dominance. Jeannie overhears Ronald say that the last of the evil spirits has been exiled, so she believes Trilby must have been found innocent by whatever spiritual powers were to judge him. Trilby's seductive speech, she thinks, was a temptation which she had to resist successfully in order to prove herself worthy of eventual reunion with him. Calmer now, she goes to the shore to empty Dougal's nets. But when she returns she finds that Ronald has discovered Trilby hidden in the casket. The monk is engaged in his third and decisive act of exorcism. He will seal Trilby for a thousand years into l'Arbre du Saint, a giant beech tree associated with Saint Columba, standing in a graveyard. (The tree, representing both tomb and chrysalis in archetypal symbolism, promises rebirth.) Running to help Trilby, Jeannie herself falls into an open grave and dies of shock. She must perish when Trilby does; their destinies (as Nodier implies by using the word "destiny" to explain her death) are one.

As she dies, a sudden insight allows Jeannie to understand the spiritual love Trilby spoke of, a love which can embrace all creatures without disloyalty. She looks at Trilby and her husband in turn. Her conscious and unconscious having been reconciled, Trilby is no longer her husband's rival. She realizes that *she* must take the initiative by introducing into her relationship with Dougal the tenderness she had yearned for. Perceiving him as a spiritual child needing guidance and consolation, she addresses him directly, affectionately using his first name for the first time in the story. With words he surely does not understand, she promises an afterlife together in another world: "Dougal, Daniel, mon bon Daniel, mille ans ne sont rien sur la terre . . . rien!" ("Dougal, Daniel, my good Daniel, a thousand years are nothing on this earth . . . nothing!" [p. 144]). In death, the dream that never ends, Jeannie's desires shall be innocently fulfilled. And, as the last believer in Trilby's vanished race, she attains in death the heroic stature of an embodiment of the poetic principle.

Upon Jeannie's individual drama, *Trilby* superimposes the collective tragedy of a society that forfeits an earthly paradise by sinning against the imagination. At the beginning of the story, the fisherfolk believe in fairies and spirits as much as they believe in the saints. Jeannie, at her spinning wheel, unself-consciously sings the canticle of Saint Dunstan together with the ballad of the ghost of Aberfoil (p. 104). But the malediction directed against the fairies, "cet ennemi inconnu qui ne s'était manifesté que par des bienfaits" ("that unknown enemy who had made his presence felt only with good deeds" [p. 123]), expels them from Scotland forever, and destroys the Scottish peasants' once idyllic communion with nature. Self-exiled from paradise unawares, they must henceforth toil to earn their bread with the sweat of their brow. And the romantically individualistic, self-sufficient life of the rural fisherman whom Nodier portrays will soon be overwhelmed by the urban civilization looming in the background of the story.[17]

Nodier's authorial comments make it clear that he would have preferred things otherwise. He felt a generalized distaste for the post-Revolutionary world and for its commercialized literature. The first preface to *Trilby* sarcastically explained that the material progress of Nodier's day had made it impossible for the sophisticated Parisian public to appreciate folk literature (*C*, p. 97). As Balzac's *Contes bruns* and many other contemporary accounts suggest, Nodier did nevertheless come to terms with his milieu: he contributed actively and impressively to the "oral tradition" of the Paris salons.[18] But even toward the end of his career, he could not suppress his intense nostalgia for the lost world of folktales: "Those verbal enchantments, which recall to mind the happy existence of a bygone, untutored, virtuous age" (*C*, pp. 783–84). In opposition to commercial modern literature, he steadfastly upheld the folktale as an ideal:

> Pour en retrouver de faibles vestiges de la poésie et de l'âme, qui menacent de s'éteindre dans la littérature imprimée de nos jours, il faut . . . s'asseoir dans quelque village écarté, au coin du foyer des bonnes gens. C'est là que se retrouvent de touchantes et magnifiques traditions . . . qui passent de génération en génération, comme un pieux héritage, sur la parole infaillible et respectée des vieillards. . . . Hâtons-nous d'écouter les délicieuses histoires du peuple, avant qu'il les ait oubliées, avant qu'il en ait rougi, et que sa chaste poésie, honteuse d'être nue, ne soit couverte d'une voile comme Eve exilée du paradis. [*C*, p. 784]

> [To rediscover some faint traces of poetry and spirituality, which are threatened with extinction in the printed literature of our day, one must sit down at the good folks' fireside in some remote village. It is there that one finds touching, magnificent traditions . . . passed on from generation to generation, like a pious heritage, through the infallible, respected words of wise old men . . . . Let us hasten to listen to the delightful stories of the people, before they have forgotten them, before they learn to blush at them, and before their chaste poetry, ashamed of its nakedness, covers itself with a veil like Eve exiled from Paradise.]

The wisdom Nodier finds in folk traditions, and tries to recapture in his *Contes*, makes him a reactionary in terms of literary history.[19] At the same time, his attitude expresses an intuitive awareness of a collective unconscious which leads to innovation in the literary depiction of depth psychology. From a Jungian viewpoint, *Trilby* employs folk traditions in such a way as to situate the struggle between a woman's moral sensibility and her instinctive desire in the context of rural Scottish myths. By interweaving the dramas of the personal and the collective unconscious, Nodier inaugurates in France the kind of psychoanalytic narration on two levels which, together with Goethe's *Faust* and German romanticism, will help inspire, and reach its culmination in, Nerval's *Sylvie* and *Aurélia*.

CHAPTER 4

Projection as Ego Defense:
Flaubert's *Tentation de saint Antoine*

Pas un atome de matière qui ne contienne la pensée.
—*Flaubert to Louise Colet, March 27, 1853*

The earliest recorded products of Flaubert's imagination foreshadow *La Tentation de saint Antoine.*[1] The saint, perhaps the most imaginative of Flaubert's characters, was temperamentally close to his author. Both men withdrew from society (Flaubert only intermittently, of course) in response to an overwhelming vocation; both struggled to control an exuberant fantasy life by means of austere self-discipline. Flaubert confessed that he wanted to castrate himself when he was nineteen and that for two years around that time he didn't touch a woman. "There comes a moment when you need to make yourself suffer, to loathe your flesh, to throw mud in its face because it seems so frightful to you. Without my love of form, I might perhaps have been a great mystic."[2] In later life, Flaubert liked to style himself as a spiritual descendant of Saint Polycarp—a bishop of Smyrna who frequently inveighed against his age. From 1877 on, a series of annual banquets honored Flaubert and this patron saint together.[3]

On first consideration, one might expect contrasting reactions from the artist and the saint toward the feast of visions which came to each in his solitude. The saint would attempt to repress them as distractions from the thought of God: the artist would welcome them as desirable sources of inspiration. But Flaubert embraced a cult of art which saw

47

truth and beauty as identical.[4] He became extremely self-critical, believing that many of the products of his imagination derived from personal weaknesses or needs and did not point toward a transcendent aesthetic truth. The reactions of his friends and of society toward the *Tentation* encouraged him in this belief. After Louis Bouilhet and Maxime Du Camp heard the 1848–1849 version, they criticized it severely: they judged it as a self-indulgence in incoherent fantasies which, if continued, would threaten Flaubert's career as a writer. The episodes from the second version, published in *L'Artiste* in 1856 and 1857, were received by the public with indifference while being used as supporting evidence by the government prosecutor Pinard at Flaubert's trial for subverting public morals with the publication of *Madame Bovary.* Flaubert took these negative reactions to heart. To prevent himself from merely wallowing in the slough of his own emotions as he wrote, he subjected his creative process to the threefold discipline of a faithful depiction of real places; a serious effort at historical documentation; and a careful identification of plausible sources in the external world for his characters' wild imaginings.

From late 1849 to 1851, Flaubert's journey to the Middle East with Maxime Du Camp brought the physical setting of the *Tentation* to life for him. They chartered a boat for a five-month trip up the Nile. Flaubert saw the region of Thebes where Saint Anthony had lived and the holes in the cliffs formerly inhabited by hermits. He discussed the saint with local scholars, and from a Carmelite priest heard reminiscences which may have inspired Anthony's memories of his youth.[5] As soon as he left home, he began to keep a travel journal. These experiences made the settings of the 1856 and 1874 versions of the *Tentation* more precise and concrete than they had been before.

Flaubert's continuing readings in church history led him to remove from the *Tentation* many of the anachronisms present in the first version: the image of the Virgin, the rosary, the crucifix, the pig. As each successive version became shorter, the documentary sections concerning the heretics and pagan gods were enriched. They increase from about one-quarter of the 1849 version to over half of the 1874 version. As late as the first three months of 1870, Flaubert's correspondence reveals his concern for learning more about the early Christian church during the Alexandrian period, when it had just been sanctioned by the state and was triumphing over paganism, only to fragment into heresies once the external pressures of persecution and competing religions had been removed. Flaubert's choice of this period allowed him to indulge himself in depicting the heretics' fantastic cosmologies and weird deities under the pretext of faithful historical reporting. As Gide shrewdly put it with regard to *Salammbô*, "Does Flaubert really share Theophrastus' belief that carbuncles are formed from lynx's urine? No, of course not, but he's delighted that a citation of Theophrastus authorizes him to believe it—and the same with the rest."[6]

Neither historical scholarship nor direct observation of physical settings, however, could ensure the coherence of the work. Flaubert repeatedly expressed dissatisfaction with the 1849 and the 1856 versions because he thought they were lacking two essential elements: an overall organization and a unifying impression of Anthony's personality.[7] His travel and the resulting distance from familiar places appear to have stimulated in him, as early as 1850, the insight which was to govern his decisive revision of the *Tentation* some twenty years later: "The earliest impressions [of childhood] do not fade away, you know. We bear our past within us throughout our life; we feel the influence of our wet-nurse. When I analyze myself, I find within me, still fresh and with undiminished power . . . my childhood reveries."[8] By presenting Anthony's memories of his past as sources of his visions, Flaubert gradually moved from a conventionally medieval Christian, comic-epic episode in the unending struggle between good and evil to an inner, psychological depiction of the saint. Near the beginning of the second of three parts in the 1856 version, Anthony recalls his parents' house and his old mother weeping at his departure. And in 1856 Flaubert added a passage (later suppressed) which demonstrates his lucid understanding of the psychic mechanism of projection, the generative principle of the hallucinations which make up the *Tentation*. Anthony exclaims: "It seems to me that outside objects are penetrating my person, or rather that my thoughts are escaping from it like lightning bolts from a cloud, and assuming corporeal form of themselves, there . . . in front of me! Perhaps that's how God conceived the Creation?"[9] But it was Taine's queries concerning the nature of the artistic imagination which incited Flaubert, in 1866, explicitly to link hallucinations with memory: he says his own epileptic visions occurred "suddenly, like lightning, an invasion or rather an instantaneous bursting in *of memory*, for the true hallucination is nothing other than that—for me, at least. It's a sickness of the memory, an unloosing of its hidden contents. You feel images escaping from you like jets of blood."[10]

So as he began composing the final version of the *Tentation* late in July 1869, Flaubert was able to hope to find a logical connection between the saint's various hallucinations, without sacrificing the dramatic interest of his story.[11] He described Anthony's past experiences in much greater detail than in the 1856 version. He expanded the cursory mentions of Anthony's mother and of his childhood playmate Ammonaria into detailed scenes, into the quasi-explicit indications of the sources of his fantasies of lust and death in Part VII. Three letters received from Constantine, and Anthony's humiliation in theological debate at the Nicean Council, motivate his fantasies of power and revenge in Part II. The Bible reading introduced in 1856, now shifted to the beginning of the work, provides a "day residue" (an experience remembered from the previous waking period, and incorporated into a dream) to explain the origin of Anthony's visions of Nebuchadnezzar and the Queen of Sheba. His longing for his favorite disciple, Hilarion, prepares the reader for the events of Part III. His memories of heretics preaching in Alexandria anticipates the dream of the assembly of heretics in Part IV. His memories of wall paintings at the temple of Heliopolis, and of the ranks of idols carried by the barbarians who were making a treaty with the emperor, at the beginning of Part V, announce the procession of the gods which follows. In Part VI, the Devil's supreme attempt to destroy Anthony's belief in a personal god employs, as the saint later realizes, the arguments of the pre-Socratic philosophers concerning the infinite, the Creation, and the impossibility of attaining certitude.[12] The monstrous mural paintings he had seen at Belus, and a mosaic at Carthage, announce the visions of the Sphinx and Chimera and monsters in Part VII. In sum, the 1874 version provides a source in Anthony's lived experience for almost every major vision.[13] Once the coherence of the work had been assured in this fashion, Flaubert could reintroduce the powerful episodes which he had considered omitting or truncating in 1869 because they seemed to overshadow the depiction of the personality of the saint: Simon, Apollonius, the pagan gods, the monsters.

Physiological stimuli, on the other hand, remain a constant, albeit minor, source of visions throughout the three versions. Anthony's hunger and thirst stimulate dreams of gluttony, and the final assault of La Luxure is caused by what Flaubert identified, in a note from 1849, as "la bandaison matinale."[14] He later added the moonlit Nile as the catalyst for the vision of the Ophites' serpent, and the fire which singed the saint's beard as the stimulus for his dream of the Gymnosophist's funeral pyre (pp. 106, 120). For all his belief in the Devil, Saint Anthony acknowledges at least once, in the 1874 version, that the temptations he endures derive from his own body: "Pourquoi ces choses? Elles viennent des soulèvements de la chair" ("Why these things? They come from restless stirrings of the flesh" [pp. 38–39]). But as Flaubert progressively eliminated from the work the personified, exaggerated, schematized versions of Anthony's baser instincts, strengths, and weaknesses—the pig, the virtues, the sins, the Devil—and attenuated the comical physical descriptions of these entities and the quarrels among them (see pp. 212–22, 318ff., and 357–58 in the 1849 version), he multiplied indications that preconscious memories were the sources of Anthony's visions. These changes allowed him to decrease the number of other sorts of suggestions that Anthony's was a mental drama. So the proportion of his metaphors which explicitly evoke the saint's inner world diminishes from 57 percent in 1849 to 46 percent in 1856 and 24 percent in 1874. Those which survive are the less striking.[15] In compensation, from one draft to the next Flaubert made Anthony's subjective world more predominant by carefully eliminating many expressions which overtly shifted the focus of the visions and thus betrayed the structuring hand of the author. The margins of the final 1874 version bear the reminders "too many 'then's,' and the *suddenly*"; "too many *suddenly*'s, 'but's,' 'then's' "; "watch out for *little* and *suddenly*."[16] Moreover, after 1849 he prepared the reader much more carefully for Anthony's visions. The 1849 version introduces hallucinatory voices on page two; the pig talks on page four. The considerably shorter 1856 version describes wind noises which become voices only on page twenty-three (page nine of the 1874 manuscript), and the first apparitions appear only on page forty-three.

All three versions, however, employ the *mise en abyme* construction to imply the coexistence of conscious and unconscious mental levels, and the invasion of the former by the latter. The physical setting of the hermit's hut (Level I) contains elements—Bible, river, birds and animals, bread and water, torch, pebble, knife—which lead to memories and visions of Anthony's past, of biblical characters, of Satan, temptations, and heretics (Level II). Some of these beings describe their own visions (Level III), which include pagan gods who themselves speak (Level IV). At this same level, Satan attempts to supplant them and the Christian God as the ultimate reality, but he dissolves into the twofold phantom of Lust and Death, a phantom which is itself an illusion. At last (Level V) Saint Anthony makes contact with the primordial reality of life, embodied in monsters who themselves address him.[17] Fascinated and mentally engulfed, as it were, by their seething, pulsating mass, like Jonah by his whale, Anthony undergoes a sort of Night Sea Journey which, at daybreak, restores him to the vision of Christ or the integrated personality. The spatial and temporal confines of Anthony's visions, which have steadily expanded during his arrogant attempt to apprehend the transcendent through reason, suddenly retract to the minute scale of the biological cell, the ultimate secret (p. 275). Contemplating the cell finally opens before Anthony's gaze a heaven no longer void, but charged with meaning.

Those historical inaccuracies which Flaubert allowed to stand in 1874 enrich the psychological implications of the *Tentation*. That this Anthony can read, although the real saint could not, creates a secondary source of fantasies through Constantine's letters and the biblical passages. The exaggeration of repellent behavior in the depictions of the heretics expresses Anthony's resistance to heretical thoughts within himself. His location on a cliff above the Nile, though not historically correct, dramatizes the alluring terror of self-destruction. The poignant scene of family rupture at Anthony's departure—the weeping mother, reproachful sister, and desperate playmate (whom some sentimental critics inaccurately identify as Anthony's fiancée)—emphasizes the drama of self-definition and the quest for independence in Flaubert's version of the saint's life. In reality, Anthony's parents died before he left his native village, and he continued to live there for some years after their death. When his parents died, he arranged for his sister to be lodged in a religious establishment, and he had no known romantic attachment, nor any surrogate father to lead him away.[18]

Increasingly from one version to the next the Devil functions as a Jungian "Shadow," as the repressed "unworthy" part of Anthony's personality embodying all his repressed doubts and resistance to the will of God. Anthony's need to dissociate himself from his own impulses calls the Devil into being.[19] Once one recognizes the Devil as part of Saint Anthony, and the series of temptations as an inner debate, one can dismiss such literal-minded complaints as those of Paul Valéry, Jonathan Culler, and Michel Butor. Valéry complained that Anthony as a character is weak and uninteresting, overwhelmed by a mass of historical detail: "he scarcely exists. His reactions are disconcertingly weak. . . . He is tediously passive. . . . His responses are defeats. . . . It's as if Flaubert had been intoxicated by secondary issues at the expense of the main subject"; he missed his chance to be profound by studying the psychology of temptation.[20] Butor concurs, adding that nothing in particular happens to Anthony; his situation does not change; the next night the same temptations will no doubt return. Flaubert, claims Butor, arranged the incidents like a parade, aiming for a contrast and variety which would have the maximum effect upon the reader rather than upon the saint. He makes the Seven Deadly Sins return repeatedly in approximately the same order, creating a "spiral" structure.

On the contrary, however, Anthony's paralysis throughout most of the *Tentation* results from and expresses his inner conflicts. The Devil embodies his *libido sciendi* and rebellious mental surge toward self-sufficiency which clashes with his desire to submit to God. In the guise of Hilarion, the Devil grows in stature and impressiveness throughout the work. The setting of the visions, too, expands steadily from the local to the cosmic, from the historic to the mythic, from the personal to the universal, reflecting the hubristic efforts of the human intellect to subject externality to a system of thought. Having renounced active involvement with the world, the saint unconsciously craves a compensatory mastery of the world of ideas. When he achieves self-understanding, which includes the recognition of his mental limitations, the temptation ends (in its 1874 version) with the successful integration of the two sides of his personality. Having served his function of crystallizing Anthony's self-dissatisfaction, issuing an imperative call to self-examination, and being the catalyst for a constructive personality change, the Devil becomes expendable and disappears, like those devils who appear to Goethe's Faust and Dostoevsky's Ivan.

The earlier version of the *Tentation* had three parts: first the apparition of the personified sins and the heresiarchs; then Anthony's resulting fantasies of power, lust, and self-abasement; and finally the direct confrontation with Satan. The 1874 version has seven parts to suggest the Seven Deadly Sins. In Part I there are internal assaults on Anthony's virtue, arising from tendencies in his own personality. Voluntarily removed from society in the desert, then visually isolated from his surroundings by descending night, he weakens in his religious resolve. He regrets the lost possibilities for involvement with others in the past; nostalgic memories of companionship overwhelm him. Then he begins to hear hallucinatory voices. In Part II external assaults on Anthony's virtue begin. Temptations suggesting the Seven Deadly Sins assail him (they are defensively dissociated from himself through the psychic mechanism of projection). Sloth prepares the way for the others. Hallucinatory visions begin. In Part III internal assaults on Christian doctrine begin. The saint's own weakness in the face of temptation makes him doubt the faith he holds. Disguised as Anthony's favorite disciple, Hilarion, the Devil comes forward to ask insidious questions about the foundations of the saint's belief. Part IV depicts external assaults upon Christian doctrine. Projected outward, Anthony's doubts assume the form of heretics preaching their doctrines. Distressingly similar to Christians, they too have their martyrs and their scripture. Therefore Saint Anthony's ego ideal is threatened in Part V. His attempts to personify the guiding forces of the universe (in the form of the Holy Trinity) are mocked and parodied by a grotesque procession of barbaric gods. In Part VI Satan completes Anthony's alienation from the supernatural by taking him on a voyage through outer space to show that the transcendent has no personality: it cannot be apprehended by the human intellect. Thus, in Part VII, Anthony must confront the human condition without God—no grace, no afterlife—as represented by the twin phantoms of Lust and Death. But he succeeds in recognizing them as illusions concealing the continuity of all life. He renounces pride, associates himself with this continuity, and finally achieves psychic wholeness through a vision of Christ's face in the rising sun.

Flaubert's initial description suggests a polarity between Anthony's ascetic ambition and his weakness. The saint's cabin of mud and reeds—the baseness and frailty of the human condition—is located at the summit of a cliff—a precarious attempt at spiritual elevation. The empty desert below the cliff and the prominent book on a lectern within the cabin suggest that this will be an intellectual drama divorced from a social context. The river running through the desert below hints at mental depths from which unexpected thoughts may emerge; the absence of a door on the cabin implies that Anthony will have no way to shut these thoughts out. The opposition of spiritual aspiration and human frailty recurs in the third paragraph, which describes a tall cross planted in the ground—the idealized self-image—and a twisted old tree leaning over the abyss.[21]

Characteristically for romantic literature, sunset in the opening scene creates a change in lighting which corresponds to a transition from rational waking thought to an *état second* of involuntary impressions. But mentions and metaphors of dryness show that Anthony has lost contact with his unconscious—his tenderness and need for companionship. In his first speech he says that upon arising he used to pray; then he descended to bring back water from the river; then he prayed again: "Les deux bras étendus je sentais comme une fontaine de miséricorde qui s'épanchait du haut du ciel dans mon coeur. Elle est tarie, maintenant" ("Praying with my arms outstretched, I felt a fountain of mercy, as it were, flowing down to my heart from the heights of heaven. Now that fountain has run dry" [p. 3]). At the beginning of Part II we learn that Anthony's water jug is empty and his water pitcher broken (p.24). In short, the saint is undergoing the final crisis of human development: the struggle to achieve a sense of integrity rather than self-contempt. In old age, looking back over his entire life, he must convince himself that all his sacrifice has been worthwhile; that, despite his isolation, he exists in meaningful solidarity with other men, including those of other times and places; that his own life, a limited cycle which gives way to future generations, still contributes something irreplaceable to them.[22] The text states each alternative. Formerly, says Anthony, "mes moindres actions me semblaient alors des devoirs qui n'avaient rien de pénible" ("my least actions seemed to me at that time like duties which were not the least bit arduous"[p. 3]). But at the depths of his crisis, when Death says "Tu dois être fatigué par la monotonie des mêmes actions, la durée des jours, la laideur du monde, la bêtise du soleil!" ("You must be tired of the monotony of the same actions, the length of the days, the ugliness of the world, the stupidity of the sun!"), he answers "Oh! oui, tout ce qu'il éclaire me déplaît!" ("Oh! yes, everything it shines on displeases me!" [p. 252]). Chronic displeasure with the world masks disgust with oneself.

Adrift in the present, the saint seeks an identity in the past. He recalls the first, decisive suppression of the instinctual in his life: his departure from home and the three women—mother, sister and Ammonaria—who loved him. The well beside which he met Ammonaria each evening, and her tears, associate her with the symbolic motif of water as emotional fulfillment. Because Anthony repressed all feelings about women after he left home, his feelings for the three he remembers from childhood will assume an enormous importance in his psychic life.[23] His next association, between Ammonaria and a memory of a voluptuous naked woman being flogged (pp. 6, 40) reveals his unconscious connection between asceticism and repressed sexuality. Hilarion later draws an explicit parallel:

> Hypocrite qui s'enfonce dans la solitude pour se livrer mieux au débordement de ses convoitises! Tu te prives de viandes, de vin, d'étuves, d'esclaves et d'honneurs; mais comme tu laisses ton imagination t'offrir des banquets, des parfums, des femmes nues et des foules applaudissantes! Ta chasteté n'est qu'une corruption plus subtile, et ce mépris du monde l'impuissance de ta haine contre lui! [P. 59]

> [Hypocrite, you bury yourself in solitude the better to yield to your superabundant lusts! You deny yourself meat, wine, bathhouses, slaves, and honors; but how complaisantly you allow your imagination to offer you banquets, perfume, naked women, and applauding crowds! Your chastity is merely a more subtle form of corruption, and your contempt for the world, the powerlessness of your hatred for it.]

In response, the saint breaks into sobs.

Saint Anthony feels intensely lonely. The escapism at first embodied in his reminiscences becomes more explicit when he longs to join the passing birds or to sail on the boats he used to watch. As his desire for companionship grows, his fantasies become increasingly secular. At first he wishes that he had joined the monastic community at Nitria; then he thinks of being a priest among lay persons; finally he dreams of wordly occupations. After imagining a merchant kissing his wife, his desire for physical affection becomes so strong that he wishes to caress one of the jackals in a passing troop. In this first phase of temptation, Anthony acknowledges his own weakness as the source of his unworthy thoughts (p. 10) and reads the Bible in an attempt to redirect them. But his repressed impulses of gluttony, anger, pride, and avarice return through the very instrument of their repression: the passages Anthony notices seem to justify these impulses. So a new flood of fantasies wells up. They culminate in a series of lustful memories of the wealthy female penitents who used to visit him.

In the second phase of his temptation, Saint Anthony unwittingly exteriorizes his thoughts and dissociates himself from responsibility for them. This makes them less controllable. He imagines that the sound of the wind is harness bells tinkling in a procession which is bringing a female penitent to him. Momentarily ashamed when he calls out and then realizes the procession was imaginary, he quickly loses self-awareness again: the wind noise becomes hallucinatory voices cajoling him. Sharply defined visual hallucinations follow, bright and isolated against the night sky, very like the epileptic visions which Flaubert himself experienced and described. Anthony collapses into helpless passivity.

He enters a third phase of temptation as the second section of Flaubert's dream narrative begins. With the appearance of the Devil as "a vast shadow, more insubstantial than a natural shadow" while Anthony's eyes remain closed, Flaubert signals a modulation in the saint's perceptions from the natural-external to the supernatural-internal. No longer do the visions have an ostensible cause in the real world, yet their origin has now been personified as Satan, an external figure with whose activities the saint can deny any voluntary connection. At the same time, by dreaming that he is an Egyptian hermit—as he is in fact—he attempts to deny his real situation.

Incited by desire and consummated by repression, the resultant doubling of the self progressively becomes more marked. First the saint hallucinates rich food: his desires direct part of himself toward an external object. As soon as he manages to reject this temptation, a cornucopia of coins and jewels replaces it. More an intellectual than a sensualist, the saint becomes intoxicated with this false wealth. But when he throws himself upon it, it vanishes. This time he does not have the excuse of physical need, and the second stage of succumbing to temptation, the delectation of the mind, has given way to the third, the consent of the will.

As Saint Anthony realizes what he has done, his self-contempt becomes unendurable. He must project it outward, in the form of hostility against others more wealthy and comfortable than he: "On n'est pas plus imbécile et plus infâme. Je voudrais me battre, ou plutôt m'arracher de mon corps! Il y a trop longtemps que je me contiens! J'ai besoin de me venger, de frapper, de tuer! c'est comme si j'avais dans l'âme un troupeau de bêtes féroces" ("You can't be more stupid and vile. I'd like to strike myself, or better yet, tear myself out of my body! I've been holding myself in too long. I need to avenge myself, to lash out, to kill! It's as if I had a pack of wild beasts in my soul" [p. 29]). He seizes his knife to lash out at an imagined crowd, but collapses, "cataleptic" (p. 29), and the same movement through greed to vengeful repression recurs in another form. Anthony dreams that he is enjoying the rich novelty and diversity of city life in Alexandria. Then an invading army of desert monks destroys the city and massacres the inhabitants. He himself becomes one of the monks, meets all his enemies, and slaughters them. Trembling with pleasure, he wades in blood. He inhales its vapors and delights in feeling the bloody folds of his tunic clinging to his legs. His longing for civilized luxuries and his violent repression of this longing are successively enacted.

But repression creates frustration. This feeling is relieved by fantasies of power which transform the saint into the chief confidant of the emperor Constantine, while his rivals are humiliated. He then becomes the heathen king Nebuchadnezzar, planning to rebuild the Tower of Babel and dethrone God. Waking abruptly, the saint realizes he has sinned in thought. He flagellates himself, but the return of the repressed transforms the pain into voluptuous delight. First he imagines himself being beaten next to the naked woman he had remembered earlier; then the apparition of the amorous Queen of Sheba transposes the chain of visions from history to legend. She is simultaneously an archetypal *anima*-figure who can take the form of all women (p. 51) and the first incarnation of the Devil which is directly visible to Anthony. When the Shadow has been repressed, Shadow and *anima* combine in the unconscious. Their union may be expressed as a rape, as a kidnapping, as a marriage of the heroine by the villain (as in *Aurélia* and generally in melodrama), or, as it is here, by presenting woman in the guise of a demonic temptress.[24] The saint makes the sign of the cross and drives her away.

A dwarfish *puer senex* from the queen's train remains behind. The dwarf symbolizes the emerging contents of the unconscious. As child, he embodies the potential future self, here implying the hope for personal immortality through one's influence on others. His aged, wretched appearance threatens this hope. As Part III begins, he identifies himself as Anthony's former disciple Hilarion. This episode was added in the 1874 version, absorbing conversations with La Logique and La Science. It provides an effective transition between the erotic temptation of Part II and the heretical temptations of Part IV: it suggests that Anthony's potentialities for loving women and raising children were sublimated as affection for his disciples. In his first reminiscences he says Hilarion was like a son to him (p. 7). That Hilarion has emerged from the saint's preconscious through psychic projection is underlined by Flaubert, who has Hilarion say: "Apprends même que je ne t'ai jamais quitté. Mais tu passes de longues périodes sans m'apercevoir" ("Know, indeed, that I have never left you. But you spend long periods without noticing me" [p. 55]).

The disciple embodies an apparently harmless and even admirable form of Saint Anthony's pride in his intellect and desire to influence others by providing a model of religious devotion and an understanding of Christian doctrine for his pupils. But insofar as he wishes his disciples' loyalty and admiration to remain attached to him personally, he risks becoming infatuated with his own singularity at the expense of his service to God. Ahistorically, Flaubert makes pride in intellect and an excessive intellectual curiosity be Anthony's weakest point. When Hilarion tries to stimulate Anthony's vanity by denigrating his prominent disciple and biographer Athanasius, the saint vigorously rejects all the slanders. But Hilarion then calls Athanasius so limited intellectually that he admits he can understand nothing concerning the nature of the Word. In response, Anthony smiles, pleased at his own superiority, and agrees that Athanasius' mind is not very profound (p. 58).

So Hilarion encourages a debauchery of the mind. With specious humility, he points to internal contradictions in Christian dogma and revelation. Anthony admits that he has long been struggling against the doubts Hilarion has raised. They return so persistently, he says, that at times he fears he is damned. Hilarion promises that once Anthony employs his reason rather than trusting in revealed religion, the face of the unknown shall be revealed. He claims that mortification of the flesh in an attempt to obtain God's mercy is inferior, as a spiritual discipline, to efforts to understand the nature of God; that the religious person's only merit is his thirst for truth; and that outside the purview of dogma, there are no restrictions on intellectual speculation. Anthony responds eagerly that he senses his thought straining to burst free of the prison of the body. He thinks it may succeed. The saint does not yet realize the dangers of the Gnostic temptation of knowledge: reason may lead him into the sin of demanding that the transcendent God reveal himself and justify his ways to man, under penalty of ceasing to exist. This danger will emerge slowly.

Throughout Part IV, a parade of representatives of the heresies of the early Christian period addresses the saint. Hilarion uses them to attack tradition as a basis for belief. The heretics embody Saint Anthony's doubts: Flaubert locates this scene inside a building (an immense basilica), which suggests that the entire spectacle is happening inside the saint's head. He evokes all the major Gnostic heresies one by one, while disclosing their devastating influence on faith and morals.[25]

The general movement of the beginning of the fourth section reproduces that of the second one: repression; yielding to the flesh; a disgusted reaction of redoubled restraint; self-contempt destructively projected upon the outside world. But the visions are transposed from an individual and predominantly physical plane to a collective, intellectual one. The Manichean heretics' denial of the flesh (pp. 71–74) is justified by a series of spokesmen for other heresies who condemn the physical order as the creation of the Devil or of a deranged god (pp. 76–77). This same conviction leads still other heretics to debauchery until Tertullian appears. He harshly insists on subduing both body and mind: "Priez, jeûnez, pleurez, mortifiez-vous! Pas de philosophie! pas de livres! après Jésus, la science est inutile!" ("Pray, fast, weep, mortify yourselves! No philosophy! no books! after Jesus, knowledge is useless!" [p. 84]).[26] The vision culminates in the Circoncellions' frenzy of universal destruction. The heretics join in a howling chorus. Challenged by Anthony, they produce their apocryphal, uncanonical gospels to refute the claim that they possess no revelation.

The heretics surround Anthony and close in as if demanding that he acknowledge them as a repressed side of himself. Then the swelling coils of the serpent whom the Ophites believe is Christ fill the room where Anthony finds himself, and start drawing tightly around him. Rather than recognize this Shadow, he faints and drifts into a defensive countervision of Christian self-sacrifice in which he is among Christian martyrs at the Roman coliseum. The weeping, imprisoned martyrs suggest Anthony's condition of self-imposed sequestration in the ascetic life, in contrast to the joyous, active crowds outside the arena. The encircling animal menace has been transformed from the serpent into pacing, expectant beasts of prey. At first Anthony, transported with love, is eager to face them and die for the Lord. But his resolve weakens until he feels he would prefer any other death (pp. 108–11). The lion, which in conventional iconography can represent either Satan or Christ, stands for the morally ambiguous, indeterminate nature of one's own unrecognized unconscious.

This motif of the protagonist surrounded by animals, which may be either benevolent or hostile, recurs throughout Flaubert's career.[27] The heretics crowding around Anthony in Part IV, and the monsters in Part VII, constitute similar invitations to self-knowledge. At times the *anima*-figure is added at the center. For instance, in an 1845 dream Flaubert and his mother are taking a walk when monkeys suddenly surround them. After Flaubert, repelled by the creatures, has shot and wounded one of them, his mother reproachfully identifies them as his brothers. A similar image recurred in the *Tentation* from draft to draft, and was removed only at the last moment (NAF, 23667, fol. 73, which would have appeared on p. 143, line 12): Apollonius says that at the world's end he found monkeys gorged with milk (perfectly fulfilled in union with the feminine principle), with the Indian Venus dancing quite naked amidst them. The protagonist must realize that the *anima*'s bond with the animalistic Shadow expresses his own desire for her: then his unconscious may be integrated with ego consciousness.

The following scene, added only in April 1871, shows a visit of surviving relatives to the martyrs' graves, which degenerates into a sexual orgy. Fantasies of martyrdom by animals followed by an orgy symbolize a defective relationship between ego consciousness and the Shadow (perceived as a dangerous beast intent on devouring one), superseded by self-knowledge and the union of "male" and "female" principles of the psyche. But on the conscious level, the event signifies that exemplary self-sacrifice does not ensure that one's followers will be worthy and persevere in the faith. This is precisely what Anthony, who has withdrawn from society in order to regenerate it, has been worried about. He attempts to escape his dilemma, in fantasy, by imagining the self-sufficient gymnosophist, whose voluntary self-immolation does not depend on the behavior of followers to preserve its full meaning (pp. 117–19).

Yet Anthony has become calmer and more enlightened through this encounter with his unconscious. Rather than rejecting the heretics with horror as he did at first, he now recognizes the quest for God as a unity underlying all their extravagances (p. 121). The temptation of doubt gives way to that of pride. Apparitions of the supreme heretics Simon the Magician (rival to Saint Peter) and Apollonius of Tyana (rival to Christ) embody his ambition to become a miracle worker and to possess ultimate truth. Apollonius boasts of knowing all gods, all rites, all prayers and prophecies (p. 154). This claim provokes Anthony's curiosity concerning the pagan gods, leading to the parade of these in Part V (p. 161). And until the 1869 version (which preserves a trace of it on fol. 28), Flaubert gave Anthony a prideful reaction as he watched Apollonius depart which clearly anticipated the flight through space in Part VI: "Une ambition tumultueuse m'enlève à des hauteurs qui m'épouvantent, le sol fuit comme une onde, ma tête éclate" ("A tumultuous ambition raises me to fearsome heights; the ground is rushing away like a wave; my head is bursting").[28]

By moving the procession of the gods from the end of the *Tentation* to the middle in 1874, Flaubert freed Anthony's personal drama from its subordination to the sweep of religious history. The saint comes to represent human religious experience in general, not just one phase of it. He reflects the interest of Flaubert and his contemporaries, particularly since Chateaubriand and Constant, in the relativity of religious beliefs and their underlying resemblances. Non-Christian religions are seen not as impostures, but as the provisional forms of an eternal ideal. Such was the opinion of Parnassian poetry; of Renan (a major influence on the *Tentation*); of the opening pages of Quinet's *Génie des religions* (1841); of Jacobi's *Dictionnaire mythologique* (translated in 1846); and of the major source for Flaubert's Part V, Creuzer's *Les Religions de l'antiquité considérées principalement dans leurs formes symboliques et mythologiques* (translated in 1825 to 1851). Flaubert's *Tentation* reflects the ever-increasing influence in his day of the discipline of comparative religion: in 1849, the saint's only reaction to the dying gods is to say "so mine will pass also"; in 1856 he makes comparisons among them; and in 1874 Hilarion offers a virtual course in comparative mythology.[29]

In that final version, the chief of the Roman gods himself exclaims, "Tant qu'il y aura, n'importe où, une tête enfermant la pensée, qui haïsse le désordre et conçoive la Loi, l'esprit de Jupiter vivra!" ("As long as there exists anywhere at all a thinking being who hates disorder and conceives of Law, the spirit of Jupiter shall live!" [p. 207]). Any particular image of God, then, is an illusion—like Félicité's parrot—created by "our soul projected onto objects."[30] Flaubert's own *Correspondance* proves how completely he had freed himself from projected images of God, "demythologizing" his religious attitudes:

The way all the religions speak of God disgusts me: they treat Him so self-assuredly, frivolously and familiarly . . . *God's kindness, God's wrath, to offend God,* those are their words. That's thinking of Him as if He were a man, and worse yet, a bourgeois. And then they're hell-bent on decorating Him with attributes, the way savages put feathers on their fetiches. All that's barbaric. . . . Mankind's idea of God hasn't evolved beyond the notion of an oriental potentate surrounded by his courtiers. So the religious idea is lagging several centuries behind the political one.[31]

Flaubert tentatively considered reducing the procession of the gods sharply in the 1869 version, cutting the scene from forty-one to about three pages, so as not to divert attention from his characterization of the saint. But he managed instead to integrate the individual with the general by removing descriptions of gods which the little-traveled saint could not possibly have known, and by providing sources for the procession in Anthony's personal experience (pp. 161–62). This prevents an obvious authorial intrusion.

Anthony's reflection that matter must contain a spirit to have so much power, inspired by the pagan idols (p. 162), in effect constitutes an invocation to Hilarion, who reappears grown to colossal size. He serves as master of ceremonies, introducing a procession of idols at first ludicrous, then fearsome, and drawing parallels between beliefs concerning them and Christianity. The grotesque forms of the first, primitive gods in the procession reflect Anthony's initial shock and fear at encountering these products of his unconscious—personified pride, lust, rapacity, and rage. His resultant repression culminates in a polarization of good and evil: Ormuz, the Persian god of light, and his forces combat the legions of Ahriman, the god of darkness (pp. 182–84). But this compartmentalization is too artificial to be maintained—"the distance between the two of us is disappearing," says Ormuz in despair—and Anthony intuitively realizes that what he has repressed may be good. This clears the way for the *anima*-figures, manifesting the unconscious in their positive guise of Great mother goddesses, to appear: Diana of Ephesus, Cybele, and Isis. Besides bringing potential enlightenment, however, they also stimulate Anthony's desire to regress to a child-like closeness to his mother. "Comme c'est bon, le parfum des palmiers, le frémissement des feuilles vertes, la transparence des sources! Je voudrais me coucher tout à plat sur la terre pour la sentir contre mon coeur; et ma vie se retremperait dans sa jeunesse éternelle!" ("How good it is, the scent of the palm trees, the trembling green leaves, the limpid springs! I'd like to lie flat on the earth, feel it next to my heart; and my being would be immersed once again in the earth's eternal youth!" [p. 185]). The possible danger of this impulse to fuse with the *anima* emerges when Atys appears and emasculates himself in order to resemble sexually the goddess who loves him. He vanishes, and a coffin appears with a veiled figure which Anthony fears to recognize: the body could be himself, but it turns out to be made of wax—only the image of a tendency in his personality.

The Roman gods, greatest rivals of Anthony's Christianity, then march by and fall into the void. But Anthony feels no joy at their passing. Their very multiplicity and pervasive association with human activities, as Hilarion points out, had imparted a sacred character to human life (p. 203). For them to fade and die implies the de-sacralization of man's world. The last of them, the ahistorical Crepitus, god of flatulence, is juxtaposed with the Old Testament Jehovah in order to provide a derisive diaphoric commentary on the God of Moses. The latter's appearances of might and virtue are reduced to a mere evil-smelling void.

Generally speaking, the despair of the dying gods reflects Anthony's own despair at being unable to impose a structure on the universe through his imaginative and rational mental processes. To fill the void of the cosmos with his own personality is the saint's supreme temptation (one joyously embraced by Hugo in "Le Satyre"). Thus Hilarion at last identifies himself as "La Science" (p. 229), a way to knowledge that no religious myth can match. Anthony now recognizes Hilarion as the Devil, but at last agrees to confront him rather than trying to drive him off. Only thus, he realizes, can he be freed (p. 230). In the 1874 version, for the first time the ensuing journey through space results from Anthony's own choice. And he now sees that this Devil comes from within himself: he acknowledges the familiar demonic voice as an echo of his thoughts, a response from his memory (p. 232).

As Anthony ascends, the comforting structures and personalities projected onto the universe by the cosmologies of the ancients—the harmony of the spheres, the crystalline roof of the heavens, the spirits of the dead inhabiting the moon, the angels supporting the stars—all disappear (pp. 232–35). At first the saint feels a great joy at being enlightened. Scornfully he recalls his former ignorance, his mediocre dreams (p. 234). But then the Devil preaches a compound of Spinozistic doctrine and Kantian exposition of the limits of empirical knowledge.[32] The universe has no purpose. God is not a person. He is indivisible, contained in all things. Therefore the transcendent cannot be apprehended; Anthony must renounce hope for union with a personal God. He feels the entire meaning of his existence threatened:

> "Comment? mes oraisons, mes sanglots, les souffrances de ma chair, les transports de mon ardeur, tout cela se serait en allé vers un

mensonge . . . dans l'espace . . . inutilement—comme un cri d'oi-
seau, comme un tourbillon de feuilles mortes!"

Il pleure:

"Oh! non! Il y a par-dessus tout quelqu'un, une grande âme, un
Seigneur, un père, que mon coeur adore et qui doit m'aimer!" [Pp.
239–43]

["What? my prayers, my sobs, the sufferings of my flesh, my
transports of zeal, has that taken wing toward a lie? . . . in the
void . . . uselessly—like a bird's cry, like a whirlwind of dead
leaves!"

He weeps:

"Oh! no! higher than all, there is someone, a great soul, a Lord,
a father, whom my heart adores and who must love me!"]

"Perhaps there is nothing," the Devil replies. "So worship me! and curse
that phantom you call God!"

In the earlier versions, Anthony is saved by accident: his hand
brushes against his rosary as the Devil is about to devour him. In the
1874 version, Flaubert consistently reorients the work by giving the saint
a more active role: he is saved by an impulse of hope as he raises his eyes
for help. When the Devil departs, Anthony recognizes his insidious
words as restatements of the pagan doctrines which he had once studied
with the sage Didymus.[33]

In Part VII Anthony once more attempts to reestablish contact with
the *anima*-principle of tenderness within himself. He deplores his spiritual dryness. No longer can he pray. He tries to defend himself against
having lost God as a person and an object of love by recalling past
moments of camaraderie with other religious men, which had brought
him emotional satisfaction. But these emotionally charged memories
evoke the still stronger ones of his family and Ammonaria, whom he
abandoned to follow his own destiny. His adult sexuality combines with
his memories of childhood dependency and physical closeness to subvert
them and make them sources of guilt. First, in a disguised fantasy of
sexual violation of his mother's body, he imagines a hyena poking its
muzzle through a hole in the wall to sniff at her corpse and then devour it.
A metaphor in the Chimera's speech a few pages later proves that
Flaubert associated the hyena with lust: "Comme une hyène en chaleur,
je tourne autour de toi, sollicitant les fécondations dont le besoin me
dévore" ("Like a hyena in heat, I circle around you, soliciting the
impregnations I desperately desire" [p. 262]). Here, devouring of course

suggests the most infantile form of sexual contact—suckling—but the incest prohibition causes the desired suckling to be represented as cannibalism (cf. Nodier's *Smarra*).

Sobbing and overcome with horror, the saint breaks off his fantasy and transfers cathexis to Ammonaria. He lets himself imagine her undressing until he has an erection, but immediately reacts with disgust and contemplates suicide. An instinctive defense of psychic distancing, modulated by intellectualization, transforms his unacceptable thoughts concerning his mother and Ammonaria into the stylized twofold vision of Death and Lust, whom at their first apearance he takes for his mother and Ammonaria, respectively (pp. 248, 250). The transition is not accidental. Anthony's longing to return to his mother transforms death into something desirable: it is where she can now be found. And the impulse to rid the organism of inadmissible needs also generates the death instinct as a way of striving toward biological equilibrium and the cessation of libidinal tension.[34]

Directly confronting the death instinct frees Anthony from it and leads to theological enlightenment. He recognizes that both Eros and Thanatos—the destiny of the body and of the soul without God—are illusions masking the continuity of life: the immortal soul (p. 257). This realization marks the dramatic climax of the *Tentation*. One can see that it was critical to Flaubert because he first crossed out the entire manuscript page and then restored it as if he had found nothing better.[35] Nowhere else in NAF 23667 did he change, even provisionally, more than a few lines. He abruptly rescues Anthony from the impasse of psychopathological regression by shifting from the individual perspective to a general, philosophical one, and thus he can win through to a conclusion.

No longer afraid of the Devil, convinced of his immortality, Anthony diverts his attention from the question of good and evil to speculate why Forms are many when Substance is one (p. 257). His preoccupations now reflect long-standing concerns of Flaubert the artist, who, thirty years earlier, had already been trying "to calm the irritability of the Idea which seeks to assume a form and which shifts about restlessly in us till we have found an exact, precise, self-sufficient one for her."[36] Anthony has renounced the hubristic attempt to repress the body so as to become pure Idea, in order to unite himself with a transcendent God conceived as pure Idea. But at this stage of his thinking, he still commits the error of trying to make matter subservient to thought. He hopes to glimpse primordial figures whose bodies are only images of some quasi-Platonic idea. The allegorical vision of the unsuccessful mating attempt of the Sphinx (matter) and the Chimera (thought) then appears to show him that one cannot subordinate the material and encompass it with the intellect. "Tous ceux que le désir de Dieu tourmente," declares the Sphinx, "je les ai dévorés" ("All those tormented by the desire for God I have devoured" [p. 261]).

The pulsating, seething mass of monsters which then appears in vague semblances of human forms confronts Anthony with facets of the Creation which the intellect cannot grasp, as Job was confronted with Behemoth and Leviathan. As Gilbert Durand says: "The 'monster' is indeed a symbol of totality, of the complete inventory of what is possible in nature."[37] At length the animal entities blend with plants, and plants with stones. Anthony overcomes his initial fear of these apparitions and lies down flat on the ground to contemplate the biological cell, the basic unit of life (pp. 274–75). In earlier versions Anthony's fascinated desire "to be matter myself, to know its thoughts" was followed by Satan's exclamation "You'll know them!" as he seized Anthony and carried him off. Thus matter was identified with evil or at least with imperfection, since Anthony's desire for communion with it was what gave the Devil power over him. But in this 1874 version, Satan has disappeared. Anthony feels great joy after his vision of the monsters: "Je voudrais me blottir sous toutes les formes, pénétrer chaque atome, descendre jusqu'au fond de la matière—être la matière!" ("I should like to huddle within all forms, penetrate each atom, descend to the depths of matter—be matter!" [p. 276]).[38] He does not condemn himself for these words, as he condemned himself earlier after the visions of temptation. For pantheistic ecstasy is not a sin. It reveals God's presence in the physical world: the Deity and matter are not incompatible. As Flaubert expressed it in 1857, "I don't know (and nobody knows) what these two words mean: soul and body, where the one begins and the other ends."[39] Anthony's final cry, "être la matière," could be considered a defeat for the orthodox Catholic, subjugated by an overwhelming experience of hylozoism. But from Flaubert's viewpoint, it implicitly grants Anthony a final wisdom shared with Spinoza, whom Flaubert had called the most religious of men.[40] Once Anthony renounces his arrogant attempt to comprehend the transcendent God, the immanent God is restored to him. For the spiritual is not what is left over when the material has been taken away, by means of rationality or asceticism: the spiritual is anything in a right relationship to God.

Critics who interpret the ending of the 1874 version as a defeat for Anthony forget that Flaubert's manuscript notes show he always intended to have the saint win, exhausting by his resistance all the Devil's stratagems.[41] Flaubert knew that the historical Anthony, as Harry Levin points out, "emerged from his trials in the desert to strengthen the faithful and confound the heretics of Alexandria. In the monastery he had organized, among those who were attracted to the stringencies of his rule, he died a serene and natural death at the age of a hundred and five."[42] In the final draft, Flaubert removed the adversative "mais" which set the apparition of Christ's face against the apparition of the monsters. He also removed the phrase "la tentation est finie" which suggested that the saint's final effusion was part of the temptation. And by shifting the appearance of Christ, "the classical symbol for the unity and divinity of the self,"[43] from the procession of the dying gods to the end, where He replaced the three Theological Virtues, Flaubert made the *Tentation* more clearly a drama of personality.

For Christ to appear in the sun, of course, meant no apotheosis to Flaubert. Other gods had appeared there too, only to fade. In the 1849 *Tentation*, Uranus complained: "Saturn has mutilated me, and God's face no longer appears in the disk of the sun."[44] And until the last draft, the 1874 *Tentation* suggested a physiological explanation for such visions, in Tertullian's description of the soul: "It has a human face, and is transparent like those aerial disks which sometimes float between your eyelids and the sun."[45] What really matters is not what one sees, but how. So long as Anthony insists on trying to impose his own intellectual structures on the universe, he generates the Devil, vainglorious self-sufficiency writ large. Once Anthony renounces his secret desire for rational explanations, the entire universe becomes for him a mediator through which God is mystically knowable. He then shares Flaubert's own experience: "Are we not composed of the emanations of the Universe? . . . And if atoms are infinite in number and pass into Forms like an eternal river flowing between its banks, then what holds back thoughts or connects them? Sometimes, by dint of contemplating a pebble, an animal, a picture, I have felt myself enter into it. Communication between people is no more intense than that."[46]

III

The Simplification of Self:
Psychic Regression

CHAPTER 5

Adolescent Identity Diffusion:
The Flight from Materiality in Nerval's *Sylvie*

Il me suffit que j'aie gardé votre souvenir
—Lautréamont

Nerval is justly famous as a magnificent stylist and as the creator of a complex personal myth which rivals those of Novalis and Blake. With them he represents the purest strain of visionary romanticism, as Mallarmé, Rilke and Yeats could be said to represent the quintessence of European symbolism. But Nerval is also a keen observer and portrayer of human psychology. *Sylvie* describes the narrator's attempt to remain forever in a state of psychosocial moratorium—ritual, game, and theater—a quasi-adolescent preparation and rehearsal for adult life. By the end, both narrator-protagonist and implied author have become aware of the narrator's fear of lasting commitment to a woman. "Half-forgotten innocent old places" (Yeats) in the Valois countryside provide a setting where the oedipal rivalry is magically resolved by sharing the loved woman in the artificial idyll of a chaste ménage à trois. Her husband has her body; the narrator-as-child has her imagination. But he realizes that their mutual reveries fail to achieve anything more substantial than a pale reflection of the vanished, more passionate past.

The narrator's past, associated with the Valois countryside, progressively overwhelms the present, associated with Paris, throughout

Sylvie. The brief flashback to a rural festival in chapter 1 grows into an extended memory in chapter 2. This memory induces the narrator in chapters 3 through 8 to undertake a physical journey back toward the Valois; the description of the progress of the journey is interspersed with memories. Chapters 8 through 12 related the narrator's attempts to resurrect the past *sur les lieux*, in the Valois among his childhood friends. In chapter 13 he abandons this attempt and returns to Paris. Ten years later, in chapter 14, he revisits the Valois, now knowing that he can reexperience the past only through the mediation of frozen and symbolic forms—the archaic furnishings of his hotel room and the sentimental fictions he reads with Sylvie.

Narrative structure and the choice of verb tense consistently orient the novella toward the past. Apart from an occasional use of the historical present, the present tense is found only in the last chapter and in a single sentence of chapter 7, which casts doubt on the memories reported there: "J'en suis à me demander s'ils [ces détails] sont réels, ou bien si je les ai rêvés" ("I am reduced to wondering whether these details are real, or whether I have dreamed them").[1] And *Sylvie*'s most noticeable structural feature is the nested layering of flashbacks which repeatedly interrupt the progress of events:

Level I: present time of narration (1845) (chapter 14)
Level II: the narrator's alternating courtship of Aurélie, Sylvie, and then Aurélie (1835) (chapters 1, 3, 7–13)
Level III: reconciliation of the narrator with Sylvie, culminating in a mock-marriage (1832) (chapters 4–6)
Level IV: vague memories of Adrienne as a nun/actress (1825) (chapter 7)
Level V: the round-dance which pairs the narrator with Adrienne; her kiss and song; estrangement of the narrator and Sylvie (1823) (chapter 2)

Critics of *Sylvie* generally conclude that the novella's retrospective stance and its discontinuities reflect the narrator's quest for happiness through repeated attempts to return to times past. This interpretation frequently provokes a comparison of *Sylvie*'s narrator with Proust's Marcel. But such a comparison is misleading. Marcel's memories accumulate; one leads to the next; eventually they interconnect to form a synthetic vision which enlightens Marcel as to the present. In contrast, the narrator's memories in *Sylvie* are mutually incompatible. Regarding the single love ideal he cherishes, the narrator says that Adrienne embodies its sublime ideal aspect and Sylvie its "sweet reality." He hopes that the nun Adrienne and the actress Aurélie are the same person; but if they were, he declares, he might go mad. He finally characterizes the ensemble of his memories in *Sylvie* as "the illusions which enchant you and lead you astray in the morning of life" (p. 291) but which are destined to be dispelled by experience.

This failure results from the narrator's ambivalence. *Sylvie*'s flash-backs represent not only a turning back toward the past, but also a turning away from the present, a retreat. The narrator's elaborate attempts to explain his present behavior on the basis of past influences prevent him from recognizing the personality trends within him which by conscious effort he might modify and direct.[2] Furthermore, through his predilection for living in memory, an inherently unverifiable and uncertain region of experience, the narrator draws away from reality and isolates himself from the world—as he does through his aversion to timepieces which actually function. Even when he identifies his memory of Adrienne as a neurotic symptom, he shrouds this insight in a pall of doubt: "ce souvenir est une obsession peut-être" ("this memory is an obsession perhaps" [p. 278]).[3] In short, the narrator fails in his quests for happiness because he secretly wishes to fail. He secretly wishes not to "replace the Father" or that father substitute, the uncle, in whose house he would live with Sylvie. To understand the complex interplay of his desire with the defensive strategies designed to prevent its realization, one must consider the major structural patterns of *Sylvie* in constellation with each other. Besides the flashbacks, these patterns include the chapter divisions and the motifs of interruption, character doubling, and ecphrasis—the fictional descriptions of works of art embedded within the main narrative. The device serves writers as a "commentary on the power of art to illustrate history, create life, and frustrate time."[4]

The first chapter displays in miniature *Sylvie*'s evasive strategies. It begins: "Je sortais d'un théâtre" ("I was leaving a theater"). The imper-fect tense announces an imminent interruption by an event in the past definite. Everyday life will accost the narrator as he emerges from his cave of illusion. But just in the nick of time, a flashback intervenes, postponing the narrative flow for a hundred lines. First the narrator recounts how he has been attending the theater every evening to admire an actress from afar. Then he explains his diffidence with regard to her by characterizing the age he lives in: its sensitive spirits have retreated into a poetic ivory tower (Nerval's image). He concludes: "Vue de près, la femme réelle révoltait notre ingénuité; il fallait qu'elle apparût reine ou déesse, et surtout n'en pas approcher" ("Seen close up, the real woman shocked our ingenuous natures; it was imperative that she seem a queen or goddess, and especially that we not get too near her" [p. 262]). What the narrator actually has or could acquire is always not what he desires. Brute facts, the coarseness and vulgarity of reality, are epitomized by the Other, by the carnal woman and her lustful attendants. The narrator does not want this reality, but what he does want is elusive precisely because he lacks it. He becomes his own searching, his own aspiration.[5]

Only after this defensive prelude does the narrator allow the present moment to intrude. A friend accosts him to ask which one of the girls he is coming to the theater to see. Once the narrator is forced to name her, his love becomes socialized, burdened with his friend's expectation that he will act upon his feelings. The friend immediately points out a successful rival, one wealthy enough to gamble away gold with indifference. "Well, there was bound to be one," replies the narrator. He explains that he is merely pursuing an image; and indeed his rival's wealth affords him a pretext for avoiding active competition.

But then a fortuitous glance at the stock quotations in the newspaper shows the narrator that his inherited holdings have suddenly increased in value and made him wealthy—on paper. He could contend for Aurélie's favors after all: "My ideal was within reach" (p. 264). He quickly protests to himself that he could not bring himself to buy her; such corruption is in the spirit of a bygone age, of the ancien régime. Besides, he asks himself, who says that Aurélie is venal? But these idealistic arguments against involvement contradict what the narrator had said shortly before: he feared that the truth about the actress's private life would spoil his glorified image of her; his uncle had taught him to consider actresses in all eras as promiscuous gold-diggers (p. 262). Moreover, it does not seem to occur to the narrator that no financial considerations would preclude his expressing a respectful, uncynical affection for Aurélie. Torn between guilt, fear, and desire, the narrator abruptly finds an occasion to direct his attention elsewhere. In the same newspaper he spies an announcement of the Festival of the Bow (the bow is a classic symbol of the tension between material and spiritual) at Loisy, some twenty miles outside Paris. His childhood sweetheart Sylvie will be dancing there all night long. There still is time to meet her before dawn. He turns from the corrupt Parisian lady (i.e., from her image, which has been "contaminated" by his own projected sexuality) to the innocent country girl. In other words, the ensuing return to Sylvie—and indeed the novella's title itself—constitutes a defensive diversion.

So the narrator regresses. He moves toward the scene of his childhood summers and of the pastoral childhood of human society. Indeed, the end of chapter 1 identifies the country festival at Sylvie's village as the survival of the Celtic substrate, antedating the Roman and Christian monarchies and religions.[6] But at each level of time, the same pattern recurs: the narrator finds perfect happiness only in rituals. These include the round-dance with Adrienne; the festivals and mock marriage with Sylvie; and the theatrical performances of Aurélie.[7] As Erik Erikson explained, such "institutionalized rites and rituals . . . grant youth a world between childhood and adulthood; a psychosocial moratorium during which extremes of *subjective* experience . . . and potentialities of *realistic commitment* can become the subject of social play and of joint mastery."[8] The narrator of *Sylvie* suffers from identity diffusion, from uncertainty concerning his "ability to maintain inner sameness and continuity (one's ego in the psychological sense)" and uncertainty concerning "the sameness and continuity of [his] meaning for others."[9] Through stylized, and if possible, repeated activities, he attempts to acquire a sense of personal stability.

Passing beyond this adolescent stage of rehearsals for adulthood which they have temporarily shared with the narrator, the three women he loves proceed to adult life: Sylvie and Aurélie marry; Sylvie bears children; Aurélie and Adrienne discover vocations; Adrienne dies. But the narrator wishes to remain behind forever because he fears a practical and physical commitment to any woman. One might represent the action of *Sylvie* schematically in this way:

1) **In Time**: reality, represented by marriage (C)
2) **Intermediate Zone**: mock marriages at Othys (B) and in the narrator's play (D)
3) **Outside Time**: childhood memories (A) and theatrical illusion (E); death (F)

Or, in diagrammatic form:

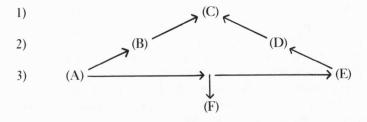

1)

2)

3)

Sylvie moves from childhood memories to reality (represented by marriage) as she grows up. Aurélie moves from theatrical illusion to the same sort of reality. The narrator, a perpetual adolescent, can follow them only as far as the intermediate zone—mock marriages at Othys and in the narrator's play, respectively: the pretend marriages which combine fantasy with a rehearsal for reality. The narrator's play is an attempt to recapture in adulthood the magic of the round-dance ritual of his childhood. Actually, the narrator is attempting to reach a central point at which time, eternity, illusion, memory, and reality blend. His dubious, obsessive and at times unconscious memories of Adrienne are kept alive by his attempts to achieve this impossible synthesis. Since he cannot make Sylvie remain in the world of childhood, nor Aurélie in the world of illusion, and since he refuses to follow them beyond the boundaries of those worlds, he identifies the unattainable Adrienne with the fixed center of an unchanging identity. Only in the last scene of the novella does he realize that this center is death, when Sylvie tells him Adrienne has been dead many years.

The Quest motif which dominates the story, and the active movement of the plot through time and space, both disguise the narrator's neurotic fixation on a dead person, a mother surrogate whose enduring presence in his fantasy life makes him incapable of commitment to a real woman. The novella's most obvious structure, the chapter divisions, seem determined by the narrator's decisions to go in search of happiness. The transitions effected by his journeys correspond to his delusion that he can act freely to obtain what he desires, and can bring about a harmonious synthesis of past and present. Child-like, he believes instinctively in the omnipotence of his thoughts and feelings, while his ego gently derides this confusion between wishing and acting. So chapter 1 ends with his resolve to substitute reminiscence for present reality. Chapter 2, and several of the later ones, end with his decisions to journey to meet his past, particularly to seek out Sylvie and to renew their childhood affection as if nothing had happened to her in the interim. Chapter 12 ends with his return to Paris to court Aurélie, since Sylvie's plans to marry a rival force him to realize that she no longer belongs exclusively to him.

Superficially, these chapter divisions seem to reflect a commonsense acceptance of reality: when a successful rival materializes next to one woman, the narrator sets out toward the other; when the quest to regain childhood happiness seems blocked in one direction, the narrator goes elsewhere. But two series of inner discontinuities embedded *within* the chapters betray the narrator's ambivalence. They suggest that the acts of will coinciding with the chapter divisions must be only half-hearted and doomed to failure. And they refute the unrealistic claims to perpetuate the past made by the revery, the ritual, ecphrasis, and the work of art.

First of all, the narrator abruptly changes the subject to avoid the recurring threats—which mainly arise from within—of sexuality or marriage. When he finds himself alone with Sylvie in an upstairs room of her aunt's house, he takes refuge in the long description of an old portrait, after the revealing denial: "qui donc eût songé à ternir la pureté d'un premier amour dans ce sanctuaire des souvenirs fidèles?" ("who, indeed, would have dreamed of sullying the purity of a first love in this sanctuary of faithful memories?" [p. 274]). And toward the end of his latter visit to Loisy, when he finds himself unable to recapture the sincerity of his past love feelings, he represses the strong physical attraction which remains: "Sylvie, que j'avais vu grandir, était pour moi comme une soeur. Je ne pouvais tenter une séduction" ("Sylvie, whom I had watched grow up, was like a sister to me. I couldn't have tried to seduce her" [p. 286]). His thoughts then promptly revert to Aurélie. Throughout the novella, he delays his professions of love for Sylvie until they must inevitably be interrupted. In his climactic attempt to win her, they are taking a walk together. "J'allais tomber à ses pieds, j'allais lui offrir la maison de mon oncle" ("I was about to fall at her feet [to propose], I was about to offer her my uncle's house [for us to live in together]" [p. 287]), and marriage. But by this time they have arrived at her native village, where supper is waiting. In these three examples the association of Sylvie with the mention of a blood relationship (aunt, sister, uncle) suggests a childhood incest taboo reactivated in the narrator by the proximity of his childhood haunts. This taboo debars him from the mature sexual responses which would be necessary to rebuild a relationship with the now adult Sylvie.

The two descriptions of Sylvie's room, past (chapter 5) and present (chapter 10), neatly symbolize this dilemma. On the narrator's first visit there she is making lace. This lace—like the lace, smoke, and foam in the poetry of Mallarmé—suggests the work of art: a tracery of words on a page, a structure, itself insubstantial, imposed on the void by the imagination, by the *anima*-figure weaving a fantasy. In fact Sylvie undertakes this role here, for in the next chapter she takes the narrator to visit her old aunt at Othys, where she will unite with him in a mock marriage and don costumes which re-create the past.

When the narrator returns to Loisy three years later, Sylvie is dressed "almost like a city girl" (p. 283). The furniture in her room is modern now; a mirror with gilded frame has replaced the old painted wall panel between the two windows, "où se voyait un berger d'idylle offrant un nid à une bergère bleue et rose" ("where you could see a shepherd from a pastoral idyll offering a bird's nest to a shepherdess dressed in pink and blue" [p. 283]). The panel suggests the bygone, stylized, artificial innocence of the pastoral genre, with marriage and sexuality harmlessly disguised as the nest. The combination of pink and blue represents the impossible, as in "amour, hélas! des formes vagues, des teintes roses et bleues, des fantômes métaphysiques" ("a love, alas! of vague forms, pink and blue hues, metaphysical phantoms" [p. 262]) or in

> Ermenonville! pays où fleurissait encore l'idylle antique,—traduite une seconde fois d'après Gessner! tu as perdu ta seule étoile, qui châtoyait pour moi d'un double éclat. Tour à tour bleu et rose comme l'astre trompeur d'Aldébaran, c'était Adrienne ou Sylvie,— c'étaient les deux moitiés d'un seul amour. [P. 292]

> [Ermenonville! land where the idyll of Antiquity still flourished,— translated once again (by Rousseau) in imitation of Gessner! you have lost your only star, which shone with a twofold brightness for me. Blue and pink by turns like the deceitful Aldebaran, it was Adrienne or Sylvie: it was the two halves of a single love.]

The mirror suggests vanity and self-consciousness. The wild warblers have been replaced by tame canaries, just as Sylvie's naive style of singing had given way to a more sophisticated one. The narrator is in a hurry to leave this room, where he finds nothing of the past. But before he can leave, he learns that there is no more demand for Sylvie's lace. She makes gloves instead, and she shows him the long metal tool called *la mécanique* which stretches the leather while it is sewn (p. 283). This clear association of male and female symbols implies that now a relationship with Sylvie must involve sexual intimacy (one thinks of the metal rod with which the double threatens the narrator in Nerval's *Aurélia*).[10] More generally, the artificiality to which the narrator objects in the new Sylvie reflects his subliminal sense that their relationship can no longer be completely "natural," since its now necessary sexual dimension would have to be hidden from society. When the narrator finally does enter into a sexual relationship with Aurélie, he finds it empty and flat: "What could I say now that would be any different from anybody else's story?" (pp. 289–90). "When sexuality is in the service of a flight from anxiety and desperation [our narrator has just described himself as having halted "at the edge of the abyss"], we would expect it to become mechanical, like all neurotic mechanisms."[11]

The narrator is estranged from both Sylvie and Aurélie by the phantom of Adrienne, the tall, blond, aristocratic girl briefly encountered and kissed in accordance with the traditional rules of the round-dance of the narrator's childhood. The narrator's half-dozen recollections of Adrienne's two brief appearances are themselves associated with vagueness and danger: he implores Sylvie to save him from the fatal apparition which haunts his life (p. 279), and then claims that she has done so (p. 289). The "half-dreamed memory" of Adrienne's kiss and song seems an "entraînement fatal où l'inconnu vous attire comme le feu follet fuyant sur les joncs d'une eau morte" ("a fatal attraction of the unknown, which draws you on as if it were a will-o'-the-wisp flitting over the reeds in a body of stagnant water" [p. 267]).[12]

The dream-like atmosphere suggests that both Adrienne's appearances may be screen memories, that is, a combination of fantasy and past experience in a single, representative, stylized image, pointing to a subjective rather than an objective truth. The sense of déjà vu which links Adrienne to Aurélie in the narrator's mind (see chapter 3) derives from the memory of an unconscious fantasy which the narrator attempts unsuccessfully to unearth and understand.[13] Even after the narrator has actually won Aurélie, and after she has denied any connection with Adrienne, he keeps trying to relate her to the Adrienne of the past. This fixed idea is the true dramatic mover of the novella. It ends only with Sylvie's final, reality-affirming burst of laughter, followed by her telling the narrator that Adrienne has been dead for thirteen years, approximately since the time that the grown-up narrator first returned to Loisy in chapter 3. Adrienne's persistent image vitiates the narrator's attempts to take hold of the real world.

Her latent connection with an incest prohibition is repeatedly suggested by the images of repression which cluster around her. Not only is she immured in a convent surrounded by a high, long wall over which the narrator is tempted to look until he rejects that project as a "profanation" (chapter 5, pp. 271–72); not only does she appear as an angel holding a flaming sword, like the guardian who barred Adam and Eve from returning to Eden (p. 277); not only is she compared to Dante's Beatrice, the idealized, untouchable woman (p. 266); but also thoughts of her in chapter 7 are framed by memories of historical genocide: the Druids exterminated by the Romans (p.271), and the massacre of three thousand Protestants on St. Bartholomew's Day (pp. 276–78). Thus rebellious, impious thoughts in the narrator's mind are ruthlessly suppressed.

The fragile equilibrium between fantasy and reality in the narrator's mind is threatened not only from within, but also from without. The voices of reality-principle figures, at times associated with the smell of pungent food, disrupt the narrator's musings by insisting on the physicality of life and on the social context into which the narrator must eventually integrate his daydreams. The anonymous friend's question at the outset, and Sylvie's laughter at the end, are two examples, but there are others besides. After Sylvie has put on her old aunt's wedding gown, in chapter 6, the sizzling of a pan of eggs and bacon and the aunt's voice calling them to lunch, "suddenly recalled us to reality" (p. 275). Here, cooking suggests transformation and, by association, the aging which will affect Sylvie as it has affected her aunt. The children's own contribution to this meal is the uncooked dessert, the delights of fantasy—strawberries and cream.

On his next visit to Loisy, in chapter 9, the narrator revisits his uncle's now uninhabited home, of which he has inherited a share. The furniture has been carefully polished and preserved like a cherished memory, but the only living creature that has survived from the uncle's time is an old parrot. This bird reasserts the claims of the material, "demandait à déjeuner comme en ses plus beaux jours, et me regarda de cet oeil rond, bordé d'une peau chargée de rides, qui fait penser au regard expérimenté des vieillards" ("asking for his lunch as he had done in his prime, and looked at me with that round eye, bordered with a heavily wrinkled skin, which makes one think of the worldly wise look of the old" [p. 281]). Traditional Christian inconography associates the parrot (because of its gaudy plumage) with the vanities of worldly existence. Perhaps the parrot also suggests that the narrator experiences the acceptance of the material as a parrot-like imitation of others which precludes self-realization.

In any event, the parrot associated with food and experience anticipates the episodic figure of "Le Père Dodu" (his name means "plump" and is presently used in France for a brand of frozen chicken) in chapter 12. Just as the narrator is about to propose to Sylvie, they arrive at her village. The smell of onion soup tells them that supper is being served. At table Dodu is the most prominent character. Like the parrot, he forms a link with the past—as a child, he gathered herbs for Rousseau—and like the parrot he has forsworn the past to live in the present. Among his many trades (which evoke the parrot's many colors) are the making of cooking spits (transformation) and cuckoo clocks (associated with passing time rather than frozen time, as in chapter 3, where the narrator must consult the concierge's cuckoo clock because his own clock is unwound).

By explaining how Rousseau's conversation made him renounce the country superstitions he used to hold, Dodu unwittingly shows how the narrator's two avenues of return to his lost paradise are mutually incompatible. The late eighteenth-century literary idyll of Rousseau and Gessner fostered a cult of rural simplicity and the study of nature, yet rejected, on the basis of rationalistic arguments, the simple magical beliefs which form the backbone of rural life. The attempt to return to a child-like past involves an artifice which denies the past in spirit. Dodu bluntly points out this contradiction in an ad hominem argument. He immediately identifies the narrator as an outsider and refers to his repressed physicality: "There you are, little Parisian! Have you come to corrupt our girls?" (p. 287). The narrator's original motive for returning to the country was to evade the temptation of seducing Aurélie. But he cannot return to Loisy as a child: he has become a man. Dodu reminds the narrator that his desires have followed him, and forces him to admit that "man becomes corrupt [i.e., touched by mature sexuality] everywhere." Dodu then completes his function as the messenger of materiality by making a remark which allows the narrator to infer that a rival, *le grand frisé* ("Big Curly"), is already engaged to Sylvie.

Long ago, Big Curly's mother was the narrator's wet-nurse: they were *frères de lait* and later, childhood playmates. But the narrator no longer recognizes *le grand frisé* because the latter embodies aspects of his own psyche which have been repressed. That *le grand frisé* derives from psychic projection is suggested by the fact that he has no real name of his own. A messenger of the material, he is identified only by a physical attribute. In this respect he resembles both Dodu and the ultimately successful rival for Aurélie, known only as "le jeune premier ridé" ("the wrinkled young romantic lead"). These three characters all possess names which denote a concentration of matter—plumpness, curliness, and wrinkles fold more stuff into the same space than slimness, straightness, and smoothness would do. The tag names therefore make the materiality of the body intrusive, even a bit oppressive. Big Curly's chosen trade of pastry cook connects him also with physical transformation (the baking) and genital sexuality (putting loaves in and taking them out of the oven).

The curious anecdote twice associated with *le grand frisé* symbolizes how the narrator's flight from materiality fixates him in fantasies where childhood may be preserved. When both were children, *le grand frisé* tricked the narrator into stepping into water over his head. He then pulled him out, but the narrator's watch was ruined: "La *bête* est *nayée*," the narrator exclaimed, "ça ne fait plus tic tac" ("The *critter* has *drowned*; it doesn't go 'tic-toc' any more" [p. 288]). Immersion is a symbolic return to the womb. Time has halted; maturation is blocked; the female symbol of periodicity has been immobilized; and the beast of libido silenced. In various forms, this emblem of refusal of the responsibilities of maturity will accompany the narrator throughout the work: as his uncle's empty house, with gleaming, unused furniture; as his ornate clock in Paris, adorned by the chaste Diana, and unwound for two hundred years; as the association of Aurélie on stage with a dancing goddess of the hours on a fresco at Herculaneum. Here time has been doubly immobilized: the frozen image was itself encapsulated by the volcanic eruption which buried the town in A.D. 79.[14] The narrator might dig through the hardened lava which paralyzes him, but he cannot resurrect his past.

As a reality figure, Sylvie's brother plays a similar role to that of *le grand frisé*. In earlier texts, in fact, he, Sylvain, tricked the narrator into deep water. In *Sylvie*, during the narrator's reconciliation with her, he interrupts their sharing of childhood memories to say that it is time for them to go home (chapter 4, p. 271). Later, while drunk, he reactivates the narrator's obsession with an unattainable ideal by taking him on a wild ride to attend the religious drama in which Adrienne appears as an angel (chapter 7). And when the narrator returns to Loisy again, his tender declaration to Sylvie is broken into by Sylvain, who comes up, raucously laughing, drunk once more, and calls over *le grand frisé*. In all these scenes, Sylvain acts friendly, but he serves (except at the outset of chapter 4) to distance the narrator from Sylvie. His drunkenness symbolizes Sylvie's physicality, which repels the narrator. He takes upon himself the coarseness—or, more accurately, the humanity—which the narrator does not wish directly to acknowledge in Sylvie herself. The virtual absence of Sylvie's parents from the story (they once are mentioned as present, but they never speak and never are described) removes any authoritative social obstacle from the path of the narrator's courtship. The obstacle is internal. That Sylvain's name echoes Sylvie's implies that he is an offshoot from her in the narrator's mind, a repository for her physicality. His drunkenness also reflects the narrator's fear that his own body, impelled by biological drives, may go out of control.

In short, the warring forces in the narrator's psyche determine not only the narrative's pendulum-like movement through time but also the nature and function of the secondary characters. At the outset the narrator worships Aurélie as actress, but remains willfully ignorant of her private life. "Je craignais de troubler le miroir magique qui me renvoyait son image" ("I was afraid of disturbing the magic mirror which reflected her image back to me" [p. 261]). This mirror metaphor reveals that she must be his own *anima*, a soul-image exteriorized and projected onto an appropriate vehicle in the outside world. When the psyicality of real people imposes itself upon the narrator's awareness to the point where it no longer can be assimilated comfortably into the projected narcissistic image, the pressure of the narrator's need for idealization generates new characters to drain off and embody the all too human

components of the old ones. There results a continual splitting of iden-
tities. As the narrator explores his memories, the love vision for which
Aurélie originally served as vehicle divides into Adrienne and Sylvie,
"the two halves of a single love." Sylvain, and then Dodu, serve to
embody the physical reality which the narrator is reluctant to confront in
the adult Sylvie herself. Finally the narrator himself divides. The
anonymous, successful rivals illustrate the path not taken by the narrator. They undertake a practical and sexual commitment to the women
he loves—keeping track of finances, raising children, preparing lunch
(pp. 291, 293)—while he continues to relate to them in fantasy. The
rivals are the exteriorized forms of the physicality which both generates
and interferes with the narrator's fantasy life.

Sylvie's prominent motif of ecphrasis synthetically expresses the
import of all the other structures in the novella: both the quest for lost
time and its failure. *Sylvie* abounds in descriptions of, and allusions to,
works of art which attempt to reproduce a past era but result only in pale
imitations. These descriptions betray the mental images which the
narrator carries with him (as Proust's Swann carries in his head Botti-
celli's Venus), images which interfere with his ability to apprehend
reality. A recent study of human personality development has described
the way in which a cult of the art object such as the narrator of *Sylvie*
embraces can aid in the evasion of reality:

> The aestheticist perceives images and pictures of reality, instead of
> encountering it. By thus transforming it he can avoid the full en-
> counter with a three-dimensional and alive world and, furthermore,
> selectively screen out, underemphasize, or turn against those
> aspects of reality which do not fit into his particular world of images.
> The subtle derealization which takes place in the transformation of
> the object into an image not only serves the purpose of creating a
> distance and barrier between perceiver and object; very often the
> unconscious "composition" of these images also has the function of
> magic wish-fulfillment. . . . The self in these cases becomes an
> image, too. This self-image . . . arises from narcissistic wishes and
> phantasies and usually has as its secret and sometimes unconscious
> counterpart an equally distorted negative self-image.[15]

The narrator's society, his companions, and his late uncle appear to have
been aestheticists as well as he. So we find an eighteenth-century sum-
merhouse which imitates a temple to Urania; a lake crossing inspired by
Watteau's *Embarquement pour Cythère*, itself an imitation of Antiquity
(chapter 4); the visit to Othys, filled with allusions to Rousseau's *Confessions* (chapter 6); the uncle's house decorated with large prints in the
manner of Boucher, and a whole set of framed engravings of scenes from

[Rousseau's] *Emile* and *La Nouvelle Héloïse*, by Moreau" (p. 280). Near the end, Aurélie wastes her talents on "verses feebly inspired by Schiller" (p. 289).

Such a pale reflection of Sturm und Drang passion recurs in the final phase of the narrator's relationship with Sylvie, now married and with two children. While *le grand frisé* fixes lunch, Sylvie and the narrator sit under the trees reading sentimental literature together: "Je l'appelle quelquefois Lolotte [the married woman Werther loved] et elle me trouve un peu de ressemblance avec Werther, moins les pistolets, qui ne sont plus de mode" ("Sometimes I call her 'Lolotte,' and she thinks I slightly resemble Werther, except that I don't have the pistols, which have gone out of fashion" [p. 293]). So they relive, with conscious artifice, the unreal idyll of a chaste ménage à trois as it was depicted in the eighteenth-century novels of passion *The Sorrows of Young Werther* and *La Nouvelle Héloïse* (the latter is itself a softened version of *Werther*). But their pale copy of love lacks sufficient intensity to admit of "les pistolets"—the tragic possibility of suicide. Our final view of them is also calculated to evoke Paolo and Francesca, except that the situation of Dante's lovers is reversed. "We read no more that day" becomes "we no longer did anything but read."[16]

The lingering, disillusioned longing of their relationship at the end is covertly duplicated by the implied author. He deliberately echoes another eighteenth-century work, *Les Confidences de M. Nicolas*, by Restif de la Bretonne.[17] There the dream of finding simple happiness by marrying a peasant girl also expresses keen nostalgia for lost childhood, and the vain hope of miraculously merging this lost childhood with the present. So both the characters and the implied author reach, at last, the self-same destination: a sophisticated but desperate lucidity.[18]

Attracted to three women, *Sylvie's* narrator has lost all of them: Sylvie and Aurélie to rivals, and Adrienne to God. But Adrienne's attractiveness depends on her unavailability, and the narrator loses Sylvie and Aurélie because, with part of himself, he secretly wishes to.[19] Despite their being sublimated, his normal emotional needs and sexual desires drive him into situations where he must risk encounters with reality. And commitment, as Axël and Marcel also were to realize, risks reducing the narrator's grandiose fantasies to a common denominator of mediocrity. But his half-conscious identification of commitment to the ordinary with mediocrity betrays a secret lack of faith in his ability to transform reality, to mold it into a unique expression of selfhood. *Sylvie* is a drama of blocked maturation: the narrator's self-doubts imprison him at an adolescent's level of emotional development.

CHAPTER 6

Absorption by the Terrible Mother:
Nodier's *Smarra*

Non licet omnibus adire Corinthum

Nodier's setting leaps capriciously
from modern Italy to Athens and Thessaly under the Roman Empire to
the same places in ancient Greece three centuries earlier. The adventures
of three couples—Lorenzo and Lisidis, Lucius and Myrthé, Polémon
and Méroé—are tenuously, confusingly intertwined. But Nodier's
preface to the original edition claims that *Smarra*'s haphazard array of
places and episodes conceals a drama as coherent as the plot of a classical
tragedy (*C*, pp. 34–35).

Nodier himself provided the essential clues to the hidden unity of
his fantastic tale. He called *Smarra* the faithful account of a nightmare (*C*,
p. 34). Elsewhere he defined the nightmare as a drama with a thousand
actors, in which the dreamer himself plays all the roles (*REV*, p. 169).
Applied to *Smarra*, Nodier's definition of the nightmare means that all
six major human characters and the monster Smarra can be interpreted
as fragments of the protagonist's total self, exteriorized through the
psychic mechanism of projection. *Smarra* has at most two characters, Me
and It: It is the feminine phantom feared, desired, and woven from the
dreamer's imaginings. The women Lisidis, Myrthé, and Méroé embody
aspects of the Jungian *anima*, the feminine part of every masculine
psyche which is repressed from ego consciousness into the unconscious.

It reemerges, according to Jung, in the forms of "everything that functions like a mother" in our fantasy life.[1]

The dreamer's identity crisis dramatized in *Smarra* is not successfully resolved with the establishment of a mature personality. The recurring motif of thwarted or disastrous attempts to enter a city (Larissa; Athens; Corinth) embodies Lorenzo's anxiety about undertaking a mature sexual and emotional relationship with a woman. Whether this attempt be made in the spirit of conquest (Corinth), submissiveness (Athens), or curiosity (Larissa), it would be symbolically consummated by one of the characters entering into the city. But as the dream ends, Lucius and Polémon, beset by the Thessalonian witches, fail in their siege of Corinth.

Nodier coordinates his narrative's steady retreat into the historical past with the dreamer's psychic state. The dreamer's memories regress through earlier periods of his life toward a semblance of infancy. Lorenzo has just married, Lucius has just left school, and Polémon is associated with an imagery of helpless children during the nightmare which lies at the heart of the story. The name of Polémon's mistress, Méroé, sounds very like *mère*. As the Queen of the Witches who eventually devours Polémon's heart, Méroé plays the role of the Jungian Terrible Mother, the awesome, possessive, dominating figure who denies her children an independent identity. The regression of libido reactivates the childhood relation to the mother; but "what was natural and useful to the child is a psychic danger for the adult, and this is expressed by the symbol of incest. . . . Insofar as the mother represents the unconscious, the incest tendency . . . is really only the desire of the unconscious to be taken notice of."[2]

Nodier constructed *Smarra* like a *monde gigogne*, a world of nested boxes where a story within the story becomes the narrative frame for another story contained within itself, and so on, indefinitely, at the pleasure of the author. The five titled divisions of the story are arranged ABCBA, as it were, to form three levels of experience. Each corresponds to a phase of personality development less mature than the last: adulthood, adolescence, and infancy.

A) Lorenzo with Lisidis in their marriage bed: (Prologue, pp. 44–46)
   B) Lucius with Polémon in Lucius' pleasure palace (Récit, pp. 46–59)
      C) Polémon's nightmare of Smarra and Méroé (Episode, pp. 59–68)
   B) Lucius and Polémon again (Epode, pp. 69–75)
A) Lorenzo and Lisidis again (Epilogue, pp. 75–77)

Polémon's nightmare presents the mother-child relationship and rivalry with the oedipal father as seen retrospectively by the adult, and as it colors his relationships with all other women. Lucius' psychic state throughout his unfocused search for pleasure corresponds to what Erik Erikson has characterized as adolescent identity diffusion. Lorenzo's need to adjust to the new commitment of marriage has generated emotional stress. This stress reactivates unresolved conflicts from earlier periods of Lorenzo's life, generating feelings of helplessness and terror. By dramatizing these conflicts in what the psyche presents as dreams within dreams, Lorenzo attempts to rob them of reality. The main, initial dream represents an attempt to replace that which is rejected in the inner ones, according to Freud: "If a particular event is inserted into a dream as a dream by the dream-work itself, this implies the most decided confirmation of the reality of the event—the strongest *affirmation* of it."[3]

Each of *Smarra*'s three levels can be subdivided into its own "waking" and "sleeping" realities. Lorenzo's "waking reality" is his marriage with Lisidis, but since he begins his tale at the magichour of midnight, exclaiming, "Ah! qu'il est doux, ma Lisidis . . . de venir partager avec toi la couche longtemps solitaire où je te rêvais depuis un an!" ("Ah! how sweet it is, my Lisidis . . . to come to share with you the bed, lonely so long, where I had been dreaming of you for a year past!" [*C*, p.44]), it seems quite possible that she has appeared only as a wish-fulfilling fantasy. Lucius' condition of "waking reality"is that of a soldier camped beneath the walls of Corinth: the pleasure palaces prepared for him in Athens and Larissa are eventually identified as the "transient fortune of dreams" (p. 74). The "waking reality" of Polémon's affair with Méroé and his friendship with Lucius gives way to his nightmares, into which Lucius and then Lorenzo are ultimately absorbed.

The prologue begins in a house in Arona, beside Lake Maggiore.[4] Like Nodier's other major dream narratives, *Trilby* and *La Fée aux Miettes*, *Smarra* is set near water, as if to suggest the proximity of the unconscious depths to the protagonist's state of waking consciousness. As Lorenzo goes to bed with Lisidis, his bride of a week, he hopes her presence will ward off the terrifying nightmares which have been afflicting him. He ascribes them to his having read the first book of Apuleius, with its story of vampirism, and he attempts to dissociate Lisidis from them: "Le premier livre d'Apulée saisit l'imagination d'une étreinte si vive et si douloureuse, que je ne voudrais pas, au prix de mes yeux, qu'il tombât jamais sous les tiens" ("The first book of Apuleius grasps the imagination in such a strong and painful embrace, that I would give my eyes to prevent your ever seeing it" [p. 45]). He dares not consider that his relationship to Lisidis may be the source of his nightmares, as well as of the agreeable erotic fantasies that have preoccupied him for the past year. His psychic needs have polarized the attributes of Lisidis as he consciously and unconsciously imagines them. Consciously, he idealizes both her and himself, perceiving in each only the desirable qualities of selfless, trusting, protective love for the other. His fear of being dominated and his aggressive desire to dominate are repressed by being projected onto the characters of classical Roman literature. And then he invokes the idealized image of Lisidis, which he loves, to protect himself against the darker image of her which he refuses to acknowledge.

On the level of Lorenzo's waking reality, we learn near the end of the story that his week-old marriage has just had its first social test at a dance in the magnificent Borromeo palace on the Isola Bella.[5] The presence of other attractive women has activated Lorenzo's desires to regain his independence. He would like to be free to have any woman, without responsibility, while keeping Lisidis as a preferred but submissive servant. These feelings generate the harem fantasies, attributed to Lucius, of a pleasure palace and a favorite slave, Myrthé. But feeling similar yearnings for independence, Lisidis has danced too long with a rival. Her attention to the rival has made Lorenzo fear being dominated or rejected by her. In his dream, the surrogates Lucius and Polémon effect a partial catharsis of Lorenzo's guilt and fear by being dominated and punished in his place. From this perspective, the male rival at the dance becomes the monster Smarra, the true husband of the mother-wife Méroé in the dream. As a witch, Méroé embodies those dominating aspects of Lisidis which Lucius is reluctant to acknowledge consciously, as well as his projected fears of her anger and revenge for his unfaithful thoughts. There appears to be little communication between the actual human beings, who for the most part interchange two exteriorized fantasy projections. When Lorenzo talks to Lisidis at the beginning of the story, she has fallen asleep (p. 45). At the end, he falls asleep while she talks to him (p. 77).

At the end of the prologue, a sensitive passage describes Lorenzo's approach to the dream. As is characteristic of visionary romantic literature, the protagonist's perceptions move from gathering darkness, to sound, to a new and different light. Vision, an objective response to the outer world and to the awareness of the barriers which distinguish different roles and forms, yields to the perception of sound. Sound impressions are more resistant to measurement and categorization than are visual ones; they can be perceived, but lack weight, form, or shape. Here the perceptions of sound descend the hierarchy of consciousness from human to animal to inanimate, from rhythmic to undifferentiated: the regular tread of a townsman gives way to the hoofbeats of home-bound mules, and finally to the unmeasured moaning of the wind. This sound "devient une voix de votre âme, l'écho d'une idée indéfinissable, mais fixe, qui se confond avec les premières perceptions du sommeil" ("becomes a voice of your soul, the echo of an indefinable, but fixed idea, which blends with the first impressions of sleep" [p. 45]). A swarm of moth-like Sylphs appears, "créatures dont le grand Esprit a conçu la forme sans daigner l'accomplir, et qu'il s'est contenté de semer, volages et mystérieux fantômes, dans l'univers illimité des songes" ("creatures of whose form the Great Spirit thought without deigning to give it material existence, and which he has been satisfied to scatter in the form of fleeting, mysterious phantoms, through the endless universe of dreams" [p. 46]). The imagery of a whirling swarm suggests a fragmented waking personality, disoriented in sleep. These moth-like beings embodying potentialities for sentient existence which have remained unrealized in waking life emerge from the darkness of the unconscious to dramatize repressed fears and desires, with the dreamer as an involuntary partici-pant and spectator, in whom "an unknown faculty transforms their tales into animated pictures" (*C*, p.46).

The Récit begins. Lorenzo, now asleep, imagines himself to be Lucius, the protagonist of Apuleius' *Golden Ass*. He mounts his horse and rides away from the philosophical schools at Athens (Minerva, wisdom, rationality) to explore the magical region of Thessaly. As Nodier's *Histoire du roi de Bohème* makes plain, journeys stand for dreams, and riding a horse represents the act of love. Even the horse's name, Phlégon, evokes sexual desire.[6] Through the intermediary of Lucius' erotic fan-tasy, Lorenzo reenacts his confusing, exciting transition through adole-scence to mature sexual experience. He travels alone at night, through dark woods and beneath a foggy sky, that is to say, in a state of identity diffusion. The sorceresses reputed to haunt the forest are the imaginary women who will teach Lucius the art of love. Their magic frightens the protagonist because, as the married Lorenzo, he feels guilty and disloyal toward Lisidis; as the adolescent Lucius, he fears the unknown; and as Polémon, his mature sexual response to women remains confused with the child's forbidden attraction to his mother. Exteriorized, these fears take the shape of crippled beggars and hideous old men—potential future selves mutilated by the experiences which Lucius approaches. They embrace him with terrifying glee.

Like Lorenzo at the beginning of the story, whose thoughts move from remembered nightmares to a delighted appreciation of Lisidis,

Lucius progresses from terror to *volupté* as he approaches Larissa. Such a movement of thought is typical of dream sequences which end with a wish-fulfilling act to which the dreamer cannot give wholehearted, conscious moral consent. A preparatory dream or dreams serves to overcome the dreamer's initial resistance by veiling the thing desired through symbols, and by purging the dreamer's fear and disgust. Only then can his wishes emerge in recognizable form.

As Lucius observes the city, accumulated images of transparency in the description of the building suggest that the city is opening like a body before the eye of desire: "Qui me rendra le chant des jeunes filles de Thessalie et les nuits voluptueuses de Larisse? Entre les colonnes d'un marbre à demi transparent, sous douze coupoles brillantes qui réfléchissent dans l'or et le cristal les feux de cent mille flambeaux, les jeunes filles de Thessalie . . ." ("Who can bring back to me the singing of the Thessalonian girls and the sensuous nights of Larissa? Between the columns of a translucent marble, beneath twelve gleaming domes whose gold and quartz reflects the flames of a hundred thousand torches, the girls of Thessalonica . . ." [p. 48]). The marble columns and cupolas resemble legs and breasts. Lucius' desire, however, has not yet focused upon an object; the singing procession of girls that approaches him remains as a vague swarm, charming but evanescent, surrounded by a cloud of perfume, music, and flickering iridescent light. The description of the scene, moreover, reflects a strong effort at sublimation. Song itself, particularly in the literature of romanticism, often presents sexual pleasure in symbolic, idealized disguise (see *Atala*, *Sylvie*, etc.). And here the song inspires defensive thoughts of a pure first love and of a mother's (equivocal) devotion for her child (p. 49).

Then one figure emerges from the undifferentiated crowd. "Tall, motionless, erect," she is the "imperfect image of the beloved who is no more" (p. 49), whom Lucius claims to have mourned faithfully for seven years. Since he has just left school, it is difficult to imagine how he would have had the time to love and to remain faithful to a romantic memory for so long. The female phantom's distinctive height evokes a mother seen by her child: the "terrifying reproach" her presence communicates to Lucius might derive in part from his having forgotten his own mother while pursuing adult independence. But the number seven suggests that the principal meaning of the apparition attaches to the Lorenzo-Lisidis relationship. At the end of *Smarra*, Lisidis mentions that the day of the dance was the eighth day of their marriage. The details of the apparition to Lucius attempt to diminish Lorenzo's guilt over his fantasies of infidelity by attenuating his obligations to Lisidis and by exaggerating his fidelity. She has been transformed from a wife to a fiancée; she is now dead (an emphatic oneiric equivalent of "forgotten"); and besides, Lucius/Lorenzo has already been faithful to her for seven years (days) before he attempts to enter the pleasure city of Larissa. Nevertheless, Lucius' psychic discomfort becomes too strong to endure. The world shrinks beneath him in an affective distancing which reduces the "dead fiancée" to insignificance. And at last this world becomes no larger than the hexahedral toy which children spin along the pathways of the Céramique, a district of Athens.

So the phantasmic *anima*-figure which prevented Lucius from entering the city of mature sexual experience drives him back to child-hood. He returns to the city where he went to school, and what he first sees there is a children's game. But in attempting to regress to the condition of a child, Lucius finds himself encumbered with an adult body, self-concept, and need for self-definition. His trip to Thessaly amounted to a moratorium, obviating the need to compete and choose an occupation. Lucius' harem fantasies situated there likewise concealed a wish to postpone or evade psychosocial self-definition, since the slave girls obeyed Lucius rather than challenging him. But at length his psychic regression draws forth the devouring aspect of the *anima* from its lair in the infantile depths of his psyche.

Nodier chooses to make the transition from Larissa to Athens by mentioning the paths around the Céramique because those paths are lined with tombs commemorating warriors who, like Lucius' friend Polémon, died for their country. (This common Greek name comes from the word *polemos*, "war": as a surrogate for Lucius and Lorenzo, Polémon is placed at the center of Lorenzo's psychic conflicts and bears the brunt of them.) Inside an open square in Athens, Lucius then perceives a procession of the sorceresses' male victims, tormented by nightmares. Their bodies tremble gently like a jew's-harp, and they circle slowly like the mechanical figures on a clock. By comparing the victims to toys—small, inanimate things not to be taken seriously—Lucius as narrator controls his own fears and distances himself from their purgative reen-actment. The victims' endless circular movement suggests the ego con-sciousness in the grip of a superior force; the development of the ego has been blocked until it comes to terms with the unconscious. "The unknown woman or *anima*," says Jung, "represents the unconscious, which continues to vex the dreamer [or his surrogate] until he falls into the circular movement. This in itself supplies a potential center [the supraordinate self] that is not identical with the ego. But the latter rotates around the center."[7]

Lucius recognizes his dead friend Polémon in the procession. They had besieged Corinth together with the armies of the Achean League (244 B.C.). Polémon threw himself in front of Lucius to intercept a lance hurled at his friend and died of his resulting neck wound. Since both men will be decapitated later in the narrative, the location of Polémon's wound here foreshadows a dissociation of mind and body, brought about because the claims of the body, or instinctual self, are inadmissible by the head, or reflective self. The lance is the *anima*'s weapon, striking unexpectedly from afar.[8] *Smarra*'s major source, the first book of Apuleius' *Golden Ass*, corroborates this association of lance and *anima*, for in Apuleius it is a sorceress, not a soldier, who inflicts the neck wound. Polémon's being struck down outside a city he is trying to enter echoes the appearance of the reproachful phantom that prevents Lucius from reaching his pleasure palace in the city of Larissa. Corinth, like Larissa, was renowned for the delights of love, for its temple to Venus and its expensive courtesans. In his correspondence, Nodier cited the familiar proverb "non licet omnibus adire Corinthum."[9] Not everyone may go to Corinth, because its pleasures cost too dear. The power of the *anima*, unacknowledged by ego consciousness, debars the protagonists from a mature love relationship.

As the scene darkens, suggesting an imminent change to another level of consciousness, Lucius invites Polémon to his pleasure palace (magically transported from Larissa to Athens). They will listen to the harp and voice of Lucius' favorite slave girl, Myrthé, whose songs have the power to drive away evil spirits and nightmares. This girl is herself an archetypal *anima*-figure in its protective aspect. Her name comes from the Greek word for perfume (*muron*) and from the name of the myrtle, a plant consecrated to Venus and the token of happy lovers. The many verbal refrains in Lucius' praises of her song create a walled-in, sheltering world of regularity and thus of reassurance. But Myrthé shares some attributes with the Terrible Mother. That her father is a smith (p. 72) associates her with the underworld: she exercises enchantments and rules over familiar spirits. The nightmares from which Lucius suffers associate him with Lorenzo and Polémon, and Myrthé protects Lucius as Lisidis tries to protect Lorenzo. But Lucius' nightmares are peculiar to his state of identity diffusion. They signify a sense of inadequacy and fear of being exposed to others. He dreams of losing his teeth and nails (the battlements which protect the inner man—of course, this also suggests castration).[10] He dreams of being exposed to the crowds on the street in a transparent tunic; he fears that others can read into his soul and will find him despicable.

Nodier uses insect imagery in his description of Lucius' palace to prepare the transition to the nightmare sequences of Polémon's story. The dark-haired companions of the blond Myrthé have stolen honey from the bees; their names—Thélaïre and Théïs—not only evoke famous courtesans but are also the names of species of insects. The spirits of intoxication fill the air like fireflies. The monster Smarra later appears among a swarm of phantoms that hover like gnats. Like a mosquito, he pumps blood from Polémon's chest; later, he will lick it with a tongue that uncoils like a butterfly's. Nodier lived for a time with the naturalist Girod de Chantrans, and was co-author of a treatise on the function of antennae in insects when he was only eighteen. He chooses the names and characteristics of insects to represent nightmare apparitions because insects are part of an objective reality which can be precisely described, and yet their appearance and customs are completely alien. The social insects display a more elaborate community organization than one finds anywhere outside human society, and the semblance of purposefulness which this organization creates is analogous to the inhuman purposefulness of evil spirits. At the same time, the implied author's choice of insects as vehicles for his fantasies has a defensive element: because insects are small ("unimportant"), the fantasies appear less menacing.

Polémon's story replaces the lovemaking which would be the natural conclusion of Lucius' harem fantasy. As a soldier, Polémon will embody the impetus of male sexuality in Lucius and run the risks which Lucius fears to face directly. We are supposedly in Athens, but Polémon offhandedly situates his adventure in Larissa. So Larissa has come to Athens; that is, Lucius/Lorenzo's adult desires have pursued him despite his retreat to the place where he spent his childhood. In contrast, the adult Polémon's relationship to Méroé suggests a child's relationship to its mother. Adoringly he follows her everywhere. His love feelings reflect an ominous abdication of personal will: "Quand elle passait, vois-tu, tous les nuages rougissaient comme à l'approche de la tempête; mes oreilles sifflaient, mes prunelles s'obscurcissaient dans leur orbite égarée, mon coeur était près de s'anéantir sous le poids d'une intolérable joie" ("When she went by, you see, all the clouds turned red as if a storm were approaching; my ears rang, my eyes wandered and blurred, my heart was nearly annihilated beneath the weight of an unbearable ecstasy" [p. 60–61]). And the death of Méroé's husband, which leaves her free, disguises the dreamer's wish for the death of his father.

Wordlessly, one evening, Méroé lures Polémon into her palace. After making love they fall asleep with her head on his arm, as did Lisidis and Lorenzo (pp. 45 and 61). But when Polémon lies quite still, Méroé rises quietly to invoke her familiar spirits and to prepare a magic potion. She compounds it of the veil in which a remorseful lover hid his head after having killed a woman's husband to possess her, and of the tears of a hungry tigress who devoured one of her young. In the context of the imagery of children, mothers, and helplessness which pervades Polémon's account of his nightmare, the ingredients of Méroé's potion suggest the child's oedipal fantasy of replacing his father, and his resulting guilt, together with the child's response to his mother's love, experienced consciously as tenderly protective (the tears) and unconsciously as destructively possessive (the devouring).

The cosmic harmony symbolized by the *ouroboros* of Méroé's bracelet (a snake with its tail in its mouth) is destroyed when the creature comes alive and slithers away hissing. In Jungian terms, this manifests "a symptom of anguish expressive of a reactivation of the destructive potentiality of the unconscious."[11] The protective aspects of the mother fail, yielding up the "child" Polémon to destruction. Within the palace, colonnades open out endlessly (in this passage the columns suggest the mother's legs as seen by a small child),[12] and beside every column a new-born infant snatched from its mother is being slaughtered (p. 63). Jung explains that the child is a potential future self: "In the individuation process, it anticipates the figure that comes from the synthesis of conscious and unconscious elements in the personality. . . . Where . . . numerous homunculi, dwarfs, boys, etc., appear, having no individual characteristics at all, there is the probability of a *dissociation*" of conscious and unconscious elements of the psyche (*ACU*, pp. 164–65). Polémon's vision of numerous, undifferentiated children, separated from the protective mother, suggests such dissociation.

He cries out in horror. To punish him for spying on her secrets, Méroé releases the monster Smarra from beneath the turquoise in her ring. (This gem is associated with lead, with Saturn, and thus with the nether regions.) Smarra embodies the child's oedipal hostility toward the rival father. Through the mechanism of projection, this hostility is unconsciously attributed to the father himself, and is consciously perceived as a generalized, unidentified source of terror. As the stronger father who possesses the desired mother, Smarra has been created "for the despair of the *children* of men" (emphasis added); Méroé offers herself to him as a reward for his effectively persecuting Polémon (p. 64).

Smarra drains Polémon's blood like a vampire. In the background writhe hideous phallic reptiles and stunted, drunken women, symbols of his repulsion at the repressed incest wish, and severed heads suggesting the punishment of castration, but more generally signifying a mind dissociated from a body whose desires it can no longer endure to contemplate. Every night thereafter Polémon's dreams reenact the dreaded, desired incest fantasy. Méroé's phantoms swarm around Polémon, and "sully his trembling lips with their harpy caresses" (p. 65).

The guilt induced by Polémon's adult sexuality, superimposed on an infantile attraction to the mother, represents only an intermediate stage in his drama of regression. Méroé as Terrible Mother literally engulfs him in the womb and destroys his independent existence. The night before Polémon told Lucius his story, Méroé appeared in his dream "much taller than I had seen her before" (p. 65); that is, Polémon has become smaller—more nearly a child—in relation to her than he had been before. To show him all the kingdoms of despair, the empire she will bestow on her husband Smarra, she leads Polémon through a narrow passageway: "Imagine-toi des murailles mobiles et animées, qui se resserrent de part et d'autre au-devant de tes pas, et qui embrassent peu à peu tes membres de l'enceinte d'une prison étroite et glacée. . . . Et tous les démons de la nuit qui crient . . . 'Tu ne respireras plus!' " ("Imagine moving, animated walls, which close in on all sides ahead of you, and which gradually seize your limbs in the enclosure of a narrow, icy prison. . . . And all the devils of the night are shouting. . . 'You shall breathe no more!' " [p. 66]). For Polémon as a helpless child to penetrate this passage is not to enjoy a sexual union but to return to the womb, where all possibility of his rebirth or independent existence will be harshly denied.[13]

At the end of Polémon's journey with Méroé, "la porte sépulcrale qui nous reçut ou plutôt qui nous aspira au sortir de ce gouffre s'ouvrait sur un champ sans horizon qui n'avait jamais rien produit" ("the sepulchral door which received us or rather which inhaled us as we left that abyss opened out onto a field with no horizon, which had been forever barren" [p. 66]). In this sterile womb, Polémon finds "the corpse of the most ancient sun," the earliest form of his personal existence. On his way, he has passed "tous les débris des mondes innombrables qui ont précédé celui-ci dans les essais de la création" ("all the ruins of the countless worlds which preceded this one during attempts at creation") —memories of his past selves now all perceived as failures.[14] Here the monsters who have haunted his dreams return to dig up and devour rotting bodies. They force Polémon—"car j'étais, hélas! faible et captif comme un enfant au berceau" ("for I was, alas, as weak and incapable of resistance as a child in its cradle" [p. 68])—to participate in this cannibalism, which is equivalent to his self-destruction.[15] "Fear of incest turns into fear of being devoured by the mother. The regressing libido apparently desexualizes itself by retreating back step by step to the pre-sexual stage of earliest infancy."[16] In the last scenes in which Polémon appears, his heart actually is devoured by Méroé and her band.

Polémon finishes his story and falls asleep, but Lucius himself now sees Polémon's phantoms. Nodier elsewhere explained rationalistically that the power of suggestion accounts for the contagiousness of sleep-walking, talking in one's sleep, and especially nightmares.[17] But Polémon is also an aspect of Lucius and Lorenzo, and this contagion proves the failure of the defensive strategy of transposition in the dream work. Lucius falls under the condemnation of the superego, which manifests itself initially in its exterior form before introjection (incorporation into self-structure) has taken place early in childhood. When Lucius closes his eyes, his first impressions are regressive, recollections of his school days and his family. A murmur of hostile voices tediously repeats some verses from Aeschylus and the last advice of Lucius' dying grandfather. For in nightmares and states of pathological regression, "structures such as the superego, which have come to function automatically within the personality, seem to become fragments," John E. Mack explains. The "shoulds" directed at the child by the "significant others" in his experience, before he has incorporated them into his own superego, "then confront other portions of the ego in the dream in their original elemental form as an angry voice, noise, or other threatening or accusatory image."[18] The room seems to become suffused with blood; its rows of candelabra turn into shining lances held by two rows of soldiers; and Lucius is led between them toward his execution.

Lucius learns that he stands accused of having murdered Polémon and Myrthé. In effect this means that they are lost to him as psychic defenses. Myrthé can no longer be used artificially to embody only the protective aspects of the *anima*, and Polémon can no longer serve as Lucius' scapegoat. Lucius must assume the burden of Polémon's incest fantasy. In a final effort at sublimation, he looks up to the sky for a dove, "pour confier au moins à ses soupirs, avant le moment horrible que je commençais à prévoir, le secret d'un amour caché qu'elle pourrait raconter un jour en planant près de la baie de Corcyre, au-dessus d'une jolie maison blanche" ("to at least confide to its sighs, before the horrible moment I was beginning to anticipate, the secret love that it could relate one day while soaring near the Bay of Corcyrus, above a pretty white house" [p. 70]). The little white house recurs frequently in Nodier's fiction as the shelter for an idealized pair of child and mother or maternal figure.[19] And the dove may symbolize "chastity, the sublimation of the instincts and the dominance of mind."[20] But the dove, having lost her dearest child to a bird of prey, remains weeping on her nest. This idealized mother, unlike Méroé's weeping, hungry tigress, is not held responsible for killing her own child. Her destructively possessive aspects are detached from her and embodied in another bird. She keeps only the tears.

In the watching crowd, the elements of Lucius' psyche unite to condemn him. A dwarf, or the repressed "unworthy" side of the personality, appears and claims that Lucius has become little, like himself. The parent figures appear in both their individual and social aspects to judge their child—there is a man who resembles Lucius' father, a veiled woman, an old soldier (in this scene Lucius is described as a soldier, like Polémon), and a "femme du peuple" (compare the crowd at Michel's execution in *La Fée aux Miettes*). The dream work prevents Lucius from being directly confronted by his incestuous feelings. These regressive, guilt-provoking fantasies are implicitly attributed to the crowd rather than to Lucius himself: "Les croisées étaient garnies de curieux avides, entre lesquels on voyait des jeunes gens disputer l'étroite embrasure *à leur mère ou à leur maîtresse*" ("The windows were full of avidly curious people, among whom you could see young men contending *with their mother or their mistress* for the narrow opening" [emphasis added; p. 71]). A little girl sings of Lucius' crimes, but her madness suggests that Lucius feels partially detached from her accusations. Indeed, he sees Polémon and Myrthé still alive.

Immediately following his execution, his severed head grows wings and can fly. He becomes a bat rather than a bird. Because the incest wish has not clearly emerged in the dream, Lucius/Lorenzo cannot understand and then surmount it. His psychic development has been arrested. The bat signifies "the being definitively halted at an intermediate point in his evolution upwards: he is no longer the lower level, but not yet the higher one."[21] Nodier makes this explicit by stating that Lucius' head finds no shelter, and by comparing it to a butterfly newly emerged from its chrysalis vainly beating its wings against the windowpane which separates it from the light. As his female slaves (transformed into maenads) arrive with Méroé and Smarra, ready to tear out and devour the sleeping Polémon's heart, a band of horrible, decrepit children bind Lucius (whose head has been reunited with his body) to his bed. He is bound to his present condition, and his possibilities for future development (the children) appear withered and stunted. At this point the implied author distances himself from the protagonist with another reference to a children's toy: he compares the phantoms which beset Lucius to insubstantial, ephemeral, iridescent soap bubbles blown from a pipe (p. 74). When Lucius manages to leap out of bed, he finds himself in a warrior's tent beneath the walls of Corinth. Polémon, lying near him, is dead.

Lucius/Lorenzo slowly emerges from the dream in the epilogue. Talking in his sleep, he confuses his palace with his Italian bedroom and Lisidis' voice with the voices of the phantoms. He accuses her of having abandoned Polémon to the witches: of having withdrawn the maternal, protective aspect of her personality from the dependent child in himself. He calls on her to save him from Théïs, Myrthé, and Thélaïre; to reassure him that the compliant, subservient aspect of herself is her entire self and that his fears of her aggressive domination are an illusion. These two demands upon Lisidis, for protection and for submission, are mutually contradictory. Lucius/Lorenzo cannot enter the city of maturity because Polémon, embodying his dependent childish tendencies, has not yet been integrated with the rest of Lucius/Lorenzo's personality. So long as this state lasts, his need for protection will activate his fear of being dominated by the Other, and his desire for submission, to the extent that it may be gratified, will lessen the effectiveness of the Other as protector.

The stress of self-confrontation has become too great: Lorenzo wakes before recognizing or reconciling the conflicting elements of his complex new relationship with Lisidis: dependence, and a desire for both independence and domination. For Lorenzo, Polémon embodies the former tendency and Lucius embodies the latter. Both Lucius and Polémon serve as psychological defenses for Lorenzo: they take on feelings unacceptable to him, and satisfy his need for self-punishment. In short, the dream attempts to say: "Lucius, not I, is tempted to be disloyal. Méroé, not Lisidis, is the frightening dominant sorceress. Polémon, not I, died at her hands." Lorenzo's terrified reaction to his dreams elicits a protective maternal response from Lisidis, and she soothes him until he falls asleep. In his new dreams, the whole unresolved cycle of conflicts will presumably be enacted again, and he will remain a permanent victim of the dream.

There remains a need for the implied author, as distinguished from the protagonist, to extricate himself from the dream and to return to waking reality. He does this with a characteristically whimsical *Note sur le rhombus* (pp. 78–79). There he proudly explains that learned commentators have not identified this magic instrument used by Méroé, although it is mentioned several times by classical authors. It is, in fact, a double German top called a "devil," which spins with a loud noise and was a popular nineteenth-century children's toy. As at the end of *La Fée aux*

Miettes and at the beginning of *Jean-François les bas-bleus*, the ending here affirms that rationalistic pedants cannot destroy the pleasure of Nodier's illusions. He knows more than they, and can beat them at their own erudite game. At the same time, to place the final emphasis of the story on a child's toy serves to depreciate the seriousness of the tale and thus insulate it from criticism through a sort of romantic irony. But the vested interest of the implied author runs deeper: he wants protection not only from an unsympathetic public but from himself. The work of art has unleashed intense emotions; it is experienced by him as not entirely under his control. The element of child-like play evoked *within* the play of artistic creativity erects a second barrier of protection between the artist and his fears, the first barrier being the artificial construct which is the work of art itself. This creates a doubly miniaturized universe, where inner conflicts can be safely reenacted and effectively controlled.

CHAPTER 7

Submission to the Father:
From Chaos to Geometry in the *Chants de Maldoror*

*Il ne fallait pas avoir tant d'amours! Aigle, taureau,
cygne, pluie d'or, nuage et flamme, tu as pris toutes
les formes, égaré ta lumière dans tous les éléments,
perdu tes cheveux sur tous les lits!*

La Tentation de saint Antoine

Isidore Ducasse's *Chants de Maldoror*
were first published in 1869 under the pseudonym "Le Comte de
Lautréamont," an allusion to Eugène Sue's dark hero who rebelled
against the authority of Louis XIV. They combine an epic cycle of prose
poems in six chants and sixty stanzas with a confessional novel in
fantastic form. Nearly every chant begins and ends with a discussion of
the act of writing by the youthful author-persona, "who aspires to
glory."[1] Increasingly, his destiny becomes intertwined with that of his
superhuman epic protagonist Maldoror, who rebels against God. Writing becomes as much an act of rebellion as are Maldoror's ferocious
physical assaults on God and man. At times the shifting of pronouns
from first to third person and back again makes it impossible to tell
whether the protagonist of the moment is Maldoror, or the author-
persona, or both.[2] But at the end of the fifth chant, the protagonist is
forced to awake and to admit that his rebellion has all been a dream. The
catharsis of confession, which culminates in the fifth chant, appears to
purge the narrator of Maldoror. In the sixth chant the Maldoror persona

is formally dissociated from the narrator and sacrificed upon the altar of literary convention. Ducasse's next and last work, the *Poésies* (two short volumes of prose maxims), abandons the authorial pseudonym of the character Maldoror, condemns the violent revolt against God dramatized a year earlier in the *Chants*, and rejects as worthless the artistic personality which one can infer as creator of the earlier work.[3]

The *Chants* consist of a series of *crises de conscience*, recognitions of self-identity. These emerge more clearly if one distinguishes the artistic self (the one who communicates) from the fantasy self (the one who experiences) in each chant.

Chant I

The artistic self seeks independence by postulating his work as a morally autonomous marsh or storm. He counters social disapproval by denouncing it as hypocrisy. The embittered fantasy self, disillusioned with human society, voluntarily withdraws.

Chant II

God is unmasked as a tyrant. Both the artistic self and the fantasy self define themselves in opposition to Him. Both selves cherish an ephemeral ideal of purity. The artistic self locates this ideal in abstract mental constructs; the fantasy self seeks to preserve innocence by killing children before they can lose it.

Chant III

The fantasy self falls into crime but still defeats God in physical combat. The artistic self contemplates God's degradation in the material order with aggrieved astonishment.

Chant IV

The fantasy self rebels against the human condition both through angelism (the claim to transcend physicality) and a dream of bestiality (the claim to have abolished conscience). The artistic self rebels against the physical world and its rigid categories by invoking the free movement of metaphor.

Chant V

The fantasy self is forced to submit to God. The artistic self is forced to confess his obsessive homosexuality.

Chant VI

The artistic self submits to artistic convention (the novel form). The fantasy self is reduced to a cardboard puppet of the *roman noir*.

101

Poésies

The fantasy self has vanished. By adopting the medium of parody, the artistic self commits suicide. But by composing the drama of a failure to achieve transcendence as either artist or superman, the historical Ducasse scores an artistic triumph similar to those of his contemporaries Baudelaire, Rimbaud, or Mallarmé.[4]

The God who functions as pretext and target for the intense aggressiveness and sarcasm of the *Chants* is a complex entity. At moments he represents an inaccessible ideal of purity; the angelic emissaries of conscience who dog Maldoror throughout the work, in repellent animal forms, embody, as if in a mirror image, the self-contempt with which Maldoror contrasts his imagined depravity with his ideal. At other moments, God serves as a device for alleviating self-hatred: the intolerable self-image is projected onto God, who sanctions Maldoror's impurity with his example. In Chant III a hair fallen from God's head onto a whorehouse floor declares: "Je leur donnerai [aux hommes] la permission de rejeter leur dignité, comme un vêtement inutile, puisqu'ils ont l'exemple de mon maître; je leur conseillerai de sucer la verge du crime, puisqu'*un autre* l'a déjà fait" ("I will give [men] leave to cast aside their dignity like a useless garment, because they have my master as an example; I will advise them to suck the cock of crime, because *an other* has already done so" [III, 5, p. 151]).

Ducasse's revolt begins with his use of a pseudonym, which makes him the son of his own works rather than of his biological father.[5] In the eyes of both narrator and protagonist, writing is power. The subversive book or lecture and the seductive letter serve as the instruments of domination over others throughout the *Chants*.[6] And the text itself rebels against the literary fathers of Ducasse through parody; it emits mocking, distorted echoes of Lamartine, Musset, the Gothic novel, Byron, and Michelet. But both direct revolt and its reincarnation as parody leave the rebel dependent on the father for his sense of self. Worse yet, revolt often fails to disturb the father's indifference, so that the hero is compelled to condemn himself in hopes of attracting the father's attention. As Rollo May explains, "*condemning ourselves is the quickest way to get a substitute sense of worth.* . . . The self-condemning person is very often trying to show how important he is that God is so concerned with punishing him. Much self-condemnation, thus, is a cloak for arrogance."[7] Nevertheless, the father's rejection, added to self-condemnation, takes hold in an enduring sense of personal worthlessness, which intensifies until it becomes intolerable.

Maldoror, the narrator's monstrous self-image, emerges from the confrontation of his obsessive homosexuality with his middle-class sexual values. When not paralyzed by guilt, he incarnates the purity for which he longs, and which he feels he has been denied, in the forms of innocent children and virgin adolescents. He struggles to recapture this innocence by embracing those who enjoy it with an altruistic friendship; the next moment he sadistically destroys his idealized companions.[8] The mode of his assaults, stabbing with a pointed instrument or hurling his victims against a wall (a symbolic representation of the male body)[9] or a tree (a phallic symbol), clearly suggests sexuality masked by aggression. His descriptions of rhythmical movement, swimming or galloping on horseback with some of these same companions, likewise suggest veiled sexual activity. So do the dogs who try to devour the body of one little girl (II, 5) and who rape another (III, 2); so does the intimacy of Maldoror's wrestling matches with an angel, with God, and with a dragon, licking and sucking and burrowing into his adversary's body (II, 11 and 15; III, 3). But by destroying children, who represent a privileged condition of innocence preceding the polarity of good and evil, and of male and female,[10] Maldoror preserves them from corruption, from what he experiences as the sullying sin of adult sexuality and procreation. But his desire degrades its objects and transforms them into animals, who confront him with the image of his own degradation. This is the meaning of the angelic emissaries of conscience who are, at the same time, crabs, spiders, or worms. The union of Maldoror with the objects he has depraved is consummated in the delusional zoopathy of Chant IV (the fantasy that his body is inhabited by animals who have devoured parts of it), and by the vampire-spider who nightly sucks his blood in Chant V. After the overt confession of homosexuality in Chant V (here an expression of the misunderstood need for paternal guidance),[11] God the father can himself appear for the first time as an animal—a rhinoceros—who is promptly shot by Maldoror's pistol. At length, when the energy of his revolt motivated by disgust at the parents and disgust at himself dissipates, Maldoror will submit to the paternal power and be reintegrated into the dependency of childhood.

Publicly to confess homosexuality is an indirect act of allegiance to the mother: it assures her that she will have no female rival. The sea ("la mer," homonym for "la mère") follows Maldoror everywhere; once he is even metaphorically identified with it ("la mer maldororienne"). The adjective "céleste," a word close to Ducasse's own mother's middle name, Célestine, also appears often.[12] Maldoror's hopeless yearning for love seeks consolation in "des fictions célestes" (III, 1, p.131). His only successful matings, with a female shark and with a female louse, suggest a disguised union with the mother. Not only is this intercourse of human with beast "against nature," as is incest, but it also reflects the secret thought that "among animals, incest is not forbidden." The incestuous mother condemned in Chant IV or the nunnery transformed into a brothel with God as customer in Chant III mainly reflect the hero's disappointment at his childhood recognition of his own mother's sexuality, which means that he cannot have her entirely for himself.

A coherent structure of interconnected imagery, rather than plot, provides the major unifying force of the work. Temporally, the narrative is discontinuous and self-contradictory. Maldoror hurls waves of lice at humanity every fifteen years (II, 9), but also he has been rooted for four centuries in the earth (IV, 4). He has not slept for thirty years (V, 3), but a magnetic slumber has held him enthralled at night for the last ten years (V, 7). In Chant VI he claims to have ravaged mankind with carnage from time immemorial, crushing entire generations, but all the allusions there are contemporary.[13] The imagery itself "disrupts, by bringing together in one syntactical structure concrete and abstract words and literal and figurative usages, the reader's expectation of clearly defined categories of the sensual and the mental as well as of reality and imagination."[14] Nevertheless, the predominant imagery clusters around two well-defined polarities of order and disorder, geometry and chaos. Wild beasts, wilderness, and storm evoke the inexplicably imperfect material order and the amoral instincts of creatures. A constantly recurring vocabulary evoking geometry, mathematics, and logical processes refers to and implies the notion of a remote spiritual perfection, source of moral standards.[15] Frequent references to a whirlwind evoke a temporary, unstable equilibrium of the mutually opposing psychic forces in Maldoror: centripetal force, the desire to find security by submitting to externally imposed judgments, and centrifugal force, the drive toward autonomy which preserves the hero's identity at the cost of propelling him into a void.[16] The outcome of this conflict is self-destruction: the hero tears himself to pieces and devours himself in the stanza of the dogs (I, 8) and of the self-consuming heart (III, 1). The romantics frequently alluded to intense self-destructive feelings with similar metaphors (Balzac speaks of a heart that devours itself in *Le Lys dans la vallée*; Gautier describes the lover as a beast of prey devouring its object in *Mlle de Maupin*); but Lautréamont acts them out in fully developed fantastic episodes. The two famous series of *beau comme* similes (VI, 3, pp. 224–25; VI, 6, p. 235) reproduce on the rhetorical plane the interaction of centrifugal and centripetal impulses. The unchanging center of the repeated *beau* corresponds to the artistic ideal and also to God, creator and center of the universe. The grotesque vignettes of deformity which follow evoke the inadequate, distorted manifestations of the ideal which can occur in the material order; they also constitute a form of higher sarcasm by implying "this is the universe that God has made: is it not beautiful?" And finally, of course, the *beau comme* series proclaim artistic autonomy by dissociating the aesthetic from the utilitarian or moral.

From the outset, the narrator insists on his artistic independence. The first stanza reverses the conventional strategy of the *captatio benevolentiae* (the attempt to win the sympathy of the audience, usually through affectations of modesty) by stressing the probable inadequacies of the reader in relation to the work. He compares his book to an unexplored, poisonous marsh—a conventional Christian image for the state of sin, as contrasted with the road of spiritual progress. The timid reader hesitating at its edge will need the protection of a rigorous logic, of a sustained capacity for moral judgment, to cross it unscathed. (By attributing his own timidity to the reader, the implied author frees himself of his own hesitation at embarking upon a dangerous and shameful confession.) The prudent reader confronting the work is advised to behave like the leader of a V-shaped formation of flying cranes at the approach of a fierce storm—to shun the approaching moral chaos which might engulf him, nimbly diverting the "geometrical figure" to "a safer and philosophic road." The triangle suggests a world ordered by the Trinity: marsh and storm are a free world where social conventions and God's moral precepts no longer apply.[17] The wind which sweeps through the first chant at frequent intervals reinforces the sense of unpredictable, uncontrollable change promised by the author.[18] And as Suzanne Bernard has elegantly explained, the nineteenth-century prose poem was itself an act of revolt against generic conventions.

It takes some time for the narrator to find his own voice. In the early stanzas he remains close to the tone of Baudelaire's "Au lecteur"; he expresses a delight in premeditated sin and in the *mauvaise foi* of false repentance; he unmasks the reader's hypocrisy and claims him as a brother. Then halfway through the second chant the narrator reveals that he was born deaf, learned to speak only with difficulty, and recovered his hearing when he screamed with revulsion at the spectacle of the sadistic demiurge. He means, among other things, that he is conscious of having just discovered an original stylistic vehicle for his artistic personality (II, 8, pp. 96–99).

As for Maldoror, when his insurgence attains its greatest intensity, he claims to be altogether outside the Christian cosmos; a voluntary visitor, immortal, and of extraterrestrial origin (p. 77). Speaking of Maldoror, an archangel admits that "moi, je ne suis qu'une substance limitée, tandis que l'autre, personne ne sait d'où il vient et quel est son but final. A son nom, les armées célestes tremblent. . . . Satan lui-même, Satan, l'incarnation du mal, n'est pas si redoutable" ("I myself am only a limited substance, whereas nobody knows where the other comes from nor what is his ultimate purpose. The heavenly legions tremble at his name. . . . Satan himself, Satan, evil incarnate, is not so formidable" [p. 241]). The hero's hubris transcends nemesis: as in Sartre's *Les Mouches*, the powerful grandeur of his revolt temporarily transforms guilt into something superior to the principle by virtue of which it *is* guilt.

But since Maldoror is in fact limited, finite, confined within the imperfect universe which God has made, his self-glorifying fantasies break down in the face of the onslaught of paralyzing, recurrent nightmares and delusions of being spied upon (see pp. 66, 99, 195–98, 210–12, 217). God as judge (i.e., personified self-contempt) strives to invade Maldoror's mind with the scalpel of conscience, to force his repentance and submission, and thereby to destroy his independent identity. Freud remarks:

> There actually exists in the ego an agency which unceasingly observes, criticizes and compares [the actual ego with an "ideal ego"], and in that way sets itself over against the other part of the ego. . . . the patient is betraying a truth to us. . . . when he complains that he is spied upon and observed at every step he takes and that every one of his thoughts is reported and criticized. His only mistake is in regarding this uncomfortable power as something alien to him and placing it outside himself.[19]

A revolt against the "censoring agency" of conscience, Freud explains elsewhere, arises from the patient's desire to liberate himself from all influences of authority figures, beginning with paternal ones. The patient then withdraws homosexual libido from the authority figures in his preconscious: "His conscience then confronts him in a regressive form as a hostile influence from without." In delusions of persecution like Maldoror's, "the persecutor is usually of the same sex as the persecuted patient, and is the person the patient loves most."[20] A father may be replaced by a schoolmaster (as he is, episodically, in the *Chants*)[21] or by some superior—here, God himself. "*Paranoia persecutoria* is the form of the disease in which a person is defending himself against a homosexual impulse which has become too powerful."[22] The guilty conscience embodied in God and His angels is "incomprehensible if traced to real misdeeds. . . . It is motivated from the point of view of unconscious thoughts, but not of intentional acts"[23] because in his primitive unconscious thinking the neurotic believes in the magical omnipotence of thoughts and considers them as tantamount to deeds. And more generally speaking, even for the normal adolescent the social system generates a secular analogue of original sin. The adolescent becomes guilty by virtue of the inevitable maturation which progressively differentiates him from the family unit in which he was brought up, yet he also becomes increasingly guilty if he remains within that unit because his maturing transforms him increasingly into a rival of the father. The family becomes guilty whether it wishes to keep him within itself or to drive him out. The *Chants de Maldoror* are framed by stylized scenes (I, 11; VI) which depict a close-knit family group with the hero on the outside looking in and trying to lure the son outside the family. From this perspective Maldoror represents the awareness of differentiation growing within the son.

The general movement of the first chant illustrates the protagonist's retreat from confronting his own emerging sexuality. Initially (I, 2) his aggressive fantasies are projected onto the reader, whose ostensible timidity is denounced as a hypocritical mask. Maldoror is superior to this reader because he is sincere in admitting to the amoral instincts of his unconscious (I, 3). The self-portrait which expresses his delight in cruelty is the image of all men (I, 4). But then the same lucidity which serves as the instrument of his dominance forces him tacitly to recognize that his disgust at humanity is also self-disgust. His resulting suffering makes him feel once again inferior to other men, who seem fatuously self-satisfied: his condemnation of their hypocrisy here becomes an appeal for brotherhood. This appeal is finally directed toward a "God of mercy" (I, 5). Still isolated, Maldoror abandons himself to his sado-masochistic instincts. He sees both good and evil as excesses by which man, enraged at his inferiority to God, tries to gain heaven. But since it is God who defines "good" and "evil," man, by accepting these notions, is competing with God on God's own terms, and must fail (I, 6). Maldoror becomes increasingly isolated from humanity when the unresisting sexual partner of I, 6 is replaced by the allegorical female figure of Prostitution (a transient, artificial, commercial relationship) and condemned by the glow-worm of Conscience (disgusted fascination with one's own sexual organ [I, 7]). There ensues the self-destructive masturbatory fantasy of the dogs (I, 8), and finally a retreat into the ocean of the unconscious (I, 9).

107

Seeking liberation from conscience, Maldoror in the second chant begins to assume animal forms. A powerful latent death wish against the parents generates the force behind the delusional truth of the assumed identity.[24] Through metamorphosis Maldoror descends the Great Chain of Being toward a state of pure instinctual aggression and un-self-conscious sexuality, or, as he puts it, toward "the whirling vortex of the unconscious faculties." In an allegory of metamorphic liberation from the superego, Maldoror admires the ferocity of a huge female shark as she devours the victims of a shipwreck; he fights off other sharks which have attacked her; finally, he swims out to embrace her. The two fuse into an undifferentiated glaucous mass smelling of seaweed: "Emportés par un courant sousmarin comme dans un berceau, et roulant, sur eux-mêmes, vers les profondeurs inconnues de l'abîme, ils se réunirent dans un accouplement long, chaste et hideux" ("Borne by an undersea current as if in a cradle, and rolling over and over toward the unknown depths of the abyss, they united in a prolonged, chaste, and hideous embrace" [II, 14, p. 123]). Maldoror explicitly characterizes such liberation as perfect happiness in the fourth chant when he dreams of himself as a conquering swine: "Il ne restait plus la moindre parcelle de divinité: je sus élever mon âme jusqu'à l'excessive hauteur de cette volupté ineffable . . . Les lois humaines me poursuivaient encore de leur vengeance . . . mais ma conscience ne me faisait aucun reproche" ("Not a scintilla of divinity was left [within my mind]: I was able to raise my soul to the excessive elevation of that ineffable delight. . . . Human laws still pursued me with their vengeance. . . . but my conscience reproached me not at all" [IV, 6, pp. 176–77]). In the rare moments when he is completely freed from conscience, Maldoror becomes mightier than God. As a gigantic octopus in the second chant, with tentacles long enough to encircle the planets, Maldoror defeats God in single combat and forces Him to beat an ignominious retreat (II, 15, p. 127).

But metamorphosis, during the course of the work, gradually loses its efficacy and slips out of Maldoror's control. Already in the fourth chant he discovers that his fantasy of being a swine was not a real, effectual revolt, but rather an involuntary dream imposed by Providence as a degrading punishment. Driven from this shelter of guiltlessness, Maldoror must reassume his vulnerable human form: "Revenir à ma forme primitive fut pour moi une douleur si grande, que, pendant les nuits, j'en pleure encore. . . . Combien de fois, depuis cette nuit . . . ne me suis-je pas mêlé à des troupeaux de pourceaux, pour reprendre, comme un droit, ma métamorphose détruite!" ("To return to my original form was so painful for me that I still weep over it at night. . . . How many times, since that night . . . have I mingled with herds of swine, in order to reassume my former shape which was destroyed and which is mine by right!" [IV, 6, pp. 177–78]). When Maldoror and other sympathetic characters like the Amphibian take to the air or water, they do so more to escape social hostility and to find consolation from kindred spirits than to enjoy the freedom of movement in three dimensions. In particular, bird flight, that conventional emblem of liberty and transcendence, appears strikingly fettered in the *Chants*. The cranes of I, 1 stay in formation with a leader; the starlings of V, 1 remain bound together in a compact mass; Maldoror with angel's wings is bound to the spectacle of his revenge upon mankind (II, 9); the great birds of prey in V, 2 are imprisoned by their rivalry over the woman they both loved; Maldoror as swan carries an anvil (VI, 8). In the sixth chant, metamorphosis can no longer serve the purposes of aggression. Maldoror takes the form of a cricket merely to lurk in a gutter (VI, 2). As a swan, he cannot even conceal himself successfully: God makes him black so that the other birds will shun him. The trajectory of the work impels Maldoror steadily away from the refuge of metamorphosis toward a confrontation with his emerging guilt and remorse.

For a time, the strategies of the confessional novel insulate Maldoror from this increasingly obsessive remorse by transferring responsibility for his sins elsewhere. The Maldoror of Chant II postulates two gods. One is inaccessible, pure spiritual essence, the supreme judge and source of moral standards. This perfection is knowable to the human intellect in the form of the abstract systems of mathematical thought:

> O mathématiques sévères . . . j'aspirais instinctivement, dès le berceau, à boire à votre source, plus ancienne que le soleil. . . . Il y avait du vague dans mon esprit. . . . Vous avez mis, à la place, une froideur excessive, une prudence consommée et une logique implacable. . . . Arithmétique! algèbre! géométrie! trinité grandiose! triangle lumineux . . . reflet puissant de cette vérité suprême dont on remarque l'empreinte dans l'ordre de l'univers . . . la propre image du Tout-Puissant. [II, 10, pp. 105–6]

> [Oh austere mathematics . . . even in the cradle I instinctively aspired to drink at your springs, more ancient than the sun. . . . My thoughts were vague. . . . In their place you put excessive coldness, consummate prudence, and implacable logic. . . . Arithmetic! algebra! geometry! magnificent trinity! luminous triangle . . . powerful reflection of that supreme truth made manifest in the order of the universe . . . the very image of the All-Powerful.]

Maldoror recognizes in himself an innate instinct for purity which makes his moral judgment superior to the contingencies of the created order.

Maldoror then compares his idealized image of God made manifest in mathematics with the inferior creator God whom he deduces from the imperfect material world. This comparison unmasks the inadequacies of the demiurge.[25] With the poisoned spear of logic, Maldoror explains, "je fis descendre, de son piédestal, construit par la lâcheté de l'homme, le Créateur lui-même! Il grinça des dents et subit cette injure ignominieuse; car, il avait pour adversaire quelqu'un de plus fort que lui" ("from his pedestal, built up by man's cowardice, I made the Creator himself come down! He ground his teeth and submitted to that degrading insult; for his adversary was stronger than He" [II, 10, p. 108]). Maldoror is evil only because this inferior God, source of all physical being, is himself corrupt. Worshipping Him is useless: "Il n'est pas reconnaissant . . . car, les tremblements de terre et les tempêtes continuent de sévir depuis le commencement des choses" ("He is not grateful . . . for earthquakes and storms have continued to rage since the beginning of things" [II, 9, p. 102]). So Maldoror assumes the role of judge to condemn the demiurge. "N'est-ce pas lui qui me fournit des accusations contre lui-même? . . . Ma poésie ne consistera qu'à attaquer, par tous les moyens, l'homme, cette bête fauve, et le Créateur, qui n'aurait pas dû engendrer une pareille vermine" ("Is it not He who provides me with accusations against himself? . . . My poetry will consist entirely in attacking, with every available means, man, that wild beast, and the Creator, who shouldn't have begotten such vermin" [II, 3, p. 84; II, 4, p. 87]).

For men, inevitably imperfect owing to their imprisonment in matter and their separation from pure spiritual essence at the moment of creation, become more imperfect as they evolve from asexual to hermaphroditic to distinct male and female beings. In this fallen state, sexual desire is a snare; it promises reunion of male and female, but in fact perpetuates disunity through the propagation of the species in its most debased—sexually differentiated—form. When Lautréamont was composing the *Chants*, this complex of ideas was becoming widespread. Nourished by Schopenhauerian pessimism and by Hartmann's fantasies of race suicide, it achieved its most striking expression in the early poetry of Laforgue. Therefore Maldoror as rebel naturally refuses to propagate the human species, since that would amount to abetting the demiurge's plans for perpetuating the unjust material order. All Maldoror's sexual acts are associated with the destruction of life. He often substitutes a knife for a penis (II, 3; III, 2; V, 7). Fellatio, sometimes disguised as vampirism, pervades the work: both activities are consummated by devouring vital fluids. Maldoror only once yields to heterosexual desire when he rapes a sleeping child. "Somber and dissatisfied" after his momentary weakness, he sends his bulldog symbolically to repress his normal sexual instincts by killing the little girl. Instead, the dog imitates his master and rapes her.[26] This episodic companion functions as a scapegoat who assumes Maldoror's desires to purge his master of them. Maldoror promptly condemns the animal for having "yielded to its baser instincts": with the symbolic castration of a kick that knocks out one eye, he drives the dog away. Then he undoes the possible consequences of his rape by thoroughly eviscerating the girl, in a hyperexaggerated abortion. Maldoror elsewhere tries to prevent others from participating in God's act of creation: he exalts bisexual and homosexual beings (see II, 4, 5, 7; IV, 7; and V, 5); in the first and last chants—and less explicitly in all the others, he attempts to divert virtuous adolescents from normal sexual development into homosexual relations with himself (see I, 11; II, 6; IV, 8; V, 7; VI, 5, etc.). This project explains why Lautréamont prophesies that men "s'avanceront à grands pas, conduits par la révolte, contre le jour de leur naissance et le clitoris de leur mère impure" ("will go forward with great strides, led by revolt, against the day of their birth and the clitoris of their impure mother" [III, 5, p. 155, cf. I, 5, p. 48]). He hopes they too will rebel against the procreation of the species.

To serve the demiurge is to become an accomplice in the tyranny of the imperfection of the material order, which excludes us from the ideal. Passively to suffer the injustice of the demiurge, as Maldoror and Mario attempt to do at the beginning of Chant III, is to be ignored. If one tries to attack the demiurge, he withdraws. So Maldoror tries to destroy the demiurge's flawed world. Since prehistoric times, Maldoror claims, he has crushed countless human generations beneath his heel as an elephant crushes an anthill (VI, 2, p. 223). His mating with a female louse to beget a deluge of parasites for the destruction of mankind is a demonic parody and refutation of the demiurge's creative act (II, 9). But such acts of violence resemble so closely the sadistic cruelty of the demiurge that the rebel Maldoror cannot condemn the tyrant he opposes without condemning himself. He tries to take refuge from this dilemma, posed by his moral consciousness, by evading self-recognition (see the mirror- and telescope-breaking episodes of IV, 5 and IV, 7[27]) and by plunging into the irresponsible freedom of metamorphosis and the dream. Expelled from these Edens of unawareness, he must finally hide behind the mask of hypocrisy in the *Poésies*.

Nor can he find real social acceptance or companions to alleviate his loneliness. The first chant consists in a series of unsuccessful attempts at alliance between Maldoror and humanity in general (through laughter), Prostitution, the ocean, the gravedigger, the *fils de famille*, and the toad (stanzas 5, 7, 9, 10, 11, and 13), not to mention the reader (stanzas 1 and 14). (The androgyne and the amphibian are in and of themselves symbols of union.[28]) Maldoror's only friends are "ces êtres imaginaires . . . qu'enfantera le débordement orageux d'un amour qui a résolu de ne pas apaiser sa soif auprès de la race humaine. Amour affamé, qui se dévorerait lui-même, s'il ne cherchait sa nourriture dans les fictions célestes" ("those imaginary beings . . . who shall be engendered by the stormy overflowing of a love which has determined not to quench its thirst among humankind. A famished love, which would consume itself, if it did not seek its sustenance in heavenly fictions" [III, 1, p. 131]). These fictions incarnate Maldoror's yearning for purity, but his yearning can be satisfied only by acceptance by the remote god of purity. This god communicates with him only in nightmares, through the voice of conscience. The voice invites submission—Maldoror must admit his inferiority to an ideal which is inaccessible to him—but it never promises pardon or grace—i.e., the restoration of his innocence. "Isolé comme une pierre au milieu du chemin," says Maldoror, "je couvre ma face flétrie, avec un morceau de velours, noir comme la suie qui remplit l'intérieur des cheminées: il ne faut pas que les yeux soient témoins de la laideur que l'Etre suprême, avec un sourire de haine puissante, a mise sur moi" ("Isolated like a stone in the middle of the road, I cover my branded face with a scrap of velvet, black as the soot on the inside of the chimney: no eye must bear witness to the ugliness which the Supreme Being, with a smile of powerful hatred, imposed upon me" [I, 1, p. 55]).

The third chant illustrates in dramatic form Maldoror's conviction that for God to create the physical world was in itself a degrading act. God appears brutishly drunk after and because of an act of creation (III, 4). Then God visits a whorehouse. His intercourse with a prostitute is both allegory and metaphor. As allegory, "cette profanation . . . l'alliage forcé de ces deux êtres dont un abîme incommensurable séparait les natures diverses" ("that profanation . . . the unnatural alliance of those two beings whose different natures were separated by an immeasurable abyss" [III, 5, p. 149]), represents the unnatural union between matter and spirit which generated the physical world. Then God summons an "innocent" adolescent (who also has been visiting the whorehouse) and flays him alive. This vignette combines both the homosexual touch—all over the body—and horror at that touch, as at the beginning of Chant IV. The narrator's own desires lead him to imagine the contact; repression makes him see it as disgusting. Afterward, God's forehead remains ineradicably stigmatized with a drop of sperm and a drop of blood. As allegory, these stigmata symbolize the demonic proliferation of suffering, inferior beings in the material world. As metaphor, the stigmata mean that the inner state of purity desired by the narrator has been irremediably lost because of his (possibly imaginary) homosexual experiences, in which he has played both the passive and the active role. (The drop of sperm suggests fellatio. Blood, sperm, vampirism, and fellatio are even more clearly associated in V, 5, p. 203, at the conclusion of a hymn of praise for pederasts.) Remorsefully, God bows his head, fearing men's scorn "quand ils apprendront les errements de ma conduite . . . dans les labyrinthes boueux de la matière" ("when they hear about the wanderings of my behavior . . . in the muddy labyrinths of matter" [III, 5, p.154]).

But God, however debased by the act of creation, still can retreat to heaven. His creatures must remain imprisoned on earth, "that rocky chamberpot on which writhe the constipated anuses of the human cockatoos" (III, 1, p. 133). Descriptions of chaotic and confining matter accumulate with compelling force at the beginning of the fourth chant. The architectural forms of a temple, suggesting order and justice, are obscured by buzzing swarms of black wasps—the teeming life of material existence. Although Maldoror claims voluntarily to share man's imprisonment, he continues: "Les dentelures d'un horizon aride et morne s'élèvent en vigueur sur le fond de mon âme. . . . Notre sort . . . reste enchaîné à la croûte durcie d'une planète . . . l'homme et moi, claquemurés dans les limites de notre intelligence . . . chacun reconnaît dans l'autre sa propre dégradation" ("The crenelations of a barren, depressing horizon rise forcefully in the depths of my soul. . . . Our lot . . . remains chained to the hardened crust of a planet . . . man's and mine, each of us walled up within the limitations of our intelligence . . . each sees in the other the image of his own degradation" [IV, 1, p. 158]).[29]

Bound to the material order, Maldoror tries to resist the human condition through angelism: denying normal physical needs, struggling against cold, fatigue, and sexual impulses. Thus he attempts to prove that God has no control over the human bodies which He has made. With the aid of the voluntary suffering which results from physical deprivation—and from the masochistic acceptance of life itself— Maldoror passively condemns a God he can no longer assault directly. He confronts God with the tormented human flesh which is the physical image of His moral corruption. "J'ai reçu la vie comme une blessure," says Mario, one of the episodic, imaginary companions to Maldoror, "et j'ai défendu au suicide de guérir la cicatrice. Je veux que le Créateur en contemple, à chaque heure de son éternité, la crevasse béante. C'est le châtiment que je lui inflige" ("I've received life like a wound, and I have forbidden suicide to heal the gaping hole. I want the Creator to contemplate, during each hour of his eternity, its yawning crevice. That's the punishment I inflict on Him" [III, 1, p. 136]). Mario's declaration illuminates the otherwise enigmatic scene of Maldoror's supposedly "voluntary martyrdom" in IV, 4: "Les pourceaux, quand ils me regardent, vomissent. Les croûtes et les escarres de la lèpre ont écaillé ma peau, couverte de pus jaunâtre. . . . J'avais fait voeu de vivre avec la maladie et l'immobilité jusqu'à ce que j'eusse vaincu le Créateur" ("Pigs, when they look at me, vomit. The crusts and scabs of leprosy cover me like scales, and my skin is covered with yellowish pus. . . . I've made a vow to live with sickness and immobility until I've conquered the Creator" [IV, 4, pp. 169–70]). Beneath the posture of defiance, both Mario's words and Maldoror's reflect the pathetic spite of a rejected lover. Yearning for a god of purity but ignored by Him, they pray with their whole body for attention, acceptance, and love.

Almost imperceptibly, the center of gravity in the *Chants de Maldoror* has shifted from physical to verbal action by the beginning of the fourth chant. So Maldoror now tries to arouse his audience's disgust at heterosexual love by offering *exempla* which present such love as odious. A mother and wife torture a man who refused to commit incest with the mother (IV, 3); a sea captain kills his unfaithful wife by forcing her to take a long midwinter walk just after she has given birth to an illegitimate child (V, 2); a beetle takes vengeance on a sorceress who has transformed him and three other human lovers into animals, binding her and dragging her along the ground until she has been transformed from an "amorphous polyhedron" (irregularity, injustice) to a sphere (perfect order, retribution [V, 2, p. 193]). This last *exemplum* echoes the myth of Circe: sexual enslavement turns men into animals. Their metamorphosis is degrading because it is involuntary. The misogynous refrain of these *exempla* retrospectively explains the second image in the series of three with which Lautréamont characterized the *Chants* at the outset: the timid reader was advised to turn aside like a traveler from a marsh; like a son from his mother's face; like birds from a storm. The mother—woman as creator—is the human analogy to the demiurge and the feminine counterpart to the author of *Maldoror*. If one explores the mystery of the creativity of any one of these three figures, one will find an amoral chaos.

So that the reader may become attuned to his work, the narrator now prescribes two medicines: the arm of the reader's mother or sister to be torn off and devoured, and a basin of pus in which the diseased reproductive organs of both sexes have been dissolved. "Si tu suis mes ordonnances, ma poésie te recevra à bras ouverts, comme un pou résèque, avec ses baisers, la racine d'un cheveu" ("If you follow my prescription, my poetry will receive you with open arms, as a louse drains dry, with its kisses, the root of a hair [V, 1, p. 190]). In other words, the text urges its reader to absorb women's identity so as to become self-sufficient; to destroy all women, inherently evil because they are the instruments that perpetuate imperfect material existence; to regard reproduction with disgust; and to join the narrator in fellatio instead. A psychoanalyst would interpret this obsession with fellatio as a secret desire to acquire the paternal phallus by ingesting it: to become pregnant with it by the father and thus to assume the mother's role.[30] Revolt against God the procreator conceals the wish to be the passive sexual object of God's fecundations. The author nearly says so himself: "Quelques-uns soupçonnent que j'aime l'humanité comme si j'étais sa propre mère, et que je l'eusse portée, neuf mois, dans mes flancs parfumés" ("Some people suspect that I love humanity as if I were its own mother, and had carried it, for nine months, within my perfumed flanks" [IV, 2, p.164]).

As the energy of Maldoror's revolt decays, the narrator displaces him more and more, until the last chant reduces the superhero to a grotesque puppet maneuvered by "the strings of the novel *genre*." For a time, the weapon of words preserves the narrator's own independence. Immediately before the oppressive concentration of prison imagery which opens the fourth chant, he exploits the rhetorical equivalent of the free movement of metamorphosis in order to transcend fixed definitions. The narrator refuses to forswear this subversive exercise of metaphorical freedom, "quand même une puissance supérieure nous ordonnerait, dans les termes les plus clairement précis, de rejeter, dans les abîmes du chaos, la comparaison judicieuse . . ." ("even if a higher power should command us, in the most explicit terms, to throw back, into the abysses of chaos, the judicious simile . . ." [IV, 2, p. 159]). Starting with the fourth chant, long, involved sentences take over from equivocal moral situations part of the task of disorienting the reader, who is further confused by a pedantic "critic-voice" which interrupts to comment with romantic irony on the *Chants'* stylistic improprieties.[31]

But the metaphorical freedom invoked at the outset of the fourth chant quickly becomes suspect under examination, if one adopts the viewpoint of the psychiatrist Jacques Lacan, who equates metaphor with repression.[32] Maldoror's announcement that "its a man or a stone or a tree who is about to begin the fourth chant" (IV, 1, p. 157) betrays an attempt to dehumanize, to desensitize the implied author by means of the passage from man to stone. The tree, ostensibly a compromise between man and stone (living but insensitive), is also a phallic symbol, which, through a return of the repressed, will become part of a gibbet from which the tortured phallus-man is seen hanging two stanzas later (IV, 3). The narrator's ostensible assertion of the right to appear in any guise he chooses gives way to a metaphor of the violent contact of two hard objects—narrator and reader—which shatters the former "like the flakes of a block of mica smashed by the blows of a hammer" (p. 157). The stone itself then becomes subject to suffering: Maldoror envies the brief death agony of families killed by explosions of mine gas: "as for me, I exist forever like basalt!" (p. 158). And the narrator's long-winded uncertainty, in IV, 2, about whether two objects in the distance are pillars, baobab trees, pins, or towers becomes subject to the laws of optics (p. 161) and arithmetic (p.163), and at length does not protect him from hearing the creak of chains and the groans of pain of the human condition (p. 163).

With this perspective, one can recognize as equivocal the ostensible reassertion of artistic autonomy which opens the fifth chant. There the *Chants de Maldoror* are compared to a swirling mass of starlings, in a striking simile which tries to absorb the antitheses of chaos and geometry in a single synthetic definition of the work's thematic and verbal structures. Each bird is instinctively drawn toward the center of the flock, but the rapidity of his flight continually carries him past it,

> en sorte que cette multitude d'oiseaux, ainsi réunis par une tendance commune vers le même point aimanté . . . forme une espèce de tourbillon fort agité, dont la masse entière, sans suivre de direction bien certaine, paraît avoir un mouvement général d'évolution sur elle-même . . . les étourneaux n'en fendent pas moins, avec une vitesse rare, l'air ambiant, et gagnent sensiblement, à chaque seconde, un terrain précieux pour le terme de leurs fatigues et le but de leur pélerinage. Toi [the reader], de même, ne fais pas attention à la manière bizarre dont je chante chacune de ces strophes. [V, 1, pp. 187–88]

> [so that this multitude of birds, thus united by a common tendency toward the same center of attraction . . . forms, as it were, an intensely turbulent whirlwind, whose entire mass, without clearly advancing in any direction, seems to revolve around itself . . . none the less the starlings cut through the ambient air with uncommon

rapidity, and perceptibly, every moment, gain ground toward the end of their labors and the goal of their pilgrimage. You, likewise, don't pay any attention to the bizarre way in which I sing each one of these stanzas.]

This description of the birds' whirling flight was taken verbatim from an assistant's article in an encyclopedia of natural history, edited by one Dr. Chenu. But the plagiarism enriches rather than diminishes the signification of Lautréamont's definition of the *Chants*. For the borrowing represents objective validation for his dynamic model of the human psyche—scientific observers have reported natural analogs to the mind's interplay of conflicting forces as he understands them. And he adds a declaration of intent: the apparently aimless movement of his poem conceals an arduous pilgrimage toward a desired goal, the conquest of purity.

In particular, the starling simile functions to explain the form of the immediately preceding Falmer stanza (IV, 8), with its recurring phrase fragments and its desperate attempt to suppress a tormenting memory. More generally, it helps explain the function of refrains and even of metaphors in other stanzas: they are not only the instruments of formal lyricism but also the foci of an obsession. For the centripetal force acting upon the starlings suggests a desire to submit to God and to conventional moral judgments; the birds' flight away from the center suggests a struggle for untrammeled self-realization. Brought together in dynamic equilibrium, these two strong opposing forces generate the predominant whirlwind image. After the starling passage, Lautréamont again separates the whirlwind into its components. With sarcastic deference, he claims he has no intention of imposing his extreme tastes on those readers "who tremble with fear at the sight of a shrew or the eloquent expression on the surfaces of a cube" (p. 189). The shrew, which daily devours a greater percentage of its body weight in living prey than does any other mammal, stands for the voracious animal instincts of the realm of moral chaos: the cube implies moral discrimination, discipline, and order (cf. the bizarre use of the word *cubique* in VI, 5, p. 233).

With the metaphors of shrew and cube, Lautréamont has analyzed the psychic dynamism of his work to prepare its dramatic climax. Separated, the drives toward revolt and submission can be embodied in Maldoror and in God. The latter, in the form of a huge serpent of remorse, approaches Maldoror, who threatens to crush the creature's triangular head and the ground beneath it into a formless paste with his heel, that is, to reduce both Trinity and creation to chaos (V, 4, p. 199).

God retorts by demanding obedience and allegiance in return for "the free gift of an existence which I drew forth from chaos." Maldoror resists, denouncing God's unjust rule. Reversing the roles of God and Serpent in the book of Genesis, he tries to expel God from the universe of the *Chants*.[33] He curses God and condemns him to wander endlessly through the wilderness (perhaps an echo of Quinet's *Ahasvérus*). For a moment Maldoror even takes the part of his victims in I, 11; III, 2; and Chant VI: he casts himself as an outraged father whose wife, son, and ancestors God has unjustly killed. But at length it is he rather than God who turns aside, under the pretext that, suffocating with indignation, he seeks "a more tranquil and virtuous spectacle." It seems more likely, however, that Maldoror no longer can endure a confrontation which threatens to reactivate his guilt. He takes refuge in contemplating an imaginary legion of "incomprehensible pederasts." Maldoror claims they are "the crystallizations of a higher moral beauty" because they transcend the limits of man's logic and woman's sensibility alike (V, 5, p. 202). Actually, Maldoror has evoked the pederasts in order to arouse his own sexual desires. He hopes that their intensity will blot out his awareness of divine justice, as did the aggressive impulses liberated by metamorphosis earlier in the work. He then admits that the pederasts are beings who resemble him; fantasies of anal intercourse combine with dreams of world mastery; and the scene culminates in a frantic vision of homosexual anti-creation—a supreme guiltless refuge from God:

> Oh! si au lieu d'être un enfer [i.e., had his impulse been acceptable, without guilt], l'univers n'avait été qu'un céleste anus immense . . . j'aurais enfoncé ma verge, à travers son sphyncter sanglant, fracassant, par mes mouvements impétueux, les propres parois de son bassin! Le malheur n'aurait pas alors soufflé, sur mes yeux aveuglés, des dunes entières de sable mouvant; j'aurais découvert l'endroit souterrain où gît la vérité endormie, et les fleuves de mon sperme visqueux auraient trouvé de la sorte un océan où se précipiter! [V, 5, p. 203]

> [Oh! if instead of being a hell, the universe had been only a huge heavenly anus . . . I would have stuck my cock through its bloody orifice, shattering, with my impetuous movements, the very walls of its basin! Then misfortune wouldn't have blown, over my blinded eyes, entire moving dunes of sand; I would have found the underground place where truth lies sleeping, and the rivers of my sticky sperm thus would have found an ocean to hurl themselves into!]

Like Rimbaud's drunken boat, Maldoror breaks through the walls of the known universe, which condemns him, to discover the hidden ulterior truth of his innocence.

But Maldoror immediately acknowledges that such permanent liberation is impossible. And after this climax of his epic, the force of his revolt is spent. The climax of the confessional novel—full self-disclosure, shame, and submission—follows at once. His open admission of homosexuality makes the pressure of guilt so strong that he first attributes his sexual nature to Providence (men find the odor of his semen so attractive that they kill each other to be near him [p. 205]), and then seeks the sanction of God's example of spending the night with a pederast (p. 206). This double abnegation of responsibility effectively restores Maldoror's God to his place of leadership. In the following stanza a priest representing human society comforts the mourners at a funeral for a ten-year-old boy by telling them that Maldoror, who gallops past, is "the only true dead person" (V, 6, p. 210), dead in sin and deprived of grace. Maldoror's fantasy refuge disintegrates: "We are no longer in the domain of narration," the narrator exclaims. "Alas! now we have arrived at the real" (V, 7, p. 212).

Conventional moral order reimposes itself in V, 7 with the geometrical imagery of the refrains describing the spider who is God's agent, bringing God's commands to Maldoror after having punished him by sucking his blood nightly for ten years. Emerging from its hole "at one of the intersections of the angles of the room," the spider unhurriedly approaches its victim. It awakens Maldoror, driving him out of the amoral wilderness of dreams and forcing him to march along "the road of memory." Maldoror has claimed that he never sleeps (IV, 3, p. 196). The spider, suddenly reversing this perspective by situating Maldoror's adventures in a dream world ("You have been asleep all the time"), discredits the revolt. The independent identity which Maldoror thought to have elaborated during ten years of dreams is dead (the dead boy in the previous stanza symbolized that identity). Here, the room denotes the body; the spider's lair where two walls meet, a bodily orifice; the spider itself, guilt emerging from the tormenting intensity of sexuality. More precisely, the spider represents "the *phallic* mother, of whom we are afraid. . . . the fear of spiders expresses dread of mother-incest and horror of the female genitals."[34] For a spider continually spins material out of its insides, as if giving birth; it snares insects in its sticky web, as an overpossessive mother snares her offspring. That this creature soon breaks apart into two male youths whom Maldoror has loved shows that the mother fixation has diverted the hero's libido from other women onto boys: they are recognized as objects of attraction, while the mother is not. Maldoror's unconscious fascination with the mother as potential sexual object is his sin toward the Father. Banned from the "sanctuary of sleep," broken in spirit, facing the cold dawn, the hero must admit his sins, repent, and submit to the implacable decrees of "the Being who is stronger than you" (p. 217).

Such inability to escape divine authority uncovers beneath Maldoror's revolt a fundamental, countervailing intention: self-immolation. He turns to the demiurge and exalts him to purity by assuming his guilt; that is to say, he identifies himself as a sinner in order to justify the punishments God inflicts on him. Instead of claiming, as before, that he suffers because a sadistic deity delights in torturing His creatures, he now admits that he suffers from remorse caused by his having transgressed divine law. The self-assertion consummated by an overt admission of homosexuality seems to terrify the narrator, who has observed this monster taking shape in his creation: he hastens to submerge his Maldoror self-image beneath torrents of contrition. The demiurge, thus restored to his pedestal of remote and inaccessible perfection, becomes one with the God of pure spiritual essence. So divine authority and the existing world order at last acquire a basis of legitimacy.

Once Maldoror has been judged and condemned at the end of the fifth chant, the narrator emotionally dissociates himself from Maldoror, who consequently becomes remote and unreal. No longer does he make physical contact with his adversaries and victims: he acts upon them from a distance. In the first five chants he had seized adolescents by the feet or hair, wrestled intimately with an angel, burrowed into a dragon's body, and enveloped God in his octopus-like tentacles. Already in the fifth chant, however, he opposed God with a curse rather than an assault. And in the last chant, he swings young Mervyn from a long rope which an accomplice[35] has tied; he kills an angel with a stick thrown from two miles away; he shoots God, who appears as a rhinoceros, with a pistol.[36] Maldoror's stature shrinks to that of a literary type, a "poétique Rocambole" (VI, 2, p. 222; cf. *Poésies I*, p. 266). His surrealistic world of fantasy becomes a realistic decor: one can follow his progress through the streets of contemporary Paris, among familiar monuments.[37] The cliff disappears from the recurring seaside landscape (VI, 8). And toward the end, no new species of animals appear.[38] The sense of involvement and danger and the creative impulse of the work have weakened: the narrator submits to literary conventions as Maldoror has just submitted to God's justice. "Je crois enfin avoir trouvé," he declares, "après quelques tâtonnements, ma formule définitive. C'est la meilleure: puisque c'est le roman!" ("After some groping, I believe I've finally found my definitive formula. It's the best: because it's the novel!" [VI, 1, p. 221]).

Humor preserves for the narrator a considerable measure of independence in the sixth chant. The *pince-sans-rire* quality of his expressed enthusiasm for the novel becomes apparent when he promises us, for example, that "every standard gimmick will be used to best advantage" (VI, 8, p. 241).[39] He emphatically reminds us, by means of the fantastic, disconnected sentences which conclude stanzas VI, 2 through VI, 6, that an author can lead literary conventions in any direction he chooses. As in the later fiction of Roussel, or Harry Matthews' recent novel *The Conversions*, these sentences are shown to be prophetic by the course of events in succeeding stanzas. Such ingenuity, however, does not keep the work from degenerating in the sixth chant into a gratuitous intellectual game. Beneath the surface, this game constitutes a compulsive spiritual hygiene intended to prevent the shameful, threatening Maldoror figure from emerging once again to dominate the narrator's personality. And Maldoror becomes effectively eclipsed by the self-deprecating young writer "who aspires to glory," already evoked at the end of the fourth chant. The concluding episode illustrates this well. Standing atop the Vendôme column, Maldoror hurls his last victim into space. But his revolt, no longer devastating, leaves only superficial, accidental traces: Mervyn's desperate hands dislodge a strip of decorative trim from the column. ("Go see for yourself, if you aren't willing to believe me" is the last sentence of the *Chants*.) The column itself, cannon-shaped and forged from melted-down cannon, suggests a gigantic phallus, but its ejaculation flies toward a dream of literary immortality: Mervyn's body lands on the Panthéon dome, as if returning to the comforting maternal breast. Only with Hugo's death fifteen years later were writers explicitly included among the "great men" to whom the Revolution had dedicated the Panthéon. When Lautréamont wrote, the building was still being used as a church. Still, Mervyn, being the moral "creation" of Maldoror, stands in the same relationship to Maldoror as Lautréamont's fictional creation stands to its author, and Maldoror aims to enshrine this creation among the gods. That Mervyn then becomes a withered skeleton demonstrates that Maldoror's revolt has been drained of its substance: in earlier episodes, the victims' bodies were described as flesh and blood, or paste.

Having thus reduced Maldoror to a poetic phantom in the last chant, the narrator now sacrifices himself by means of the indirect, aphoristic self-cancellation of the *Poésies*.[40] First he relinquishes his aristocratic pseudonym of le Comte de Lautréamont, and identifies himself on the title page as Isidore Ducasse. He then reverses his aesthetic and moral positions: "Si l'on se rappelle la vérité d'où découlent toutes les autres, la bonté absolue de Dieu et son ignorance absolue du mal, les sophismes s'effondreront d'eux-mêmes. S'effondrera, dans un temps pareil, la littérature peu poétique qui s'est appuyée sur eux" ("If you recall the truth on which all others depend, the perfect goodness of God and his total ignorance of evil, sophisms will collapse of themselves. And at the same time, so will the unpoetic literature which finds support in them" [*Poésies I*, p. 268]). He exalts "taste," "the summit of intelligence," while rejecting the notion of poetry as a marsh, a storm, or a theater for what he now sees as the cardboard devils of romantic revolt: "poetry is geometry *par excellence.*"[41] For he has undergone catharsis, and poetry as geometry has acquired a rich meaning: it is the instrument of purity. "Purity," of course, has also become more pure: no longer is it ambivalent. For the rebel protagonist of Chants I through V, it sometimes meant a state of innocence regained—acceptance by God; at other times it meant a state of independence from God the judge, and from the demiurge, and from the latter's corrupt creation. But once the protagonist assumes the demiurge's guilt at the end of Chant V, he has become a scapegoat. The narrator purges himself of his protagonist in order to reintegrate himself once and for all with the divine order. He achieves atonement with the Father, and the *Poésies* bar the door against Maldoror's return.

Ducasse's pious acceptance of self-discipline and restraint in the *Poésies* does not, however, conceal an acrid sarcasm directed against the hypocritical Second Empire society which hid its own monstrous image behind the mask of a complacent prudery.[42] With jarring platitudes, fatuous certitudes, and exorbitant exaggerations, Ducasse professes a superficial optimism that is incongruously both pseudo-Christian and postivistic (e.g., in *Poésies II*, pp. 279, 287, and 291). In frequent restatements of maxims from Vauvenargues and Pascal, the crudely reductive style and insolent reversals of meaning imply that the thoughts of these *moralistes* are jejune, trivial, whether affirmed or denied.[43] But this sarcasm betrays a loss of vital energy. As a form of aggression, it is no longer embodied in virtual action, in fantasies of world destruction. Instead, it has become abstract, embodied in the contrasts of ideas. In itself, this abstraction constitutes a desperate but unsuccessful attempt to suppress the shameful body by denying its realm, the concrete. Ducasse's sarcasm in the *Poésies* is the ineradicable phantom of the body, the body's revenge against a precarious domain of purity from which it has been excluded. But this last revolt makes itself felt only in the awkward incongruousness of the author's feigned submission. Its only support is a generalized rhetorical pressure. By merely claiming superiority and no longer dramatizing it, by assuming—however scornfully— the mask of the audience's supposedly inferior personality, the implied author presides over the destruction of his inner self.

IV

The Aggrandizement of Self: Fantasies of Power

CHAPTER 8

The Quest for Self-Actualization in Nodier's *Fée aux Miettes*

> *Vérité, fantaisie, quel est le rêve?*
> *quelle est la veille?*
> —*Beelzebub (*Quinet*, Ahasvérus)*

Nodier's most complex, ambitious fantastic tale is *La Fée aux Miettes*. It combines the sharp conflict between dream and material reality in *Trilby* with the multiple nested layers of dream in *Smarra*. Nodier's preface tells us that he first conceived the story as a fairy tale; subsequently,

> j'en avais peu à peu élargi la conception dans ma pensée en la rapportant à de hautes idées de psychologie où l'on pénètre sans trop de difficulté quand on a bien voulu en ramasser la clef. C'est que j'avais essayé d'y déployer, sans l'expliquer, mais de manière peut-être à intéresser un physiologiste et un philosophe, le mystère de l'influence des illusions du sommeil sur la vie solitaire, et celui de quelques monomanies fort extraordinaires pour nous, qui n'en sont pas moins fort intelligibles, selon toute apparence, dans le monde des esprits. [*C*, p. 171]

> [I had gradually broadened my conception of the story, by connecting it to elevated psychological notions which are not too difficult to penetrate if you are willing to pick up the key. I mean that I

125

had tried to illustrate there, without explanation, but in a way which might interest a physiologist and a philosopher, the mystery of the influence of the illusions of sleep on persons living alone, and the mystery of some fixed ideas which seem quite extraordinary to us, but which are to all appearances quite comprehensible in the spirit world.]

The "key," of course, is a reading in the subjective mode: Nodier intends most secondary characters to represent elements of the personality of Michel and aspects of his response to the world. As Michel himself says of the Fée's ideas: "J'étais étonné de les voir apparaître subitement dans mon intelligence aussi claires que si elles s'étaient réfléchies sur la glace d'un miroir" ("I was astonished to see them appear suddenly in my intellect as clearly as though they had been reflected there on the surface of a mirror" [*C*, p. 198]). Two heuristic principles of psychoanalytic interpretation can guide us through the confusing wealth of incident and detail in Nodier's narrative: (1) apparently arbitrary motifs, if frequently repeated, point to a hidden central meaning; and (2) the greater the distortion, the greater will be the affect. The person of the Fée herself, and two dreams of humanoid dogs, can thus be located at the emotional center of gravity of the work.

La Fée aux Miettes consists of an authorial preface followed by five nesting layers of narrative, each containing its own dream which anticipates and leads to the next layer. As with *Smarra*, a schematic representation provides a picture of the confusion:

Authorial preface: "this work has psychological import" (pp. 167–72)
  (I) the frame narrator in France (pp. 173–78)
  (the frame narrator's dream of Michel, pp. 179–326)
    (II) Michel relates his life in France (pp. 179–221)
    (Michel's dream of the Fée's ninety-nine sisters, pp. 215–17)
      (III) Michel in Scotland (pp. 221–43)
      (his dream of the dogs' wedding, pp. 229–30)
        (IV) Michel at the inn with the talking dog (pp. 243–77)
        (his dream of the four-headed monster, pp. 246–49)
          (V) Michel in the Fée's cottage (pp. 278–98)
          (his dreams of ecstasy with Belkiss, pp. 296–97)
        (IV) Michel combines life with the Fée and carpentry (pp. 298–318)
      (III) Michel's quest for the singing mandrake (pp. 318–19)
    (II) others tell the end of Michel's story (pp. 319–26)
  (I) the frame narrator in Venice (pp. 326–29)

Total claustration in the lunatic asylum (Level III) and in the Fée's enchanted dwelling (Level V) alternates with Michel's encounters with human society (Levels II and IV). Each time the narrative shifts from one level to another, Michel becomes increasingly alienated from society and, at the same time, more spiritually enlightened than he was before. The text alludes on page 299 to the storm mentioned on page 247 in such a way as to suggest that all the events of levels IV and V (Michel's nightmare, trial, near-execution, and marriage) may be the fancies of a single night's sleep, fancies which only he believes are real. He definitely scrambles his autobiography with the admission: "Mes impressions de la veille et du sommeil se sont quelquefois confondues, et je ne me suis jamais fort inquiété de les démêler, parce que je ne saurais décider au juste quelles sont les plus raisonnables et les meilleures" ("My impressions from the waking and sleeping states sometimes become confused with each other, and I have never been terribly concerned with sorting them out because I couldn't possibly decide exactly which are the most reasonable and the best" [*C*, p. 240]).

Nodier's preface characteristically suggests two opposing interpretations of his story—*sottise* or *sagesse*—and then tries to mediate between them. By 1830, when he returned to active creative writing after an eight-year interlude, he had come to endow with cosmic significance his attempt to reconcile the imagination with reason. He had become convinced that imaginative and rational perception reflected two opposing world principles. Only by maintaining an equilibrium between these forces could one ensure the survival of man and society:

> Il y a . . . deux sociétés, dont l'une appartient au principe imaginatif, et l'autre au principe matériel de la vie humaine. —La lutte de ces forces, presque égales à l'origine, mais qui se débordent tour à tour, est le secret éternel de toutes les révolutions. . . .
>
> Dans un pays où le principe imaginatif deviendrait absolu, il n'y aurait point de civilisation positive, et la civilisation ne peut se passer de son élément positif.
>
> Dans un pays où le principe positif entreprend de s'asseoir exclusivement au-dessus de toutes les opinions . . . il n'y a plus qu'un parti à prendre, c'est de se dépouiller du nom d'homme, et de gagner les forêts avec un éclat de rire universel; car une semblable société ne mérite pas un autre adieu. [*REV*, pp. 188–89]

> [There are . . . two societies: one belongs to the imaginative principle, and the other to the material principle of human life. —The struggle of these forces, which are nearly equal at the begin-

ning, but which gain ascendency each in turn, is the eternal secret of all revolutions. . . .

In a country where the imaginative principle became supreme, there would be no pragmatic civilization, and civilization cannot get along without its pragmatic element.

In a country where the pragmatic principle attempts to reign unchallenged over all viewpoints . . . there remains only one course to take,. which is to cast off the name of man, and to run off into the woods with a universal burst of laughter; for such a society deserves no other farewell.]

Nodier believed that a growing preponderance of the positive principle in his time threatened society with imminent disaster (*REV*, p. 186; *C*, p. 644). *La Fée aux Miettes* struggles to restore the revivifying imaginative principle to society by presenting to an overly sophisticated Parisian audience what Nodier holds to be the natural revelation contained in visionary madness, dream experience, and the collective expression of dreams in popular legends. Even the generic title of *La Fée aux Miettes* and of the other contes, the oxymoron "histoire fantastique" ("true fantastic tale"), betrays a tension between the imagination and reason. Nodier desires that the encounter he arranges between these two principles be a harmonious blending rather than a violation of the latter: "J'ai dit souvent que je détestais le vrai dans les arts . . . mais je n'ai jamais porté le même jugement du vraisemblable et du possible, qui me paraissent de première nécessité dans toutes les compositions de l'esprit" ("I've often said that I detested the true in art . . . but I've never passed the same judgment on the plausible and the possible, which seem to me of prime necessity in all mental compositions" [*C*, p. 168]). He believes that the modern skeptical reader embodies reason; his visionary protagonist embodies imagination; to make possible a communication between the two, he explains, he has created a frame narrator, "espèce équivoque entre le sage et l'insensé, supérieur au second par la raison, au premier par le sentiment" ("an equivocal species between the sage and the madman, superior to the second by virtue of his reason, to the first by virtue of his feelings" [*C*, p. 170]).

Finally, Nodier answers the potentially damning criticism that Michel's fantasies lack originality, since they derive from the libretto of Favart's comic opera *La Fée Urgèle*. He claims that he could trace Favart's sources back to Solomon, who said there is nothing new under the sun (p. 172). Ostensibly depreciating his own capacity for invention, Nodier slyly attaches his apparently frivolous tale to a venerable tradition, to the folk wisdom of the collective unconscious, and to a legendary personage who embodies wisdom itself. Through *sottise* (the childish fairy tale) Nodier's preface reaches *sagesse*, just as the fictional hero Michel does when his Fée identifies herself as the Queen of Sheba, widow of Solomon (*C*, p. 277).

Within the main narrative, this wisdom is embodied by the frequent moralizing digressions which counteract the polarization of imaginary and real. Whether Michel's story be true or no, the digressions imply that from it one can gain a moral lesson. He follows his account of each important event in his life with a commentary: an exhortation to learn a trade, work diligently, love, respect the humble, and envy no one (*C*, pp. 184–5, 188–91, 198–207, 211–13, 220–27, 230–31, 245–49, 278–84, and 304–18). These sections occupy almost a third of the text and are corroborated elsewhere by Michel's supreme project of rebuilding the temple of Solomon (wisdom) in the desert (of ignorance). Moralizing vindicates Michel's bizarre perceptions by showing that they lead to attitudes which we all could accept. And the very banality of moral exhortation compensates for the luxuriance of his visions.

The frame-narrator first appears to us as he hurls aside Livy's history of the Roman Empire, disgusted with its glorification of material success and its claims to moral utility. His imagination, embodied by his Scotch valet, Daniel, has been standing patiently by his chair, and now proposes a journey to the famous lunatic asylum at Glasgow (an article on that asylum appeared in the 1829 *Revue de Paris*, a journal Nodier wrote for often). The narrator welcomes this occasion for an imaginative escape from the real world, and praises lunatics as occupying a place higher than ordinary men on the Great Chain of Being (p. 176). Daniel and the narrator set forth just before the autumnal equinox, at 6 P.M., the time of the day and the year when the sunlit material world gives way to darkness, the realm of the dream. Within the asylum, Michel rises suddenly from the ground at the narrator's feet, as if materializing from his unconscious, to tell his life story. For Michel to pause in his quest in order to relate his past life to the narrator in itself constitutes an avowed retreat from the imminent loss of his "last illusions" to the idealized memory of childhood happiness (p. 185). He wishes to postpone the disappointment of pulling up the last mandrake root in the asylum garden; if it is mute like the others, his appointed quest has failed and his mystical bride, the Queen of Sheba / Fée aux Miettes, will perish.

Michel's oral autobiography is actually continuous, but the text divides it into many titled chapters. The titles indicate a degree of self-conscious literary artifice which militates against taking Michel's account entirely seriously. They reflect some psychic distance on the part of the implied author; they ironically juxtapose the rational-materialistic viewpoint to the imaginative one in such a way as to call both viewpoints into question: "Où l'on rencontre le personnage le plus raisonnable de cette histoire à la maison des fous"; "Comme quoi Michel fut aimé d'une grisette et amoureux d'un portrait en miniature"; "Comment Michel le charpentier fut innocent, et comment il fut condamné à être pendu"; "Ce que Michel faisait pour se dédommager quand il fut riche"; "Où l'on enseigne la seule manière honnête de passer la première nuit de ses noces avec une jeune et jolie femme [i.e., by dreaming about her], quand on vient d'en épouser une vieille" ("Where you meet the most rational person in this story in a madhouse"; "How Michel was loved by a working girl and in love with a portrait in miniature"; "How Michel the carpenter was innocent, and how he was condemned to hang"; "What Michel did to compensate himself for being rich"; "Where we teach you the only honorable way of spending your wedding night with a pretty young woman, when you've just married an old one."[1] In one way or another, all these titles re-echo the dominant idea that the imagination provides a refuge, necessary for the sensitive person, from the disappointments of material reality. "Quel infortuné, ô mon Dieu! n'a pas eu sur la terre, où tu nous as jetés pêle-mêle, sans nous peser et sans nous compter . . . dans un moment de colère ou de dérision! . . . quel homme n'a pas eu sa mandragore qui chante?" ("What poor soul, oh God! has not had on this earth, where you've tossed us pell-mell, without weighing us or counting us . . . in a moment of anger or mockery! . . . what man has not had his singing mandrake root?" [*C*, p. 185; the ellipses are Nodier's]), the narrator exclaims. But according to the order in which the elements of each title are experienced by the reader, the illusion of happiness evoked by the first half is brusquely dispelled by the hard fact of the second half. In this way the implied author gently derides the dreams to which he cannot completely succeed in surrendering his rational, critical consciousness. Deliberately flat, ironic understatement in some titles, as opposed to Michel's exotic account of things (e.g., the ravishing, legendary oriental Queen of Sheba is described as a "jolie femme"), further removes us and the implied author from Michel's vision. His definitive triumph occurs only in the narrator's imagination (Daniel's report at the end) and in a fairy tale purchased from a *colporteur* (a wandering street vendor) at the conclusion.

Within the story, however, Michel is glorified by implication. His name corresponds to that of the archangel Michael who defeated Satan. The Fée herself lives under the west end of a church, the fortress-like area commonly dedicated to the Archangel, whose might opposes the demons of death and night coming from the direction of the setting sun. Michel's choice of the carpenter's trade shows him predestined, in a sense, to reenact the life of Christ: "Le charpentier, mon enfant! c'est dans ses chantiers que notre divin maître a daigné choisir son père adoptif" ("The carpenter, my child! It's in his workshop that our Holy Lord condescended to choose his adoptive father!" [*C*, p. 190]). Several allusions to the life of Christ appear late in the story, and Michel's gift of tongues (he knows all recorded languages) suggests that he has been baptized in the Holy Spirit and charged with an apostolic mission to his fellow men.

A characteristic hero of epic or fairy tale, Michel has no parents. His mother died shortly after his birth; his father is absent on a distant voyage from which he will not return; when Michel turns sixteen, the uncle who has been caring for him leaves in search of the father. Since an identity is not gratuitously given him through his family, he must seek his own. The influence of his uncle, whose familiarity with Orientals and with "savages" has led to "a sort of systematic scorn for European society and customs" (p. 187), prevents Michel from unreflectively embracing a ready-made social role. The "father" he seeks should also be understood as his mature identity. As chief restorer of the Temple of Solomon, he ends up serving Belkiss in more or less the same way as his uncle reportedly does as her superintendent of buildings. Her alter ego, La Fée aux Miettes, is directly associated with Michel's mother (p. 212), and for Michel to marry Solomon's widow is for him symbolically to replace the father by acceding to an adult status in his turn—royal rank being a commonplace manner of representing the parents. But Michel cannot achieve his maturation without successfully passing a series of tests of his integrity and independence: the temptation to outshine his schoolmates (and later, to avenge himself for their ingratitude); the temptation to give way before the laughter of his friends, who ridicule his attachment to La Fée aux Miettes; the temptation of material security thrice offered by the twenty guineas which he has saved and by the jeweled frame of Belkiss' portrait; the temptation of irresponsible gratification offered by the flirtations of Folly Girlfree; the battle with the monster, representing fear of sexuality; and the trial by a tribunal of animals (repressed libido).

La Fée aux Miettes, a wise and ancient beggar dwarf, guides Michel during his formative years. She subsists on the remains of the school-boys' lunches, which they offer her in exchange for help with their homework. Her knowledge of all languages associates her with a universal wisdom. Her origins in the Orient and her claim to have been married to Solomon reinforce her connection with a source of illumination; but it also suggests that such illumination comes from outside the Christian church without, however, being incompatible with Christian beliefs.[2] Her residence beneath the main entrance of the local church, granted officially in 1369, reinforces this implication. Her relationship with the spiritual order is further suggested by the unique, dazzlingly white headdress she has invented, made of several square folds set horizontally atop the scarf which completely conceals her hair, "like the base or the capstone of a Corinthian column" (p. 196). The column itself, and the order in which the elements associated with it are presented (bottom-to-top), evokes a communication between earth and heaven, resulting from the headdress which captures, masters, and directs the vital force contained in the hair, according to conventional symbolism.[3] The squares suggest the earth, or libido, harmonious control of which serves the ends of spiritual ascension as bodily energies are channeled upward. The same constellation of ideas is implied by the Fée's habit of bounding up and down at moments of joy. She reaches surprising heights, particularly when her future marriage with Michel is being discussed. And her gold-headed crutch of cedar wood represents her royalty (through the attributes of the gold and the cane) and immortality (through the attribute of the wood). Later she will halt Michel's execution by extending the crutch in a gesture of command (p. 274). Her doll-like white dresses, never wrinkled or dirty, signify her secret identity as an imperishable, incorruptible component of the soul.

Her dependence on others for sustenance (and on Michel for money), her diminutive stature, and her other grotesque features show her to be an emanation of Michel's unconscious: his *anima* or soul-image. Her "phallic" attributes—the crutch and two long canine teeth which protrude an inch and a half beneath her chin—are common to the witches and fairies of many lands. They result from the disappearance of sexual differentiation in the deep unconscious, resulting from an association with memories from a period of childhood which antedates the sexual orientation of the libido.[4] Like the fairies in folktale and medieval romance, she appears first as a wrinkled old lady testing the hero's generosity, and later as a beautiful young woman who rewards that generosity. Her curious physical attractiveness, persisting despite her great age, and her incongruous flirtatiousness with Michel serves to call his attention to her so that he may become receptive to the messages of his unconscious. Her face and trim body preserve the charm of eternal youth (pp. 194–96).[5] Her beauty will reveal itself gradually, first in a dream of her sisters as lovely princesses, then in the portrait of Belkiss in the medallion the Fée gives Michel, and finally in the physical apparition of Belkiss herself as the alter ego of the Fée (chs. 9, 11, and 22).

Two apparently trivial motifs point to the central meaning of Michel's story. These are the anniversaries, and the sum of twenty guineas. Every significant event—his graduation from school and choice of a trade; the departure of his uncle; his two rescues of the Fée and betrothal to her; his marriage; the telling of his life story; the successful completion of his quest when he finds the singing mandrake and is reunited with the Queen of Sheba—coincides with the days when Michel becomes fourteen, sixteen, eighteen, twenty, twenty-one, and twenty-two.[6] And on Michel's sixteenth, eighteenth, and twentieth birthdays, he gives his savings of twenty guineas to the Fée and hesitantly commits himself to her. On his twenty-first birthday, he plans to spend the same amount to book passage on a ship named after her. Finally, during the night before his twenty-first birthday, the animal president of a dream tribunal condemns Michel to hang, saying "Voilà, si j'ai bien compté, *vingt* de ces garnements que nous expédions d'aujourd'hui" ("If I've counted right, that makes *twenty* of these urchins we've disposed of today" [p. 258; emphasis added]). This obsessive "twenty" is the years of childhood. To achieve maturity, Michel must renounce them by investing a sum of libido in the Fée.[7] His coming of age, his twenty-first birthday, is the moment appointed for him to marry her, and at her command the execution magically turns into a wedding. Wedding and execution are the same: both signify the death of Michel's childish self, and both involve a spiritual elevation. Hanging suspends one between earth and heaven (at the end of the story Michel will rise into the air), and later in an unguarded moment the Fée promises to help him ascend to his rightful, higher than human place on the Great Chain of Being (pp. 309–10, 314).

When Michel becomes sixteen, the uncle who has been caring for him departs to search for Michel's father. The boy, who has completed his apprenticeship to a carpenter, will support himself by working at that trade. Learning that the Fée wants to return to her home in Greenock, Scotland, Michel sends her twenty guineas, all the money he had received from his uncle, so that she can make the journey. Michel's gift, in effect, renounces his uncle's help and sends the Fée off on her journey, expressing his newfound feelings of self-sufficiency: "My education is complete, I've proved I can work well, my health is vigorous and my resolve is firm" (p. 200). With an attitude typical of the successful child during the latency period, Michel feels proud of his factual and technical knowledge, equal to many an adult's. He does not realize that his emotional, physical, and social maturation has scarcely begun, although the Fée warns him that as yet he cannot always dispense with her advice (p. 201).

Without guidance during the next two years, Michel almost loses the sense of an independent identity. He gives all his savings to his friends in need—exhausts his psychic energies in adolescent attachments to his peers. His dependence on social approval becomes stronger than his self-image: "J'apprenais, s'il faut le dire, une vérité toute nouvelle, c'est que l'homme en société, quelque progrès qu'il ait fait dans l'exercice de la vertu, ne peut se passer de considération, pour être justement content de lui" ("I was learning, if I must confess it, a brand new truth, which is that a social being, no matter how far he has progressed in the practice of virtue, cannot get along without the esteem of others, if he is to be truly satisfied with himself" [p. 207]). Ashamed of his own old clothes, he puts on an old suit of his uncle's to wear for his eighteenth birthday. As he snips off the ungainly, coarse cloth buttons from the more attractive of two vests in order to replace them with buttons of pearl, a golden coin falls out. There are twenty louis in all. This is just enough money to allow Michel to buy a share in his friends' shore-trading enterprise. He can become a capitalist rather than earning wages only sufficient for the needs of the day.

The golden coin is a mandala symbol,[8] emblem of the personality which has successfully integrated conscious and unconscious. In the form of buttons, the coins literally hold together two opposite sides—of a garment (identity). Yet Robert Maples, who rightly says of this detail that "gold is the symbol of superior illumination" (p. 48), fails to add that identical coins, all stamped in the same image, represent such illumination debased to the level of common sense—a kind of practical understanding which seeks to come to terms with the material world. The shore-trading enterprise, which this money will allow Michel to join, channels the libido into voyages confined to the borders of one country and continually returning to it, suggesting narcissism and a blocked development of the psyche, as does the adolescent group that will engage in this trading. Carpentry, on the other hand—since wood is traditionally associated with the feminine principle—means shaping the raw material of the *anima* into a bride for ego consciousness, progressing toward individuation. By abandoning carpentry, Michel risks losing contact with his unconscious.

On his eighteenth birthday, Michel makes a farewell pilgrimage to Mont-Saint-Michel. Returning along the beach, the symbolic meeting place of conscious and unconscious, Michel hears his name amid calls for help. He thrusts his scallop rake into the vortex of quicksand which is rapidly closing over a strange white creature. After a desperate struggle he brings the Fée (for it was she who was about to be engulfed—permanently repressed) back up to the surface.[9] Michel, being more mature than before, can now partially accept the sexuality which those teeth represent: "Parbleu, dis-je, cette fois, la Fée aux Miettes n'a pas eu si grand tort que je le pensais, de conserver ces deux terribles dents qui choquaient ma délicatesse d'écolier" ("By gosh, said I, this time the Crumb Fairy wasn't so badly mistaken as I thought, in keeping those two frightful teeth that used to shock my schoolboy squeamishness." [p. 210]). But he immediately wards off the potential danger of sexuality with the banal generalization that prudence and modesty count for more than beauty—an unconsciously hypocritical reversal of meaning—and he bursts into uncontrollable laughter. He further belittles the Fée by twice comparing her to a toy. But his view of the dream situation as comical reveals that an important conflict (here, one between emerging sexuality and fear) has been portrayed by the dream, and that the dreamer is attempting to defend himself by dismissing the episode as absurd and inconsequential.[10]

He must nevertheless come to terms with the Fée. She has returned to guide Michel away from shore-trading, which she considers unsuitable for him, and into carpentry work: she says he can help restore the houses of Duguesclin at Pontorson, Malherbe at Caen, and Corneille at Rouen, and can help to build a monument to Bernardin in Le Havre. Finally, she says, ships are being built every day in Dieppe. This sequence of projects, as she describes them, has been designed to lead Michel steadily forward through historical time (toward his own maturation) and north toward the English Channel, which he must eventually cross to be reunited with her. Again he sacrifices his twenty guineas to her and quasi-involuntarily promises marriage when he becomes twenty-one. When he returns home, he dreams of beautiful princesses dancing in a circle around him. They all resemble the Fée: Michel has matured sufficiently that the *anima* can appear in his dreams as a love object. The royal rank of these figures calls Michel to a higher stage of development; their graduated sizes suggest the evolution of the *anima* in Michel over the course of time; but their multiplicity shows that Michel has not yet attached the love ideal to any single woman.

At this point Michel's uncle André's ship returns without its captain. André has given the ship and cargo to his crew; he has remained on an island to serve Belkiss, Queen of Sheba, as superintendent of building construction, joining Michel's father, who is her admiral. Michel confirms the donation and leaves his native Granville. Belkiss has protected Michel's family for generations, according to André. It is evident that under her influence, the generation prior to Michel's has spiritually evolved to the point of being worthy to serve her. Michel, the last of his race, will consummate the destiny of his forebears when he and Belkiss marry.

Michel wanders for two years seeking work as a carpenter in the towns the Fée had mentioned. He feels himself under her protection, but has no clear goal other than to find his father and uncle. When he finds a mysterious ship, *La Reine de Saba* ("The Queen of Sheba"), at Le Havre, Michel takes advantage of its offer of free transportation for skilled workers to an unknown destination. The "extraordinary journey" which ensues, "at incredible speed," represents the sexual maturation of a delayed puberty. The process seems rapid and violent to Michel because it is unpredictable, involuntary, and irreversible. The controlling rational faculties of captain[11] and crew are dissociated from the ship/body—the captain is unconcerned and the crew is asleep despite the violent storm that rises. Winds whirl the ship like a top; monstrous fishes and birds (repressed, unrecognized "animalistic" feelings) fall onto the deck; Saint Elmo's fire spurts from the tips of the masts (orgasm). At length the boat sinks and disappears.

Michel finds himself alone in the water with a sack which contains a struggling creature. When he tows it ashore and opens it, La Fée aux Miettes emerges. Michel laughs heartily; as before, this sign of a conflict is followed by the Fée's reminder of his serious obligation toward her. They are to marry in a year. For the third time he gives her his twenty guineas' savings; in return she gives him a medallion containing Belkiss' portrait. This gift of a small magical container by an old woman is typical of folktale.[12] The astounding beauty of the image completely absorbs Michel. Belkiss represents the transformation of the archetypal *anima*-figure in Michel's mind from mother figure to sexual object.[13] Yet "because an image is at a remove from the world of action, it helps [Michel] elevate earthly love to spiritual love. . . . it is she who, by actuating the instincts, animates faith."[14] The acquisition of this talisman represents a major stage of Michel's development. He now can contemplate his soul-image at will, and in a limited way, he begins to integrate elements of the unconscious with the "self" of ego consciousness: "Ce portrait de femme . . . parlait pour la première fois à un sens de mon âme nouvellement révélé. Je ne sais comment cela se faisait, mais j'éprouvais que le sentiment même de ma vie venait de se transformer en quelque chose qui n'était plus moi et qui m'était plus cher que moi" ("That portrait of a woman . . . spoke for the first time to a newly revealed sense in my soul. I don't know how it came about, but I felt that the very feeling of my existence had just been transformed into something which was no longer I and which was dearer to me than I!"[p. 226]). When he finally looks up again at the Fée, she is rapidly receding into the distance. Since dreams represent temporal relationships by spatial ones, the Fée's sudden remoteness links the *anima* in its maternal, protective aspect to a phase of Michel's development which now seems long past.[15]

Michel discovers that he has landed near Greenock, the Fée's home in Scotland. His wild journey to get there and the tag names of the Scottish characters he now meets suggest that he is submerged in a world of fantasy. The *anima*-figure splits into three separate components once the Fée has left Michel. One is the image of Belkiss, the spiritualized ideal of loving companionship; the next is the flirtatious Folly Girlfree, whom Michel encounters as soon as he makes his way toward town. She reflects the maturing body's demands for sexual gratification; she claims to know Michel, although he thinks that he never has met her before. The third component of the *anima* is Mistress Speaker, who runs the inn in which Michel seeks shelter. She revives the mother image because she provides food and comfort, and waits on Michel. She, like Folly Girlfree, believes she knows Michel—i.e., the libido continues to demand recognition from ego consciousness.[16]

There is no room at the inn: Michel cannot regress completely to childhood. He must sleep on the straw pallet belonging to the house mastiffs. Like Christ, he must humble himself by assuming man's physical nature and sleeping on the straw among animals. He must acknowledge the sexuality stimulated by his recent encounters with Belkiss and Folly. But only in his dreams, in symbolic disguise, is such self-awareness possible as yet. Michel dreams of a canine marriage. The dogs' barking, discordant at first, becomes melodious; then they pass by his resting place in an elegantly dressed procession. These details suggest that sexual impulses may be sublimated in such a way as to make them acceptable to the rest of the personality. On awaking, Michel self-protectively dissociates himself from the dogs by a retreat into pedantry, pondering "the bizarre phenomena of nature" and enumerating references to dog-headed men in classical Greek authors. But he accurately speculates that it is the Fée aux Miettes who has probably sent him the dream, for mysterious reasons of her own.

The next day Michel finds work in the carpenter shop of a Master

Finewood. Throughout the next year Folly flirts with him in vain. He proves himself a supremely skillful craftsman, but nearly everyone ridicules him for his devotion to Belkiss, Queen of Sheba. Master Finewood comes to love him like a son, but on the eve of his twenty-first birthday, Michel refuses to marry one of Master Finewood's daughters, who loves him. His thoughts as he rejects this marriage reveal that he is still thinking of relations with a real woman primarily in terms of a physical communion, rather than an emotional, intellectual, and spiritual one: "Isn't the happiness I derive from this illusion [of Belkiss' animated portrait] sufficiently intense and pure to compensate me for [the loss of] a few pleasures poisoned by jealousy, weakened by possession, and unceasingly threatened in their object [the woman's body] by the inevitable passage of time?" (p. 244).

His situation becomes intolerable, and he looks for an escape. The opportunity for departure presents itself when a new and more powerful version of the mysterious ship *La Reine de Saba* appears in port. Through underground passageways, it will travel to an island in the middle of a desert: i.e., to a state which would be impossible to ego consciousness without the guidance of the *anima*. As Michel reads the prospectus of the voyage, Jonathas, a ragged, avaricious little Jew, rises from the ground at his feet (emerges from Michel's unconscious) and finishes translating the Hebrew prospectus by announcing the price of the journey—twenty guineas. Since Michel's project of renouncing the real world involves repressing the materialistic side of his personality, this side is detached from him, exteriorized through psychic projection to acquire an independent existence as Michel's Jungian Shadow, Jonathas. But Jonathas cannot be totally eradicated from Nodier's fictional world. Later, at Michel's trial, Jonathas will take the precious jeweled frame of Belkiss' portrait while Michel keeps her image, and at the end of the tale Daniel reports from Greenock that Jonathas—frail and insubstantial as he seems to have become—is not quite dead.

On the eve of the day that all Master Finewood's daughters will be married at once, and that Michel plans to depart, he finds himself dining at the inn with Master Jap, the bailiff of the Isle of Man, the creature who was married in the dream of the dogs' wedding. Although no one but Michel appears to notice it, the bailiff appears here as a man with the head of a Grèat Dane. He has come to cash in the revenues of his province. As the chief officer of justice, he represents the law of sexuality which governs all humanity, and his bulging wallet signifies a sum of libido which must somehow be channeled and spent. That only Master Jap's head now is dog-like, and that Michel can now with difficulty understand his language, suggests that Michel has evolved further toward an awareness of his own sexuality.

That night, Mistress Speaker asks Michel to share his bed with Master Jap. In the darkness a monster appears to seize the bailiff's wallet. The creature has four heads: a wildcat (female sexuality), a bulldog (male sexuality), a horse's skull (female sexuality associated with death), and a severed human head (male sexuality associated with castration). The number four is associated with the *anima*; the monster embodies Michel's fear of the sexual impulses excited by the *anima*, a fear which threatens to steal—repress—his disposable sum of libido. Michel resists, fighting with the knife (phallus, acceptance of adult male genitality) which he had recently purchased "pour la traversée" ("for the crossing") into maturity. Taking up this weapon represents his acceptance of his sexuality, and after a fight he drives the monster back into the sea (the unconscious).

The bedroom is transformed into a hearing room where a tribunal of animals meets to judge Michel for having killed Master Jap, who has fainted from terror. Michel has consciously accepted the journey to maturity, but not unconsciously: the dog in him—his sexual instincts—is frightened into a catatonic state. He can be saved from the sentence of death by marrying either the Fée or Folly. In the sphere of the unconscious, it does not matter on which level of development he relates to his mature body's demands for physical intimacy. He tries unsuccessfully to deal with his crisis in terms of ego consciousness, defending himself before the tribunal on the basis of his youth, his hard work, and his innocence.[17] He also tries to marshal the forces of his superego in his defense, asking to have his surrogate parents Master Finewood and Mistress Speaker summoned as character witnesses. But Michel's lawyer declares that those persons have never been in the jurisdiction of this court (p. 255). At length it is revealed that Michel is accused of having broken his promise to marry La Fée aux Miettes (p.257). The judge recognizes the portrait of his sovereign in Belkiss (who as *anima* presides over the unconscious), but lacks the wisdom to connect her with La Fée aux Miettes or to realize that her image is worth more than its jeweled frame. The latter is confiscated, and Michel is led out to be hung.

As in *Smarra*, Nodier's description of the crowd at the execution shows that Michel has exteriorized and thus provisionally circumvented the primordial incest fantasy which had colored with apprehension his feelings toward all women. As he marches toward the scaffold, girls distribute among the crowd the freshly printed history of his supposed crime. This is again described as the murder of Sir Jap, thus implicitly related to the crime of an imperfect relationship to the *anima*, as charged during the trial. The printed sheet symbolizes the transfer to others, through projection, of Michel's regressive feelings, which hinder maturation: "D'autres jeunes filles se disputaient la feuille tout humide d'impression, afin de la reporter plus vite *à un amant ou à un père*, qui les soulevaient d'un bras *caressant* pour leur montrer un homme qu'on allait tuer" ("Other girls were quarreling over the still-damp leaflets, in order to bring them back all the faster *to a lover or a father*, who lifted them up with a *caressing* arm to show them a man who was about to be killed" [p. 268; emphasis added]). "Either a father or a lover" means "the father/lover" in dream language. Michel has reversed the sexual roles of his own situation (mother/son) by way of a secondary disguise added to that of projection. Nodier as author had become sufficiently sophisticated to do this because eleven years earlier he had used "straight" projected disguise (young men watch Lucius' execution in the company of their "lovers or mothers") in *Smarra*. The presence of one sympathetic old man in the crowd watching Michel suggests the approval of the Wise Old Man archetype in his unconscious and promises a successful integration of the personality. And one sympathetic blond girl foreshadows the triumphant emergence of the *anima* in the form of La Fée aux Miettes.

The sheriff pauses to announce that, by virtue of an ancient Scottish custom, Michel can be saved if a girl will consent to marry him. Folly rushes forward to offer herself. From the social viewpoint, she represents Michel's last opportunity to recover his sanity and live as others do. But in the mystical perspective, she constitutes the final, most seductive temptation for Michel to remain fixed in the material order. Gradually, obliquely, and with difficulty, Michel admits that this temptation has existed for him. When he manages openly to acknowledge it to himself, he becomes free. First he totally rejects the notion of loving Folly. Then he admits that he could imagine a person who would love her. Finally, he admits that he has had fantasies of loving her himself: "Je n'avais jamais eu d'amour pour Folly . . . Et cependant, monsieur, je concevais qu'un homme autrement organisé . . . pût être heureux de l'amour de Folly. . . . Les heures de délices que Folly pouvait me donner, je les avais rêvées aussi" ("I had never loved Folly . . . and yet, Sir [Michel's address to the frame-narrator betrays his defensive self-consciousness], I could conceive that a man of a different temperament . . . might be happy with Folly's love . . . The hours of delight that Folly could give me, I had dreamed of them too" [p. 272]). Thus when the Fée appears to tell Michel that he has been found innocent, he can assure her that he can honor his engagement to her without effort because his heart is bound to no earthly creature. And as he departs arm in arm with the Fée, for the first time the derisive laughter of the spectators does not embarrass him. He has affirmed himself to be independent of society (pp. 275, 277). Earlier, he had repeatedly felt abashed when others mocked his attachment to the Fée. At times he admitted to himself that their laughter was reasonable, and that only prideful stubbornness made him persist in his fixation. But now he has become totally alienated, or, in positive terms, autonomous.

Having married the Fée, Michel accompanies her to a tiny house at the foot of an arsenal wall. It expands enormously once he steps inside. Nodier probably encountered this motif, common in fairy tales, in Antoine Hamilton's *Les Quatre Facardins*. Himself librarian of the Arsénal in Paris, Nodier seems to imply that for him access to the imagination is always near at hand, and offers infinite resources. Michel adjures the vain pretensions of reason and gives himself over to the Fée's teaching, which is informed by imagination and sentiment. Her miraculous garden, a commonplace symbol of the female sexual organs, suggests sublimation because it is filled with rare jewels (spiritual wisdom) and butterflies (the promise of resurrection). Filled with tenderness by the Fée's maternal solicitude, Michel kisses her hand. At once a gentle, expressive, musical growling is heard outside. It is a canine servant of Master Jap, bringing, in tribute to the Fée, the revenues of the Isle of Man, the sum of libido which Michel had defended against fearful repression the night before. Now the integration of Michel's conscious and unconscious selves is almost complete. The Fée tells him that he has become as rich as she because she has wisely invested his earlier gifts, and that his father and uncle—his mature identity—are alive. Soon he will be able to rejoin them.

The narrative continues on two levels. During the day, the Fée chastely takes care of Michel; at night she takes refuge behind her locked bedroom door, and Belkiss, Queen of Sheba, appears to bring him sexual ecstasy in his dreams. The language describing the setting of this union, and Michel's bliss ("all illumination was extinguished"; "nearly fatal delights," pp. 296, 297), hints at a foretaste of death, the dream which never ends and the only state in which Michel will be able to achieve perfect happiness. When he expresses the fear that living with the Fée may cause him to lose his reason, she replies that madness may be a higher form of wisdom. In any event, when Michel returns to Master Finewood's workshop the next morning it becomes clear that, beginning with his last night at the inn, he has entered a world different from that of his employer and of ordinary human beings. He has heard nothing of the previous night's "terrible storm" which is the talk of the town; Master

Finewood has heard nothing of Michel's battle with the monster, his trial, and his near-execution. Yet Michel in waking life symbolically assumes the functions of a father, taking charge of Master Finewood's shop and arranging for the marriage of his six daughters. At the same time he tells the Fée that the world of men is alien to him and that nobody but she can understand him (p. 312).

After six months of happiness, Michel learns that the Fée will die six months later, on his twenty-second birthday, unless he finds the "singing mandrake root" before that time, while remaining faithful to her. This plant is rich in legendary associations. Nodier describes it as a powerful narcotic, hinting that it may provide access to visionary perception. The plant is associated with both love and death. It is reputed to be an aphrodisiac; it is said to emit a piteous scream when plucked, killing whoever hears it.[18] And most important for Nodier's story, the mandrake's shape, which resembles the human body, represents the soul in its negative, minimal aspects. Picking it means freeing the undeveloped soul from its prison of clay and raising it to perfect love experience in an afterlife. This motif of love after death, common in romanticism, reflects an unconscious yearning for reunion in death with the mother, ideally kind and beautiful, as she is remembered from earliest infancy. Indeed the Fée identifies the mandrake's song as "that refrain of your childhood." If Michel's quest succeeds, she will be reborn as Belkiss. On the eve of Michel's departure, the Fée's door at last remains open. Michel enters her room and bed. She and Belkiss become one, to provide a foretaste of his eventual reward. But to undertake his quest he must abandon his carpenter's work, his final link with social reality. Ultimately, like Saint-Exupéry's Little Prince, Michel will have to accept death to escape his terrestrial exile and regain his spiritual home.

At this point the story returns to the frame narrator in the Glasgow asylum. The sun is about to set; Michel runs to his mandrake patch to complete the quest before its appointed end. To avoid seeing Michel's imminent despair, and to preserve the memory of a dream to which he could not ultimately surrender himself, the frame narrator retreats precipitously. At once, a pedantic doctor, representative of the material principle as Michel was representative of the imaginative one, accosts him, seizes his jacket, explains ponderously that the mandrake cannot sing because it has no vocal organs, and then expounds the brutal treatment he plans for Michel. The frame narrator escapes only by leaving a button in his interlocutor's hands.[19] The resulting separation of the two sides of his jacket implies that he can no longer reconcile the material and imaginative principles in his personality.

The narrator retires to his bed to dream, after sending Daniel, his imagination, to discover what has happened to Michel. On his return, Daniel reports that Michel escaped from the asylum at sunset. Ascending with the singing mandrake flower in his hand, past the side of a Catholic church, he vanished into the upper air. In other words, Michel's spiritual development follows the same course as that associated with orthodox religion, but he goes further. Everyone in Greenock, Daniel reports, misses Michel. Folly Girlfree and all of Master Finewood's daughters have had children marked with the sign of the mandrake: Michel's exemplary kindness and self-abnegation, at last understood, have inspired the birth of a new, spiritually revitalized society.

Now that Michel's disappearance has eliminated the narrator's opportunities for a vicarious escape from reality in Scotland, he flees to what was another place of enchantment for Nodier—Venice, the setting of his *Les Fiancés* and *Franciscus Columna*. There the material principle promptly assails him again. An Italian academician asks his opinion concerning certain trifling factual details of ancient history. The second one of these questions, concerning the disposition of Pompey's troops at the Battle of Pharsala, refers to an incident reported in Book CXI of Livy, thus bringing us back full circle. The narrator turns brusquely aside to purchase Michel's just published autobiography from among the fairy tales offered by a strolling street vendor. There the archetype of Inversion ensures Michel's triumph. Although Michel has given up the inheritance of his own family and of Master Finewood, the love of two attractive women, and a respected role in society in exchange for incarceration in a madhouse, he has become the prince consort of the Queen of Sheba, Empress of the Seven Planets (the solar system). Such a book, the narrator assures the astounded academician, could better advance the moral instruction of a sensitive people than could "toutes les babioles pédantesques de quelques méchants philosophastres brevetés, patentés et appointés pour instruire les nations" ("all the pedantic trifles of those wretched pseudo-philosophers delegated, commissioned, and appointed to instruct the nations" [p. 329]). He would prove this by demonstration (by citing Michel's book), he tells us, had not a band of gypsies stolen the pamphlet while he slept beside Lake Como. The printed word, manifestation of the material principle, can never achieve more than a transient and uneasy alliance with the imagination, Nodier believed. The gypsies, wandering free creatures from a world of fantasy, have reclaimed their own.

CHAPTER 9

The Myth of Atonement in Nerval's *Aurélia*

> *L'art poussé à un certain degré,*
> *produit de ces illusions.*
> —*Beelzebub* (*Quinet*, Ahasvérus)

The dream is a second life," Nerval begins, "where the *self*, in another form, continues the work of existence."[1] The author proceeds to equate the dream with the visions of madness. Unequivocally he describes two of his involuntary confinements in an insane asylum, with at least some of their indignities—the straitjacket, the attendants. The details of his language reveal a consistent attempt to be rational, scientific, and objective. Knowingly he employs his writing as a form of autotherapy.[2] At last, he believes, this effort at self-cure, combined with the care he had received, has succeeded, "and I could judge more sanely the world of illusions in which, for a time, I had lived" (p. 824). Yet he does not dismiss his experience of that world as meaningless: *Aurélia*'s last sentence declares: "Nevertheless, I am happy in the new [quasi-Christian, syncretistic religious] convictions I have acquired, and I compare the series of ordeals I have undergone to what, for the Ancients, was represented by the idea of a descent into Hell" (p. 824). In other words, he has lived through the archetypal pattern of Withdrawal, Enlightenment, and Return. At the end, the narrator no longer identifies himself with the hero, whom we

last saw riding through heaven with Christ and Aurélia at his side. The
hero embodied the psychic energy needed to impel the narrator to and
through the visions that changed his life. Now that change has trans-
pired, the hero can disappear.

Obviously the drama of the interrelationship of narrator and hero is
the central intended meaning of the work, and *Aurélia* is extraordinarily
successful in sustaining an equilibrium between illusion and detach-
ment. Here Nerval's text is its own best critic. But two other, admittedly
incomplete, perspectives, which tilt *Aurélia* violently toward one side or
the other, are needed more fully to bring to light the richness of the text.
One of these approaches takes the hero's triumph at face value, and
studies how he reaches apotheosis, through the chaos of incident in the
text. (Since Béguin and Richer have already done this well, my own
version shall be brief.) The second, unbendingly skeptical, treats the
hero and his adventures as an elaborate tissue of delusions whose true
meaning can be read only between the lines. Where other romantic
dream narratives are concerned, it usually is possible to treat the mythic
and the delusional simultaneously: such is the complexity of *Aurélia*,
however, that two successive readings will be necessary. They are
mutually incompatible: ego-defensive strategies have created a rigid
compartmentalization separating wish-fulfilling myth from repressed,
rationalized anger.

(I, 1)   As *Aurélia* begins, the hero must descend into the underworld of his unconscious to reestablish contact with his soul-image or
anima. The sun of psychic wholeness has disappeared; all the visions
of Part I will be nocturnal.[3] The *anima* has been lost because the hero
has erroneously identified it with a single woman, the title character.
Once she rejects him, and all the more once she dies, his entire identity
is threatened.

> Chacun peut chercher dans ses souvenirs l'émotion la plus navrante,
> le coup le plus terrible frappé sur l'âme par le destin; il faut alors se
> résoudre à mourir ou à vivre. [Since I did not choose suicide, yet
> could not endure my loss,] il ne me restait qu'à me jeter dans les
> enivrements vulgaires. [I, 1, p. 754]

> [We all can recollect our greatest trauma, the most terrible blow with
> which destiny has struck our soul; then we must resolve either to die
> or to live. . . . All that was left to me was to throw myself into
> commonplace diversions.]

He has not yet realized that to survive and suffer constitutes a necessary series of ordeals which must be successfully undergone to make him worthy of his beloved (union with whom constitutes self-actualization). But the narrator's retrospective comparison of his dream transcriptions with three other initiatic texts—Apuleius, Dante, and Swedenborg—anticipates the syncretistic tendencies of the forthcoming quest, which will receive enlightenment from pagan, Christian, and occultist traditions all together.

(I, 2) Eventually the hero discovers the correct orientation of his quest, towards the east and the rising sun, source of enlightenment (p. 758). But he meets two obstacles: he does not yet realize that his quest for illumination must be an inner, spiritual one rather than an outer, physical one (he strides through the streets of Paris toward the star in which he thinks the mystic She resides), and his desire for illumination seems incompatible with Christianity because it still involves a yearning to possess the loved woman.[4]

(I, 3) From the moment that the hero cries out, rejecting Christianity as he contemplates the star, the narrator recognizes that the interpenetration of dream and waking life has begun. By rejecting a ready-made, collective religious solution to the search for individuation, the hero commits himself to the exploration of his own unconscious. When he strips off his clothing to become free of the earth, a night patrol surrounds him. He is arrested and led off to prison, which swallows him up like the dragons of older legends: "The hero is the symbolical exponent of the movement of libido. . . . The journey to the East (the Night Sea Journey in the monster's belly) with its attendant events symbolizes the effort to adapt to the conditions of the psychic inner world. The complete swallowing up and disappearance of the hero in the belly of the dragon represents the complete withdrawal of interest from the outer world."[5] The hero's inner world at once presents him with a vision of the *anima* which is no longer limited to a single person:

> Le destin de l'Ame délivrée semblait se révéler à moi. . . .
> D'immenses cercles se traçaient dans l'infini, comme les orbes que
> forme l'eau troublée par la chute d'un corps; . . . et une divinité,
> toujours la même, rejetait en souriant les masques furtifs de ses
> diverses incarnations, et se réfugiait enfin insaisissable dans les
> mystiques splendeurs du ciel d'Asie [P. 761]

> [The destiny of the liberated Soul seemed to be revealed to me.
> . . . Vast circles, like the ripples of water disturbed by a falling
> object, formed in the infinite; . . . and a goddess, always the same,
> smilingly cast aside the furtive masks of her various incarnations,

and at last took refuge out of reach in the mystical splendors of the Asian sky.]

Because the hero has not yet successfully confronted his Shadow or undesired characteristics, however, his encounter with the *anima* can only be temporary. She fades; the Shadow then appears, in the form of a double who seems to be taken for the narrator, and who is released from prison in his stead. The narrator becomes disoriented: his perceptions of the real are mingled with fantastic images, and all that he perceives is fragmented into a myriad of fleeting shapes. He is taken to an asylum and the next five chapters record his visions there.

(I, 4) Because the hero has just failed to ascend to his Star, and because he now requires psychic guidance, the images of ancestral figures enter his dreams. Jung explains that in men's dreams, wise advice, prohibitions, and decisive convictions emanate from the father figure. This spiritual guide is frequently represented not by the dreamer's real father, but by an authoritative old man, a ghost, or a talking animal. Real persons are ordinarily not used to embody the archetype of Spirit in dreams because this archetype must speak through our own unconscious. This archetype appears when the dreamer requires insight, determination, and planning which he cannot muster on his own resources.[6] Here the hero dreams that he has been transported to an ancestral home beside the Rhine. On the wall, the tutelary fairy of the region is represented by a mere sketch, suggesting that as yet only a faint image of the *anima* is accessible to the hero's consciousness as he attempts to build up his personality (p. 764). But the soul of his departed ancestor, in the form of a bird, speaks to him and shows him a portrait of the fairy in color. The eventual union of hero and *anima* now is symbolically foreshadowed by the streams of molten metal (a marriage of fire and water, "male" and "female" principles) which carry the hero to an underground country where he will receive further illumination. When he arrives, another Wise Old Man leads him to a gathering of his ancestors, one of whom explains that he must undergo years of trials back on earth. These sufferings, however, are not to be understood as symptoms of unworthiness and nothing more: they will lead to redemption. This redemption is also foreshadowed when the hero has a vision of all his ancestors and himself forming an unbroken chain of souls. These consist of only seven different beings, a number which corresponds to the number of the planets, to the notes of the musical scale, to the days of the Creation, and thus, by implication, to a universal harmony restored.

(I, 5) The vision of a cosmic order represented by the family group leads to an intimation of personal regeneration. The hero finds himself wandering through the streets of an unknown city, above which a mountain rises to symbolize his goal: the self-actualized personality. The goal is then personified. Scattered among the crowds, the narrator notices, are certain individuals who seem to belong to a race apart. They are lively and resolute, with vigorous features and an air of uncompromising individuality which recalls the war-like, independent tribes of the mountain highlands (p. 768). Now the narrator is accompanied by a guide, who leads him steadily uphill to lofty gardens and a mountain home. There he sees the Wise Old Man of his previous dream engaged in a mysterious handicraft (the construction of the personality); but as he tries to draw near to observe, his way is blocked by a man in white whose face is obscured and who threatens him with a weapon. As earlier, when the double had his back turned to the narrator (in I, 3), and later, when the double again menaces him with a weapon whose nature is unclear, the narrator's imperfect perception of this figure shows that he is not yet aware of the nature of the difficulty which debars him from full spiritual development. He remains divided between the consoling dreams of night and his mental illness during the day.

(I, 6)   In his next dream the narrator again returns to his ancestral house and to childhood, but this time his need to reestablish contact with religious beliefs becomes more specific. He meets three gracious women whose features flicker and interchange. They dress him in a gossamer suit like a spider web, and he stands timidly before them "as if I had been no more than a little child in the presence of beautiful great ladies" (p. 772). His dress is a symbolic return to the womb: the spider is a common mother symbol, and here what was spun out of her internal organs envelops the narrator. The group of three sister beings suggests the Greek Moira, looked upon as spinners and as goddesses of vegetation, and associated with the Horae, goddesses of time.[7] One leads him into a grape arbor with arched trellises arranged to form a barrel vault ("en berceaux"): the French word also means cradle. The narrator is being spiritually reborn. The trellis forms a network of crosses, and the latticework with the sky showing through also suggests the union of material and spiritual. The old garden paths, cut in the shape of a cross, are nearly effaced, as Christianity, the religion an aunt tried to teach him in childhood, has become effaced in the narrator's mind. He must cultivate it again, in order to merit reunion with the *anima*-figure. That is the implicit message of the garden, whose symbolic fountain and hollyhock (a perennial with many successive blooms on the same stalk) promise immortality. But the lady disappears.

(I, 7)   The hero learns of the death of the real Aurélia, whom he now hopes to rejoin in an afterlife. A birth dream combines the hero's personal destiny with a cosmic regeneration: "I thought I had been transported to a dim planet where the first germs of creation were struggling." Plants and then monstrous reptiles rise from the clay, while Aurélia, deified as a star, shines over them.

(I, 8)   The hero is one of the monsters. A sudden harmony modulates their shrieking, hissing, and roaring into a heavenly tune. In universal symbolism, the monster represents "the cosmic forces at a stage one step removed from chaos."[8] A radiant goddess (the star of the previous chapter) descends to earth to guide the monsters' transformations into people and animals. Their evolution suggests the underlying unity of all being. For the individual, they represent the self which one must surpass to develop a superior self, and their changes depict "a personality in the course of individuation, which has not yet truly acquired the totality of selfhood, nor actualized all its powers."[9] This progress is interrupted by a battle between two armies of elemental spirits. According to Jung, such a dream conflict between two peoples signifies that "the conscious mind is defending its position and trying to suppress the unconscious."[10] The ensuing deluge engulfs Aurélia herself; to suppress the "unworthy" unconscious also breaks contact with the *anima*. The hero's inner conflict is thereby speciously calmed, and he leaves the asylum. Actually, his psychic disharmony merely is frozen in irresolution, to erupt anew ten years later.

(I, 9)   Strolling in the country, the narrator hears a bird who seems to speak a few words. He can no longer understand them as he had earlier (I, 4). Contact with the unconscious has been lost. But this is the first time in *Aurélia* that the narrator refers specifically to his unworthiness, i.e., acknowledges his need and responsibility for change (p. 781). Is it too late? A mystical marriage between Aurélia and the returned double seems about to take place; the double has convinced Aurélia and the narrator's friends that *he* is really the narrator.

(I, 10)   The dream itself has lost its efficacy as a means to self-discovery and salvation. The narrator's steadily diminishing sense of personal worth is shown in the ensuing dream series by the shrinking physical settings, compensated for by the narrator's increasingly desperate self-affirmation. Each reduction in scale seems to offer an assurance, which is quickly dispelled. The narrator feels himself sliding down an infinite thread (subliminal associations of ideas) into the interior of the earth. He arrives at a beach covered with reeds withering at their tips: at the juncture of conscious and unconscious, growth has been halted. The division of the hero's personality recurs in the presence of *two* slopes in the landscape before him (rather than one, as in I, 4). Atop one is a chateau; atop the other, a city. Darkness halts the narrator's climb toward the chateau. He goes back down into the city and enters a casino, inside which some workers are forming a giant winged llama out of clay. The building's function suggests chance and magic; the spectacle of the artificial creature, animated by the same primordial fire which gave life to the first beings, leads the narrator to hope that the workmen have discovered the secrets of divine creation. Implicitly, to construct a beast (instincts) with wings (sublimation) suggests the blending of id and superego to form an integrated personality. But when the narrator asks whether men too could not be created in this way, he is told that men come from above, not from below: we cannot create ourselves (p. 785).

Still in search of himself, the narrator wanders through other rooms. The crowds of strangers in them scarcely notice his presence. For the dreamer to be surrounded by strangers, according to Jung, shows that "the unconscious has won considerable ground"[11] in its struggle against an ego consciousness which is seeking enlightenment. As the sphere of self-knowledge shrinks, the dreamer's acts and impressions are increasingly governed by forces in his psyche unknown to him. A crisis ensues: the narrator hears of a marriage celebration soon to occur, and imagines that it must be the wedding of his double to Aurélia. This double is the Shadow, a repository for "all those characteristics whose existence is found to be painful or regrettable" by ego consciousness. When the Shadow is forced back into the unconscious by means of repression, it "contaminates" the *anima* whose abode is also the unconscious. This state of affairs, says Jung, is represented as marriage or the like in dreams. The *anima* can only be released for reunion with ego consciousness, as its desirable complement in the whole personality, when "the Shadow is recognized as an ego-adjunct, and the *anima* as not belonging to the ego."[12]

Here the narrator does just the wrong thing, fighting against the Shadow rather than recognizing it as part of himself. He creates a disturbance and, to prevent the wedding, he is about to make a magical sign to subjugate all in attendance (pridefully to assert the primacy of ego consciousness over the figments of the unconscious which mock his helplessness) when the scream of a woman in pain awakens him. This woman is the *anima*. At this point she embodies the humble, prayerful side of the hero, which desperately cries out "no" to the path pursued so far, the attempt at an egocentric control of the world. Ego consciousness's claim to self-sufficiency threatens the *anima* with death. Profoundly troubled, the narrator throws himself upon the ground, and prays with desperation.

(I and II) *"Eurydice! Eurydice!!"* The epigraph to the second part compares the narrator to Orpheus. His descent to the hell of the unconscious has failed: he has lost the *anima* for a second time, and now he too must die. In the opening lines he mournfully hopes that death will bring oblivion to end the pain of loss. But then he thinks of God; and when he remembers that Aurélia believed in God, he begs for the gift of prayer: "Lorsque l'âme flotte incertaine entre la vie et le rêve, entre le désordre d l'esprit et le retour de la froide réflexion, c'est dans la pensée religieuse que l'on doit chercher des secours" ("When the soul hovers uncertainly between waking life and dreams, between mental disorder and the return of cold reflection, it is in religious ideas that one must seek help" [p. 788]). Progressively throughout the six chapters of Part II, the hero's confusion and guilt will gradually be replaced by pardon and enlightenment as the personal drama acquires a universal religious significance. Roughly speaking, the hero reenacts the events of Part I in a new perspective, as a comparison of corresponding situations in the two parts reveals.[13] Aurélia changes from goal to guide; the double changes from enemy to brother; and religion illuminates the hero. In the table shown here, the Arabic numbers represent chapter numbers. Chapter 6 of Part II corresponds to chapters 6 through 10 of Part I. The spiritual enlightenment described in this concluding chapter puts an end to the fragmentation of the personality and to the incomplete visions of the supernatural which characterize the earlier chapters, an incompleteness reflected by those chapters' frequent divisions of the text.

Part I	Part II
1. Dreaming is a second life.	1. In dreams, religion orients the soul.
Guilt toward the woman.	Absence of God.
2. Her pardon.	2. The possibility of prayer.
Premonition of death.	Vision of Aurélia dispels the temptation of suicide.
3. Doubling of everything, including the self. The divinity divinity withdraws.	3. It is "too late": the hero has failed to understand religion and the poets.
4. Reunion with ancestors.	4. Hope of pardon from the dead.
5. The menacing apparition.	5. Premonition of the Deluge.
Memory of a lost paradise.	Vision of Mary-Archetype.

6. Edenic garden of childhood. Death of the Lady and Nature.	6. Edenic asylum garden. The hero accepts ordeals; their mystic meaning.
7. Chaos of world origins.	Revelation of secret voices in nature.
8. A goddess presides over the evolution of the monsters. War of the "accursed races." Suffering of the Mother.	Vision: the "infinite chain" of souls. The soldier-inmate Saturnin. Vision of the goddess.
9. The hero leaves the asylum. The armed double has struck him; he resolves to fight back.	The hero returns home. Act of charity toward the double; end of ordeals; unification.
10. "An evil spirit had taken my place in the world of souls." "I had disturbed the harmony of the magical universe."	The hero ascends to heaven with his spiritual brother, Saturnin. The hero as Christ-figure bearing the good news to men.

Specifically, in the second part the hero becomes able to obviate the double as an obstacle to his reunion with the *anima* by reabsorbing the double (the symptom of his sense of inadequacy) into his sphere of self-awareness. This development culminates in the last chapter with the reanimation of Saturnin. The hero's inner conflict between belief in Christianity (the Parent, the superego, submission to authority) and the revolt modes of paganism or Enlightenment skepticism (the id, the Child) will be resolved. Rather than remaining self-absorbed, merely wanting love and feelings acceptance or rejection, the hero becomes capable of feeling concern for others and of trying to help them: he visits the sick (II, 1); piously follows a stranger's funeral procession (II, 2); gives alms to a street singer, tries to help his father and stop a fight (II, 4); prays and feels pity for women and children (II, 5); and preserves accounts of his visions and communicates them in the hope they will aid in the salvation of others (II, 6). His longing to receive his own pardon from the loved woman, and later from God, is transformed into the hope of pardon for all men and gods. His artistic act broadens from introspection to a service for others: the hero's experience comes to appear valid and instructive for all men:

Le désespoir et le suicide sont le résultat de certaines situations fatales pour qui n'a pas foi dans l'immortalité, dans ses peines et dans ses joies:—je croirai avoir fait quelque chose de bon et d'utile en énonçant naïvement la succession des idées par lesquelles j'ai retrouvé le repos et une force nouvelle à opposer aux malheurs futurs de la vie. [P. 799]

[Despair and suicide are the result of certain situations, fatal for one who does not have faith in immortality, with its joys and sorrows:— I will believe that I have accomplished something good and useful by stating without affectation the sequence of ideas through which I found peace of mind and a renewed strength to resist life's misfortunes in the future.]

Yet his renewed search for reunion with Aurélia herself in Part II evolves only gradually toward a spiritual, religious mode. In the first phase he seeks physical reunion by contemplating suicide and by rediscovering her burial place. At length he destroys the piece of paper which bears the location of her tomb, and also her letter, realizing that through cherishing these relics of idolatry he has "preferred the creature to the creator" (II, 2). He next pursues the quest for her in the domain of memory, which culminates in the rediscovery of his letters to her. Only the intervention of his therapist "restored [him] to the world of the living," removing him from the circle of his own concerns to an interest in another patient (II, 6, pp. 814–15). The third phase of the quest, sustained and active charity toward this patient, makes him worthy to be reunited with Aurélia, who descends from her star to encourage him to tell him that his trials have ended (p. 816). The visions of mountain peaks which follow confirm that he has undergone an apotheosis (p. 817).

(II, 1) The hero's transformation begins when he thinks of God for the first time in a long while: "The fatal system [of pantheism] which had been created in my mind did not allow for that solitary royalty [of a Supreme Being]" (p. 788). Pantheism corresponds to adolescent identity diffusion, and is the theological counterpart to the aimless traveling in which the hero has indulged, "infatuated with variety and caprice" (p. 755). God, or the idealized higher self, has been forgotten. But now the hero's renewed religious sensibility helps him transcend his own suffering and excessive self-preoccupation through his empathy with others. He visits a sick friend he had neglected; illness becomes a metaphor for other-worldliness; his friend speaks like an apostle. Thirty pages earlier, the narrator had described another friend, who sought to dissuade him from his quest for the star, as an apostle (I, 2, p. 759), but he had not heeded that friend's message. This time he does. The sick person related "a sublime dream . . . a conversation with a being both different from and akin to himself" (p. 791), an encounter with the integrated self. This account strongly impresses the narrator. Reflecting on his own situation, he realizes that his own double actually is another, spiritual aspect of himself with whom he must be reunited before being reunited with the *anima*.

> Dieu est avec lui [the sick friend], m'écriai-je . . . mais il n'est plus avec moi! O malheur! je l'ai chassé de moi-même, je l'ai menacé, je ;'ai maudit! C'était bien lui, ce frère mystique, qui s'éloignait de plus en plus de mon âme et qui m'avertissait en vain! Cet époux préféré, ce roi de gloire, c'est lui qui me juge et me condamne, et qui emporte à jamais dans son ciel celle qu'il m'eût donnée et dont je suis indigne désormais! [P. 792]

> [God is with him, I exclaimed, . . . but He is no longer with me! Oh woe! I have driven Him out of myself, I've threatened Him, I've cursed Him. It was He indeed, that mystical brother, who withdrew ever further from my soul and who warned me in vain! That favored bridegroom, that king of glory, it is He who judges and condemns me, and who carries away forever into His heaven she whom He would have given to me and of whom I am ffrom henceforth unworthy!]

This is the first time that the narrator explicitly associates his unworthiness with his rejection by the double. The double's nature changes from demonic to divine because the hero now accepts him as necessary mediator, rather than considering him the obstacle to self-realization.

(II, 2) Feeling helpless, the narrator awaits inspiration. The possibilities for regression to the past have been cut off. He cannot find the tomb of Aurélia or of three relatives of his mother; he returns to scenes of his childhood in a hamlet outside Paris, but death imagery— a fiery sunset, the news of a friend's suicide, dreams of wandering in a wilderness unable to reach a familiar house which overlooks it (cf. I, 5)—bars his return. His feeling of being "left behind," "too late" to join a celebration in the distant, illuminated house is typical of the depressed state. As is characteristic of dream sequences, the indirect symbolic expression of a preoccupation now is replaced by a more overtly personal expression: he sees Aurélia, once a potential mediatrix between himself and Christ, being drawn down into Hell (his own unconscious) by dark horsemen (the Shadow), to be lost. But this dream of loss brings progress for the narrator. He comes to see himself as able to influence Aurélia's destiny. He destroys his relics of her, replacing sterile, symbolic *physical* possession of the dead person with prayer, the attempt to reestablish *spiritual* contact.

(II, 3) The theater of this new quest will be the dream. He becomes aware that his inner psychic disharmony derives from his relationship to all people, not just Aurélia. The *anima* appears in the admonitory form of a nursemaid who had cared for the hero in childhood, to tell him that he should have been affected by the deaths of his relatives as well as by Aurélia's. He imagines the faces of all those he has loved scattering and falling into the night like the beads of a broken rosary. Then the vision moves deeper, to a representation of the archetypes of the collective unconscious which he has not correctly understood:

> Je vis ensuite se former vaguement des images plastiques de l'Antiquité qui s'ébauchaient, se fixaient et semblaient représenter des symboles dont je ne saisissais que difficilement l'idée. Seulement, je crus que cela voulait dire: Tout cela était fait pour t'enseigner le secret de la vie, et tu n'as pas compris. Les religions et les fables, les saints et les poètes s'accordaient à expliquer l'énigme fatale, et tu as mal interprété. . . . Maintenant il est trop tard. [P. 797]

> [Next I saw plastic images of Antiquity vaguely taking shape, tracing themselves roughly, becoming fixed, and seeming to represent symbols which I could comprehend only with difficulty. However, I thought that they meant: all this was done to teach you the secret of life, and you did not understand. Religions and legends, the saints and the poets, concurred in explaining the fatal enigma, and you interpreted them badly. . . . Now it is too late.]

(II, 4) At last the narrator confronts the Shadow, in the course of a thorough introspective autobiography: "All the actions of my life appeared to me in their most unfavorable aspect, and in the sort of examination of conscience to which I submitted myself, memory presented the earliest events to me with startling clarity" (p. 797). The difficulty of "working through" a reorientation of his personality overwhelms him. The male figures whom he encounters in a series of brief scenes which follow, and who represent the strength of resolve he would require to carry out his program to reform, seem indifferent, inaccessible, or hostile. Again he becomes disoriented and is taken to the asylum.

(II, 5) He tries to free himself from his obsessions by representing them in artistic form. At the height of his delusions, the classical *anima*-figure appears to him in a dream, announcing, "I am the same as the

Virgin Mary, the same as your mother, the same also that in all forms you have always loved. At each of your ordeals I have removed one of the masks with which I conceal my features, and soon you shall see me as I am" (p. 805). The hero achieves a surprising and unexpected spiritual progress by recognizing "that in the realm of his psyche there is an imago not only of the mother but of the daughter, the sister, the beloved, the heavenly goddess, and the chthonic Baubo. Every mother and every beloved is forced to become the carrier and embodiment of this omnipresent and ageless image, which corresponds to the deepest reality in man."[14] This awareness dissolves the projection and frees the hero from excessive dependence on a single person.

(II, 6) The revelation in terms of persons leads to a cosmic revelation: the hero feels himself in touch with the harmonies of the entire universe. Permitted to have his personal effects in his asylum room, he arranges them and is able to reexperience his past love relationship without guilt. A delirious vision of an octagonal oriental kiosk (the shape, intermediate between the square and the circle, symbolizes a union of earth and heaven—as in the baptismal font), with a gigantic *anima*-figure severed into many separate women, gives way to waking reality. The hero spends hours beside a catatonic patient, sings to him, and brings him back to life. This Shadow (a soldier, representing the function of violence which fragmented the *anima* in the preceding vision) having been confronted, he becomes the intermediary which does ensure reunion with Aurélia. She descends to join the pair and tell the narrator that his ordeal has ended. Then mountain range imagery opens the final visions. This image of ascension to the idealized, self-actualized self is followed by images of universal pardon for the pagan gods (the "Shadows" of Christianity). To record his dreams and learn their secrets becomes the narrator-hero's artistic mission. He hopes to provide a generally useful account of human character. Sympathy and pity have elevated him above self-absorption:

> La conscience que désormais j'étais purifié des fautes de ma vie passée me donnait des jouissances morales infinies; la certitude de l'immortalité et de la coexistence de toutes les personnes que j'avais aimées m'était arrivée matériellement, pour ainsi dire, et je bénissais l'âme fraternelle qui, du sein du désespoir, m'avait fait rentrer dans les voies lumineuses de la religion. [Pp. 815–16]

> [The realization that from thenceforth I was cleansed of the transgressions of my past life gave me infinite moral delectation; the certitude of immortality and of the coexistence of all those I had

loved had come to me in tangible form, so to speak, and I blessed the brother soul who, from the depths of my despair, had led me back to the luminous paths of religion.]

At the end, the hero returns with renewed spiritual strength to his family and friends. Such is a mythic reading of the text, which takes its claims at face value. Let us turn now to a more skeptical analysis of the same events, seen as manifestations of the pathological extremes of mourning and melancholia in the implied author and in his hero.

Nerval intended *Aurélia* as autobiography—an attempt at an objective self-portrait—but he wrote an autobiographical confessional novel. And the latter dramatizes "the tension between one's self-image and the way one is seen. It is, in Shaw's terms, a final attempt to impose ourselves upon our neighbors . . . comfortable in the knowledge that the imposter seen by others—that dwarf, that usurper—has now been displaced by the imperial and genuine self."[15] Reacting to loss and failure, the protagonist of *Aurélia* tries by his fantasies to transform himself into the hero of a spiritual, mythic Quest. The mode of his discourse is continual hyperbole: claims to superhuman knowledge and power alternating with despairing self-condemnation. *Aurélia*'s narrator, as spectator of his past self, reacts to this hyperbole with attenuation and understatement.[16] He presents the diary of his admitted madness as a kind of autotherapy, recording his fantasies—like Montaigne—so as to put his mind to shame by confronting it with its own divagations. At the outset he admits that "j'ai pris au sérieux les inventions des poètes, et je me suis fait une Laure ou une Béatrice d'une personne ordinaire de notre siècle" ("I took the inventions of the poets seriously, and made a Laura or a Beatrice for myself out of an ordinary person of our times" [I, 1, p. 755]). Soon lost, this self-detachment is regained in the concluding paragraph. And throughout the story, the narrator frequently reveals self-awareness as he begins to relate fantastic impressions and visions, through the explicit indication that the viewpoint in what follows is subjective: "il semblait que; je crus comprendre; je croyais, je crus voir; j'avais l'idée que" ("it seemed that; I thought I understood that; I believed; I thought I saw; I had the idea that") and similar expressions are quite characteristic of Nerval's style.

At the core of the protagonist's memories, dreams, and visions, however, this awareness disappears. Hyperbole and understatement assume new forms in an involuntary language pointing to a tangle of unconscious psychic forces. Hyperbole now manifests itself as a sort of redundancy—as the doubling of characters and the obsessive repetition of actions. Understatement reappears as narrative discontinuity—an unexpected change of subject or break in thought, the latter often indicated, in *Aurélia*, by an ellipsis. (Similar doubling and discontinuity pervade *Sylvie*.) Such hyperbole and understatement both express a failure. The presence of a double proves that the narrator's consciously elaborated self-image has failed to encompass all the traits of his personality; obsessive repetition shows that the initial act has failed to fulfill all the actor's purpose; ellipsis implies that the preceding train of thought was leading toward an impasse or a defeat. In all these instances, the consciously accepted statement has proved inadequate to the protagonist's psychic needs. These needs derive from frustrated sexual desire and from repressed anger, the natural consequences of having been spurned by a beloved person.

For after two paragraphs of prefatory remarks, the narrator begins *Aurélia* by saying that "une dame que j'avais aimée longtemps et que j'appellerai du nom d'Aurélia, était perdue pour moi" ("a lady whom I had loved for a long time and whom I shall call Aurélia, was lost to me"). He feels "condamné par celle que j'aimais, coupable d'une faute dont je n'espérais plus le pardon" ("condemned by the woman I loved, guilty of a transgression for which I no longer expected to be forgiven" [pp. 754–55]), and accepts her judgment as definitive. "Je suis indigne" ("I am unworthy"), he repeats; he thinks of suicide. But his explanations of his "faute" are too numerous and varied for any one of them to be convincing.[17] He appears in a state of melancholia, defined by Freud as "a profoundly painful dejection, cessation of interest in the outside world, loss of the capacity to love, inhibition of all activity, and a lowering of the self-regarding feelings to a degree that finds utterance in self-reproaches and self-revilings, and culminates in a delusional expectation of punishment" manifest in his pervasive premonitions of death and apocalypse. Freud further observes:

> If one listens patiently to a melancholic's many and various self-accusations, one cannot in the end avoid the impression that often the most violent of them are hardly at all applicable to the patient himself, but that with insignificant modifications they do fit someone else, someone whom the patient loves or has loved or should love. . . . We perceive that the self-reproaches are reproaches against a loved object which have been shifted away from it on to the patient's own ego.[18]

Thus the narrator accuses himself of having insulted Aurélia's memory "in easy conquests" (I, 9, p. 781), when we can guess it was really she who was at fault for having preferred an inferior suitor to the narrator, who loved her with utter devotion.

One finds no trace of overt anger in the narrator's account of his emotions. Much, of course, has been turned back against himself in masochistic self-depreciation. Still more remains. He feels neurotic anxiety because his repressed libido and desire for vengeance cannot help him restore his damaged self-respect. Having been victimized makes one unattractive, even to oneself. He fears to express his anger openly, moreover, because he is afraid of Aurélia and not yet independent of her. His anger will seek an indirect outlet in fantasies of Aurélia's suffering, debasement, and death—*Aurélia* is quite a sanguinary piece of literature—for which he can avoid conscious responsibility. At the same time, his conscious acceptance of all the blame for her estrangement lets him avoid facing "the unpleasant and frightening realization that life is incalculable and uncontrollable."[19] Pent up in his unconscious, his hatred grows inordinately. "In such circumstances the conscious love attains as a rule, by way of reaction, an especially high degree of intensity, so as to be strong enough for the perpetual task of keeping its opponent under repression."[20] So Aurélia's love becomes all-important. Only by winning her back can he recover his sense of worth. When she actually dies not long after marrying another, the narrator elaborates a delusionary system in which she becomes a goddess instrumental in his and all mankind's salvation. This glorification not only opposes inadmissible anger with its exaggerated contrary, but also holds forth the hope of regaining on the spiritual plane what was irrevocably lost on the material.[21] The process begins as soon as the narrator first meets Aurélia after their separation:

Un jour me trouvant dans une société dont elle faisait partie, je la vis venir à moi et me tendre la main. Comment interpréter cette démarche et le regard profond et triste dont elle accompagna son salut? J'y crus voir le pardon du passé; l'accent divin de la pitié donnait aux simples paroles qu'elle m'adressa une valeur inexprimable, comme si quelque chose de la religion se mêlait aux douceurs d'un amour jusque-là profane, et lui imprimait le caractère de l'éternité. [I, 2, p. 757]

[Finding myself one day in a circle to which she belonged, I saw her come over to me and offer her hand. How to interpret that action, and the deep, sad look which accompanied her greeting? I thought I saw in it forgiveness for the past; the divine accent of pity gave an indescribable value to the simple words she addressed to me, as if something religious were blending with the sweetness of a love which until then had been profane, imprinting on it the character of eternity.]

The theorizing which serves as a preface to *Aurélia*—dream is a second life as real as waking—had already become a commonplace, eloquently expounded, for example, by Nerval's master, Nodier. But the narrator's response to this notion, his fascination with the domain of sleep (p. 753), derives from a powerful vested interest. He seeks a place to continue the quest for reunion with Aurélia. He tells himself that her rejection was only temporary. In dreams he will undergo a series of redemptive *épreuves* so as to become worthy of her (I, 4, p. 766 et passim). Purified by adversity, he shall ascend to a progressively clearer oneiric vision of transcendent Truth in the form of the bride and mother goddess Isis, of whom both the earthly and the spiritual Aurélia have been dim manifestations.

If only the narrator could lose himself in this imaginative construction, he might be content. But the drama of *Aurélia* remains long unresolved because his sublimation of libido is only partially successful. Frustrated sexual feelings, and yearnings for affection and intimacy, persist. Diverted into inappropriate outlets, they repeatedly threaten the narrator's psychic health.

His initial reactions to losing his lady seem rational. He tries to forget her in travel and flirtations. But he discovers that he has deluded himself into making to another woman professions of love which were really inspired by and intended for Aurélia. This makes him doubly faithless (p. 756).[22] And even after her death, his obsessive desire for her leads him to reproach himself bitterly for being interest in another (I, 9, p. 781).

The narrator's resulting guilt, and his desire to preserve his idealized self-image as an altruistic lover (for he still hopes to deserve Aurélia some day), periodically turn his libido back upon the self. Where else could it go so long as he wishes to remain entirely devoted to her, and she is unavailable? The consequence is megalomania: the self becomes immensely overvalued: "Parfois, je croyais ma force et mon activité doublées; il me semblait tout savoir, tout comprendre" ("At times, I believed that my strength and activity had doubled; it seemed to me that I knew and understood everything" [p. 754].[23] The narrator repeatedly generates fantasies of world destruction and redemption, in which he plays an essential part, so as to create a theater adequately vast for the now-glorified self's performances.

Premonitory symptoms of this narcissistic regression of libido have already appeared in the act of courtship itself. The narrator's favorite means of communicating love feelings is the letter. Writing avoids a conversation, a give-and-take that might threaten one's illusions; it betrays an ambivalent desire for presence/absence; it suggests a possible neurotic inability to meet real sexual demands. Finally, by presenting and preserving one's sentiments in concrete form, it makes them available as objects of self-love. The narrator of *Sylvie*, complacently recollecting his letters to Aurélie, called them "les plus tendres, les plus belles que sans doute elle eût jamais reçues" ("the most tender, the most beautiful [letters] she had probably ever received" [I, 622]). *Aurélia's* narrator rediscovers his letters to her (the word *brouillons* shows that at least some of them could not have been hers to him) and exclaims: "O bonheur! ô tristesse mortelle! ces caractères jaunis, ces brouillons effacés, ces lettres à demi froissées, c'est le trésor de mon seul amour . . . Relisons" ("Oh joy! Oh deathly sadness! These faded characters, these blurred rough drafts, these half-crumpled letters, it is the treasure of my only love . . . Let us reread them"). The letter also allows one to control and to repress one's anger at the loved person. Not only does this selective expression of feelings in writing help avoid the risk of inciting retaliatory anger from the loved person, but it also helps create an idealized self-image: patiently the lover accepts harsh treatment and asks for no reward. And in the letter imaginary conversations can dictate words to the loved person, molding her closer to the heart's desire. All the easier to do so once she is dead.

Since the narrator's overvalued self-image, which compensates for rejection, has no basis in reality, it drifts steadily further into delusion.[24] The social setting of his quest shifts from the company of his friends (real people who care about him) to a dream of his ancestors (real but dead people, only some of whom cared about him) to hallucinations of the lady (a dead person who did not care about him) to visions of supernatural, imaginary beings. In each of these situations except the last, a hallucinatory double intervenes to estrange the narrator from those with whom he wishes to be reunited. First the double rather than the narrator is released on the recognizance of his friends, who come to rescue him from a police station; then the double tries to debar the narrator from the paradisiacal city of the blessed dead; finally he deceives Aurélia into thinking *he* is the narrator, so that she will marry *him* (I, 3, 5, and 9, pp. 762, 769, 782–83). His appearance warns of the results of the narrator's psychic regression and delusionary structures: the loss of the capacity to establish relationships with others. Both the form (a hostile rival) and the function (the separation of the narrator from others) of this double have been determined by the narrator's repressed anger. The latter is at odds with himself, paralyzed with the inner conflict between love and hate.[25]

A retreat into fantasy simply displaces this conflict from the conscious to the unconscious plane, where it becomes more elusive and intractable. Soon after the narrator exalts Aurélia, he characteristically generates compensatory fantasies involving her suffering and dying, both as real woman and as mother goddess. For example, when he first meets her after their separation, he sees something of a religious pardon in her routine social courtesy (see the passage quoted above). But his next vision presents "une femme au teint blême, aux yeux caves, qui me semblait avoir les traits d'Aurélia. Je me dis: 'C'est sa mort ou la mienne qui m'est annoncée!' Mais je ne sais pourquoi j'en restai à la dernière supposition" ("a pale woman with hollow eyes, who seemed to me to have Aurélia's features. I said to myself: 'It is her death or mine which is being announced to me!' But for some reason or other I adopted the latter assumption" [I, 2, p. 757]). At first the narrator imagines Aurélia dead because he desires revenge on her for having rejected him. Then he interprets his vision as a premonition of his own death, in order to punish himself for his wish. But Aurélia's death would neatly resolve the problems raised by his ambivalent attitude toward her: he could continue to love her, free from rivals and contingencies and the obstacles of her own feelings, while enjoying a revenge for which he had not been responsible.[26] Shortly after this fantasy, the narrator continues, the dream invaded his waking life so that at times everything seemed to have a double aspect. This state of affairs results from his act of repressing his desire for revenge: his dominant feelings have been divided into unacknowledged unconscious contents, on the one hand, and on the other hand, into acceptable conscious attitudes produced by reaction formation and rationalization.

Fearing his own anger, the narrator reacts against it by glorifying Aurélia. He attaches religious feelings to her. The result is an excessive emotional dependency on her, a regression toward childhood which interferes with the narrator's adult attitudes. His ensuing dreams reflect this problem. His first nervous breakdown is preceded by a dream of wandering in a vast building with many rooms, where he believes that he recognizes his former schoolteachers and schoolmates. The series of rooms suggests a past life under review; the whole building is large because the narrator experiences it from a child's viewpoint. He cannot find his own room (mature identity): instead he sees an iridescent winged androgyne (a total Self resulting from the reconciliation of consciousness and the unconscious) who tries futilely to rise through heavy clouds, only to collapse to the ground (blocked psychic development; see I, 2, p. 758). The original manuscript described the appearance of his mother's ghost to him in the asylum to which he was taken shortly afterwards.[27] To collapse and to be cared for in a hospital is itself a de facto return to infantile dependency. And his first dream there returns him to an ancestral home on the banks of the Rhine, where he glimpses a mysterious *she*.[28] There follows a reunion with his ancestors in an underground kingdom: he learns that he must submit to a long series of ordeals.

Such visions, which multiply imaginary connections with ancestors, and later with figures in history, legend, and world religions, attempt to reconstruct a sense of identity weakened by Aurélia's indifference. For "the conscious feeling of having a personal identity is based on two simultaneous observations: the perception of the selfsameness and continuity of one's existence in time and space and the perception of the fact that others recognize one's sameness and continuity."[29] To imagine a vast family (his previous existences, as Nerval would have it) concerned with his temporal and spiritual well-being satisfies both these conditions. It also perpetuates childhood and regains the lost paradise of parental love for which the narrator weeps just before the end of this series of visions (I, 5, p. 770).

The natural conclusion is restored faith in the existence of God and the immortality of the soul (I, 6, p. 771). For one can rediscover God by reexperiencing, in fantasy, one's parents as one saw them in childhood. Freud observes:

> Biologically speaking, religiousness is to be traced to the small human child's long-drawn-out helplessness and need of help; adolescent loss of faith accompanies the young person's desire to live independent of his parents, but when at a later date the adult perceives how truly forlorn and weak he is when confronted with the great forces of life, he [unconsciously] feels his condition as he did in childhood, and attempts to deny his own despondency by a regressive revival of the forces which protected his infancy.[30]

The resurrection of one's ancestors also expresses the wish to start all over again. And it tries to palliate the narrator's self-condemnation, which led to his mental breakdown. For he secretly reasons: "My ancestors have died, but still I love them: therefore I can imagine that Aurélia has died, but still love her." But the narrator's search for reassurance, leading to increasing helplessness and dependency, proves self-defeating. The more he glorifies his lady, the less plausible seems any hope of her being interested in him. As he follows her, in his next vision, into a garden (symbolic representation of the female genitals), "she seemed to fade away into her own vastness" (I, 6, p. 773). And the more remote she becomes, the greater the narrator's frustrated infantile rage. This was already apparent in the police station, where his vision of a smiling divinity receding into the eastern heavens had been followed by the apparition of the double (image of his unacknowledged anger). This time, as he pursues her fading image,

> je me heurtai à un pan de mur dégradé, au pied duquel gisait un buste de femme. En le relevant, j'eus la persuasion que c'était *le sien.* . . . Je reconnus les traits chéris, et, portant les yeux autour de moi, je vis que le jardin avait pris l'aspect d'un cimetière. Des voix disaient: "L'Univers est dans la nuit." [I, 6, p. 773]

> [I bumped into a crumbling section of a wall, at the base of which lay the bust of a woman. As I picked it up, I was convinced that it was *hers.* . . . I recognized her beloved features, and, looking around me, I perceived that the garden had assumed the appearance of a grave-yard. Voices were saying: "The Universe is in darkness."]

Later, when he learns that Aurélia actually died, he interprets this dream as a premonition. His spontaneous initial reaction is joyful, for "she belonged to me much more in death than she had alive." But this egotistical reaction, and the apparently magical fulfillment of his repressed hostile wishes, redoubles his guilt and inspires in him "bitter regret" (I, 7, p. 774). This disproportion between the intensity of his self-reproach and its ostensible cause (his failure to respond to her death with immediate, undiluted grief) points to the unknown, unconscious feeling (desire for her death) from which his guilt really stems.[31]

So the narrator is left after her death with a permanent inner conflict between love and hate. He symbolizes it by remembering a ring he gave her when they became lovers. It had to be cut to fit her finger: "Je ne compris ma faute qu'en entendant le bruit de la scie. Il me sembla voir couler du sang" ("I was not aware of my transgression until I heard the noise of the saw. I seemed to see blood flowing" [p. 774]). In other words, he wants to possess her more closely, but this could be accomplished only by violence; by murder. Although symbolically disguised, this line of thought is still too painful to pursue, and the text breaks it off with an ellipsis.

In the asylum, the narrator works hard to get well. He seeks ways to act out his hostility without guilt by making others seem to be responsible. Thus he tries to compartmentalize his feelings: ostensible adoration, vicarious rage. On a wall he paints a series of frescoes showing Aurélia as Queen of Heaven, surrounded by a cortege of lesser gods. Beneath her feet there turns a wheel (the ring/vagina, but intact). "Que de fois j'ai rêvé devant cette chère idole!" ("How many times I have dreamed before the dear idol!"). But he also sculpts her body from the base material of earth. "Tous les matins, mon travail était à refaire, car les fous, jaloux de mon bonheur, se plaisaient à en détruire l'image" ("Every morning, my work had to be done over again, for the madmen, envying my happiness, took pleasure in destroying its image" [I, 7, p. 775]). By continually re-creating effigies of Aurélia, all subject to the same risk of destruction (compare Baudelaire's poem "A Une Madone"), the narrator knowingly invites the anonymous "fous" to express his anger for him. They may be actual fellow-inmates; they may be the narrator himself, who turns against his own idealized creation and then represses the memory of his act.

Then the narrator withdraws further from his anger by composing a cosmogony. A radiant goddess presides over the evolution of primordial monsters—among them the narrator—toward humanity (i.e., love for Aurélia makes him more worthy). But one of the creative spirits in this universe conceives the idea of adding to the four original races of spirits a fifth race, the Afrites, "composée des éléments de la terre." "Ce fut le signal d'une révolution complète parmi les Esprits qui ne voulurent pas reconnaître les nouveaux possesseurs du monde" ("composed of the elements of the earth." "This was the signal for a complete upheaval among the Spirits who did not want to acknowledge the new proprietors of the world" [I, 8, p. 777]). The same movement of thought in the previous episode has been enlarged to a cosmic scale. The creation of idealized figures (initial admiration for the loved person) is followed by the creation of bodies of earth (sexual desire). The loved woman's rejection prevents a harmonious synthesis of idealization and physical desire, generating a conflict.[32] Finally she is punished in fantasy. Here, conflict and punishment are represented this way:

> Un combat se livra entre eux [Afrites versus the other spirits]. Ici, ma mémoire se trouble et je ne sais quel fut le résultat de cette lutte suprême [in fact, it remains unresolved]. Seulement, je vois encore, sur un pic baigné des eaux, une femme abandonnée par eux, qui crie les cheveux épars, se débattant contre la mort. . . . Fut-elle sauvée? Je l'ignore [ambivalence again]. Je frémissais en reproduisant les traits hideux de ces races maudites [the narrator is drawing the grimaces of his own anger on paper]. Partout mourait, pleurait,

languissait l'image souffrante [limned by the narrator. Take that, Aurélia!] de la Mère éternelle. A travers les vagues civilisations de l'Asie et de l'Afrique, on voyait se renouveler toujours une scène sanglante d'orgie [fantasized vengeful rape] et de carnage que les même esprits reproduisaient sous des formes nouvelles. [I, 8, pp. 779–80]

[A battle took place between them. At this point, my memory becomes confused and I don't know the outcome of that supreme struggle. Only I still see, on a mountaintop nearly inundated by the deluge, a woman abandoned by them, with streaming hair, crying out, struggling against death. . . . Was she saved? I don't know. . . . I trembled as I reproduced the hideous features of those accursed races. Everywhere died, wept, languished the suffering image of the Great Mother. Throughout the vague civilizations of Asia and Africa, you could see a bloody scene of orgy and slaughter perpetually renewed by the same spirits in different forms.]

The vision concludes with the severed ring image writ large. The serpent who surrounds the earth has been sliced into segments which rejoin in a hideous kiss cemented with human blood.

By the repeated, obsessional enactment of two successive gestures which cancel each other out (creation and destruction),[33] the narrator temporarily arrests the development of his melancholia toward the ever more radical self-condemnation and eventual suicide which is its usual conclusion. But his preoccupation with the dead—Aurélia, ancestors, lost civilizations and gods—betrays his secret wish to end a world where he has been defeated, so as to substitute a new order.[34] Freud observes that in such cases,

The patient has withdrawn from the people in his environment and from the external world generally the libidinal cathexis which he has hitherto directed on to them. Thus everything has become indifferent and irrelevant to him. . . . The end of the world is the projection of this internal catastrophe; his subjective world has come to an end since his withdrawal of his love from it. . . . *The delusional formation, which we take to be the pathological product, is in reality an attempt at recovery, a process of reconstruction.*[35]

This time the narrator does in fact recover and return home.

A second psychotic episode years later (Part I, chapter 9) begins when the narrator falls and injures himself severely while descending from a high terrace on a friend's estate.

En me rappelant de quel point j'étais tombé, je me souviens que la
vue que j'avais admirée donnait sur un cimetière, celui même où se
trouvait le tombeau d'Aurélia. Je n'y pensai véritablement qu'alors;
sans quoi, je pourrais attribuer ma chute à l'impression que cet
aspect m'aurait fait éprouver. [P. 781]

[Remembering where I had fallen from, I recollected that the prospect I had been admiring looked out over a graveyard, the very one
where Aurélia's grave could be found. That didn't really occur to me
until then (*after* the accident); otherwise, I could have attributed my
fall to the impression which that spectacle would have made on me.]

The denial reveals what it was intended to hide: by hurting himself the
narrator punishes himself for his subliminal resentment and its imagined
outcome—Aurélia's death. This impression is confirmed by the dreams
which follow. They express intense hostility, only partially neutralized
by projection onto other figures.

Son image, qui m'était apparue souvent, ne revenait plus dans mes
songes. Je n'eus d'abord que des rêves confus [blurred by repres-
sion], mêlés de scènes sanglantes. Il semblait que toute une race
fatale se fut déchaînée au milieu du monde idéal que j'avais vu
autrefois et dont elle était la reine. [Pp. 781–82]

[*Her* image, which had often appeared to me, no longer returned in
my dreams. At first I had only dim visions, interspersed with bloody
episodes. It seemed that a whole deadly race had been unleashed in
the middle of the ideal world that I had formerly seen and of which
she was the queen.]

Inevitably the double (secret anger and obstacle to reconciliation) reappears. In the spirit world, he supplants the narrator and will marry
Aurélia. The narrator no longer knows whether he is the good or evil one
of the two (pp. 781–83). That is because he is both: loving *and* vindictive.
His resolve to combat the double means further repressing his feelings
and can only aggravate his inner conflicts.

The bizarre vision in the next chapter (I, 10) tries to resolve these
conflicts through sublimation. The narrator descends to a tropical (heat,
passion) underworld where workmen are constructing a monstrous,
artificial winged creature. They animate it with a jet of "le feu primitif
qui anima les premiers êtres. . . . Jadis, il [the fire] s'élançait jusqu'à la
surface de la terre, mais les sources se sont taries" ("the primordial fire
which gave life to the first creatures. . . . Formerly, it would shoot up to

the very surface of the earth, but its reservoirs have been depleted" [p. 785]). Thus the narrator indirectly tells himself that the beast of libido must be suppressed because it no longer can find an object in the real world. His attempts to divert its energies into religious devotion become manifest when he chooses to call it a "lama." In French, the animal's name corresponds in both sound and spelling to the title of the holy men (lamas) of Tibet. Moreover, both priest and beast inhabit the mountains (literal sublimation). The narrator further reassures himself—but also betrays the defensive character of his fantasy—by relegating his "lama" to the realm of the artificial. "Cet animal qui semblera vivre" ("That animal that will have the appearance of life") is merely a product of "l'art élevé au plus haut point de nos connaissances, et chacun le jugera ainsi" ("art raised to the summit of our capacities, and everyone will recognize it as such" [p. 786]).

The sublimation fails. At the end of Part I, the narrator again imagines preparations for a mystical marriage between Aurélia and the double. He vehemently protests to the assembled society. But as soon as he confronts the double, he must fantasize the suffering of Aurélia, for the double is his own repressed anger. So the scream of a woman in pain outside his window awakens him. The narrator now fears he has been accursed because his protestations have disturbed "l'harmonie de l'univers magique où mon âme puisait la certitude d'une existence immortelle" ("the harmony of the magical universe from which my soul derived an unshakeable faith in immortality" [p. 787]). Were he to allow himself to realize that Aurélia deserved his anger, she could no longer remain a goddess capable of saving him.

"Lost once again!" the second of the two parts begins. The narrator's impatience has forfeited Aurélia in the spiritual as well as the material world. He turns back to the Christian God she worshipped, in order to learn resignation and *caritas*. He visits a previously neglected sick friend, who reveals that God always is present in everyone. So the narrator concludes that the double must be of God—not a hostile rival, but the possibility of a renewed relationship with Aurélia in the spiritual realm. By fighting this mystical brother he has lost his last chance to merit her. He redoubles his self-condemnation.

He must attempt expiation. He tries to undo the result he unconsciously attributes to his anger—Aurélia's death—by following a stranger's funeral procession to the cemetery where she happens to be buried. But he cannot find her tomb; and when he does locate the directions to it later, he finds himself unworthy to pray there. For he still harbors a conflict between love and hate, disguised as "the storm that was rumbling inside my head." When he tries to escape from himself by returning to the rural setting of his childhood, a striking dream clearly expresses his ambivalence. Aurélia briefly appears and vanishes. He tells himself that

> Elle a fait un dernier effort pour me sauver;—j'ai manqué le moment suprême où le pardon était possible encore. [. . .] L'abîme a reçu sa proie! Elle est perdue pour moi et pour tous!" . . . Il me semblait la voir comme à la lueur d'un éclair, pâle et mourante, entraînée par de sombres cavaliers . . . . [II, 2, p. 795]

> [She made a last effort to save me;—I missed the very last moment when forgiveness still was possible. [. . .] The abyss has its prey! She is lost for me and for everyone! . . . I thought I saw her illuminated as if by a lightning flash, pale, dying, dragged off by dark riders . . . .][36]

He had appealed for the idealized Aurélia to intercede for him with God: instead, (the unacknowledgedly guilty) Aurélia falls into Hell. So the narrator ends by tearfully praying God to pardon *her*.

He then finds a temporary but ingenious way of integrating disguised vengeance with redemptive charity. When a beggar woman comes to sing beside his restaurant table one day, he imagines her inhabited by the spirit of Aurélia, and gladly gives her money (II, 4, p. 800). Of course it is the narrator's anger which induces him unconsciously to project her mental image onto a social outcast. By feeling a pitying sympathy for her, he neatly turns the tables, while acquiring merit to aid him in the spiritual ascension needed to win her back.

But when the narrator attempts further to translate his desire for atonement into effective charitable action in the real world, he feels crushed by the resulting mass of self-imposed obligations (p. 800). A series of incidents suggests he has been cut off from the saving female archetype. When he visits his father, his father refuses to let him help bring wood (French *bois*; a universal feminine symbol) down from the attic—i.e., to fetch lost Women back from heaven. He leaves "consternated" and tries unsuccessfully to visit a cemetery (to commune once again with the dead). Then, feeling drained of creative power, he calls on a German poet to repay the money he had been given to translate some German poetry into French. One recalls that the historical Nerval trained himself to translate German into French from the age of fifteen, as the foundation for a literary career.[37] Such translation suggests a symbolic attempt to bring the lost mother back from Germany where she died. To abandon translation means renouncing the hope of effecting this return.

A web of motifs in the passages which follow reinforce the hint of a failed quest for the *anima*. When the narrator tries to reenter the Catholic Church by confessing to the Abbé Dubois (*du-bois*) of Notre-Dame, the priest is otherwise engaged. Then he goes to Notre-Dame de Lorette to pray to the Virgin, but the hallucinatory voice (exteriorized self-condemnation) tells him that she is dead; his prayers are useless. He throws away a ring with a Mohammedan inscription (the prideful, pagan desire for physical possession), but he cannot even remember the Ave Maria. He thinks of suicide. Then in a delirious psychotic state he imagines the end of the world, and is taken to the municipal hospital, "la Maison Dubois." This is a real name (II, 4, p. 803); probably it influenced the narrator to remember the abbé's name as being the same, through an unconscious association of mental with spiritual health, and of both with the feminine principle.

The next chapter (II, 5) repeats these motifs more clearly. The narrator piously kneels at an altar to the Virgin, while thinking of his mother (p. 805). He buys another ring, and wards off a second Flood by throwing it into the street during a thunderstorm. After this act of renunciation, a vision of the lover-mother-Mary-goddess is once more granted him (pp. 805–6). Unfortunately, this reconciliation is tantamount to a withdrawal of libido from the real world: refocused on the self, libido generates megalomaniacal fantasies. The narrator imagines himself to be Napoleon, then a god. He behaves so frantically that he must again be confined in a mental hospital, in a straitjacket. There he incorporates the other inmates into his delusional system. Together they must govern the motion of the stars (a distant, disguised image of dominion over Aurélia). And through evoking the hidden forces of various religions, the narrator will reestablish universal harmony (pp. 807–9).

These grandiose fantasies fail to free him from the darker self of his own anger. So he projects it onto the outside world as an imagined, universal foe: "nous revivons dans nos fils comme nous avons vécu dans nos pères,—et la science impitoyable de nos ennemis sait nous reconnaître partout [. . .] O terreur! voilà l'éternelle distinction du bon et du mauvais" ("We live again in our descendents as we have lived in our forefathers,—and the pitiless cunning of our enemies can recognize us everywhere [. . .] Oh terror! Such is the eternal distinction between the good and the evil person" [p. 811]). The narrator's ambivalence still prevents him from knowing in which of these categories he will be classified.

The narrator has been allowed to install his possessions in his room at the asylum. As he arranges his papers, he discovers old love letters to "my only love." Here the text characteristically breaks off with an ellipsis. Vivid memories of rejection must have awakened rage more intense than ever: certainly the vision which follows the ellipsis presents anger unequivocally:

> Je crus alors me trouver au milieu d'un vaste charnier où l'histoire universelle était écrite en traits de sang. Le corps d'une femme gigantesque était peint en face de moi; seulement, ses diverses parties étaient tranchées comme par le sabre; d'autres femmes de races diverses et dont les corps dominaient de plus en plus, présentaient sur les autres murs un fouillis sanglant de membres et de têtes [. . . ; and then the saving clause:]. C'était l'histoire de tous les crimes. [II, 6, p. 815]

> [Then I thought I found myself in the middle of an enormous slaughterhouse where universal history was written in letters of blood. The body of a gigantic woman was painted opposite me; only, her various members were sliced off as if by a saber; other women of various races and whose bodies piled up higher and higher, formed a bloody, tangled heap of limbs and heads on the other walls (. . .). It was the history of all crime.]

This furious paroxysm finally relieves the narrator's feelings sufficiently for him to reach a provisional equilibrium of self-acceptance. His therapist calls his attention to a catatonic fellow-patient—emblem of affects imprisoned in the unconscious. This man has been a soldier in Africa (hot country of forbidden lust and anger), and the narrator names him Saturnin, after his own "dark side."[38] He coaxes Saturnin back to consciousness by singing him songs from Saturnin's native region in France. Thus he symbolically confronts and expiates his anger. Aurélia descends from her star to tell him his trials are over (some readers may find this resolution too abrupt and facile: in the event, it will not last). "Oh! que ma grande amie est belle! Elle est si grande, qu'elle pardonne au monde, et si bonne qu'elle m'a pardonné" (pp. 816–18; no small kindness, since he has chopped her to pieces so many times). She, the narrator, and Saturnin rise together into heaven. The chaste ménage à trois which concluded *Sylvie* reappears, translated to an empyrean frame.

The *Memorabilia* or dream transcriptions which conclude the novella round out this reconciliation with the pardon of the pagan gods (pp. 820–21). They embody the narrator's lust and wrath, and their images were activated by his defense of projecting the drama of his rejection by Aurélia to a mythic plane. (Note that the narrator himself repeatedly asserts that there are connections between microcosm and macrocosm, subjective and objective, inner and outer worlds: see I, 10, and II, 6, pp. 787, 820, 823.) Like Gretchen at the end of Goethe's *Faust*, a work which Nerval had translated, Aurélia becomes a mediatrix rather than the final object of a quest. She is literally transformed into a Messiah figure when her forgiveness is described as "the word *pardon* signed with the blood of Jesus Christ" (p. 819). By associating Aurélia with the redemptive blood of Jesus, the narrator seems implicitly to be reassuring himself. It is as if he were saying: "Men tortured Jesus as I tortured Aurélia in my fantasies; still he pardoned them." But to extend Aurélia's mercy, thinly disguised as Christ's, over all history and mythology amounts to little more than an effort rhetorically to propel this mercy toward reality. In effect, the narrator first identifies himself with all men in order to be saved; subsequently he claims that his personal salvation has won him supererogatory merit which makes that salvation valid for all men: "It is then that I descended among men to tell them the Good Tidings" (p. 819).

As Geoffrey Hartman points out, "a myth mediates a discontinuity—winter, death, paradise lost, 'temps perdu'; and its very movement, the narrative, is a series of bridges over a gulf."[39] The autotherapeutic mythopoeia of *Aurélia* tries to mediate the discontinuity created in the author's psyche by the loved woman's rejection of him and her death. It transforms the protagonist from a material failure to a spiritual success: it reinterprets the former condition as a set of redemptive *épreuves* imposed by the bride-mother-goddess, so as to make it a necessary precondition for the latter. But once the composition of the myth of *Aurélia* had been completed, its discourse lost its efficacy as sublimation because that discourse came to exist as an object of the author's contemplation, and revealed itself as alien to him. Frustration is inherent to the situation. The more the author elaborates his self-image in fiction, and the more resources he devotes to sustaining it, the more he becomes dispossessed of that self. Finally he is forced to acknowledge that his self-image is no more than his creation in the domain of the imaginary, a domain devoid of certitude. He rediscovers in the effort of fictionalization the fundamental alienation which led him to construct the self-image as an Other.[40] So the historical Nerval embarked upon a decisive "acting out": he jumped through the paper hoop of fantasy into the real. Shortly after his last release from the asylum, and three weeks before the publication of *Aurélia*, he hanged himself.

Apparently the trouble was that reunion with the lost loved ones, and the reconciliation of the hero with himself, could occur only in an imaginary world,[41] or in death. All the secret projects of Nerval's unconscious were realized through his suicide. By punishing himself, he rendered homage to "Aurélia" whose rejection had stigmatized him as worthless. Simultaneously, he avenged himself upon himself for the personal inadequacy which had led to his failure with her. And as spectator of himself, he uttered the ultimate understatement: a permanent silence in the face of an overwhelming reality. On the other hand, by willingly donning the cloak of his own destruction, Nerval bridged the gap between himself and the deceased Aurélia, and promoted himself to a high rank among the gods. For the terrible irony of *Aurélia* is that a drive toward health, resulting in the elaboration of a coherent psychotic system, is presented as a triumph of self-actualization. "The artist regards himself . . . as God, the pleasure of beauty [is] taken for the joy of paradise, and the conclusion drawn that, since all is well in the work of art, all is well in history. But all is not well there."[42]

CONCLUSION

The ultimate consequences of this study are to suggest a new definition of French romanticism, as a period during which authors' intuitive understanding of depth psychology transformed narrative structure. This definition would of course complement existing definitions, rather than supplanting them.[1] Seen as a militant literary movement in opposition to an outmoded classicism, French romanticism extends from the publication of Mme de Staël's *De l'Allemagne* in 1813 to Hugo's abandonment of the theater in 1843. Seen as a political phenomenon, French romanticism extends from the fall of Napoleon in 1815 to the coming of the Second Empire in 1851. Seen as the production of literary masterpieces and the transformation of the literary language, French romanticism extends from the publication of Chateaubriand's *Atala* and *René* in 1801 to that of Hugo's last volume of *La Légende des siècles* in 1879. Seen as a broad intellectual current emphasizing the relativity of sense perceptions and the subjective basis of knowledge, French romanticism could be said to extend from John Locke's *Essay Concerning Human Understanding* (1690) until 1918, or even until the present.[2]

My own psychological definition of the movement locates French romanticism between 1820 and 1874. It claims that an unusually abundant influx of the English Gothic and fantastic to France in 1820 and 1821 (Polidori's *Vampire*, Mathurin's *Melmoth*, Scott's *Monastery*), added to the influence of Diderot on Nodier, provides the decisive impetus for the first French monuments of psychoanalytic fantasy, *Smarra* and *Trilby* (1821–1822). The movement culminates in France in 1869 to 1874 with Lautréamont's *Maldoror* and the final version of Flaubert's *Tentation de saint Antoine*. Its outstanding artistic progeny are the surrealist films of Luis Buñuel and Jean Cocteau.

In fantasy literature, Cazotte's *Le Diable amoureux* in 1772 anticipates the major epistemological shift from Enlightenment thought to romanticism by showing the mind as no longer active, dominating and controlling the environment, but as the passive recipient of revelation flowing in from the supernatural or unconscious realm. Recurrent metaphors of volcanic eruption imply the existence of repressed unconscious forces threatening to overwhelm ego consciousness. And insofar as the male protagonist stands for the mind itself, his new role in the seduction situation reflects the same change from an active to a passive relationship with externality. Rather than acting as the seducer, as the male protagonist did in the earlier fiction of Rousseau or Richardson, he becomes the seduced, as he will remain in the later fiction of Laclos or "Monk" Lewis.[3] From this perspective, the blandishments of Biondetta represent the solicitations of the unconscious, a voice that will echo everywhere in nineteenth-century French literature. The interruptions of narrative line, however, serve not to reflect psychic repression by Alvare, the hero, but rather to create the prolonged tease of Cazotte's soft-core pornography by delaying Alvare's seduction. The devil's changes of identity, from camel to spaniel to girl, dramatize his powers of illusion rather than illuminating Alvare's psychology. And at the end, Alvare's entire experience is dismissed as a demonic delusion, in conformity with an orthodox religious viewpoint that the manifestations of the unconscious are evil, and that evil is non-being.

With the advent of romanticism, manifestations of the unconscious become morally ambiguous. Nodier's Trilby is neither saved nor damned; Flaubert's Saint Anthony sees Christ only after he has identified himself with undifferentiated forms of primordial life; Nerval's Aurélia is both rescuer and rescued in the supernatural order; Lautréamont's Maldoror resists God but distinguishes himself from Satan: "No one knows where he comes from, nor what is his ultimate purpose." To embody the kaleidoscopic ambiguity of the unconscious psyche in fictional form, the romantics employ the layering of narration, the doubling and splitting of characters, narrative discontinuity, and the archetype of Inversion.

The layering of narration implies psychic regression by suddenly shifting to an earlier time period, or periods, with or without a change in the identity of the characters, followed by an eventual return to the original time level. A model for this type of narrative structure was provided by the nesting layers of the oriental tale, popularized in France by Galland's translation of the *Thousand and One Nights* in 1704, and combined with the motifs of indigenous French fairy tales by Antoine Hamilton. The structure corresponds to the psychologist's layer-cake model of the psyche, in which an adult personality overlays multiple strata of adolescent, childhood, and infantile selves, the latter remaining dynamically active throughout life. From a purely literary standpoint, the structure has been frequently described in discussions of Nerval's novella *Sylvie*. In Nodier's masterpiece *Smarra* (1821) it can be represented thus: ABCBA. The "A" level relates the adventures of two lovers, Lorenzo and Lisidis, by the shore of Lake Maggiore sometime after 1697. It includes the Prologue (pp. 44–46) and Epilogue (pp. 75–77). The "B" level tells of Lucius and Myrthé, characters inspired by Apuleius' *The Golden Ass*, in the Roman Empire of the first century. It includes the Récit (pp. 49–59) and Epode (pp. 69–75), in which fear of adult sexuality, the incest taboo, and castration are unequivocally represented in the symbolic form of a public decapitation. The innermost, "C," level depicts a thinly veiled return to the womb, is situated in ancient Greece in the third century B.C., and involves two characters named Polémon (from the Greek word for "war"—a soldier, the thrust of libido) and Méroé (a seductive witch whose true lover, the monster Smarra, punishes Polémon for sleeping with Méroé, on pp. 59–68).

The doubling and splitting of characters functions as ego defense by detaching the narrator or protagonist from fearsome or repellent tendencies in his personality, through the mechanism of projection. A secondary character—a scapegoat—is created to embody the undesirable characteristics of the self. *Smarra* illustrates this clearly when the frame character Lorenzo dreams of Lucius, who suffers in his stead, and when Lucius dreams of Polémon for the same reason. (The most fundamental forms of such dissociation, of course, are the use of third-person rather than first-person narration and the attribution to the main character of a different name than the name of the author as given on the title page.) A more elaborate model, however, is provided by Nerval's *Sylvie* (1853). The narrator-protagonist shrinks from physicality and from

Conclusion

active commitment to a woman. Each time that he gets too close to one, a
rival conveniently materializes—a nameless young man, "the wrinkled
romantic lead," "Big Curly." And the episodic character "old Dodu"
("Dodu" means "plump" in French) serves to voice the sexual temptations which the narrator is unwilling to admit to himself. Similarly, the
initial love object, the actress Aurélie, divides into Aurélie (the worldly
actress) and Sylvie (the presumably innocent country lass), the latter
becoming the new and less threatening object of the narrator's attention.
Once the narrator actually confronts Sylvie, whom he has not seen since
adolescence, he becomes aware of *her* physicality, which must then be
incarnated in her brother Sylvain. A childhood memory of the aristocratic Adrienne, now conveniently shut away from the narrator by a
convent wall, eventually embodies the idealized component of both
Aurélie and Sylvie.

Narrative discontinuity other than layering involves changes of
focus from one set of characters to another (as in *Smarra*), or from the
present or historical to the legendary, and from the individual to the
collective, as in Flaubert's *Tentation de saint Antoine* (1848–1874). The
events of the seven numbered parts may be schematized as follows:

I. The saint alone in the desert
II. The temptations of power and sexuality, presented through
    Nebuchadnezzar and the Queen of Sheba
III. The temptation of doubt concerning revealed religion, pre-
    sented through Anthony's former disciple Hilarion
IV. The same, presented through a variety of heretics
V. The same, presented through a procession of doomed pagan
    gods and Jehovah of the Old Testament (Flaubert included
    Christ at one time)
VI. The same, presented through a journey into outer space on
    Satan's back (a personal God is nowhere to be found)
VII. A vision of teeming monsters and primordial forms of life

The levels of these seven parts may be described thus:

I.   The "real" present time of narration
II. Legendary past, individual level
III. Personal past
IV. Collective present
V.   Collective legendary past
VI. Individual, legendary present
VII. Undifferentiated, timeless collectivity

177

These shifts enhance the dream-like quality of the *Tentation*, which reports the visions of a single night.

The archetype of Inversion is prominent in Lautréamont's *Chants de Maldoror*. The hero discovers in the second of the six *Chants* that his supposedly just God is sadistic and depraved; in the third *Chant* life becomes death when a character declares: "I have received life like a wound, and I forbid suicide to heal the gaping hole." At the end of Chant V, dreaming becomes waking and revolt becomes submission when an angel orders Maldoror to arise and realize that his defiance of God was mere fantasy, itself a divine punishment. The sixth chant parodies the first five, and the *Poésies* which Lautréamont published shortly thereafter disparage and condemn the values of the chants, rejecting their praise of an amoral autonomy of life and art.

As the examples of the preceding paragraph suggest, Lautréamont's *Maldoror* initiates a transition away from the dramatization of ego defense strategies in romantic dream literature. Ego defense strategies protect the self by replacing something threatening with something less threatening. Repression, regression, projection, denial, and rationalization are substitutions. As Jacques Lacan has pointed out, so is metaphor.[4] If we say "a girl is a rose," what is the basis of the comparison? Their silky softness, their color, their scent, their delicacy, their habit of spending a lot of time outdoors? The *tertium comparationis* is a rationalization invented after the fact. But we do know that we are symbolically replacing an active, independent person with a frail, passive, decorative object, incapable of self-expression and excluded from creative, economic, and social competition. If we say "death is sleep," we are transforming physical dissolution into something restorative and harmless. Metaphors usually tend toward euphemization. Lautréamont attempts to reverse the euphemizing tendencies of metaphor. Instead of saying "death is sleep," for example, he says "sleep is death"—rendered in his more colorful language as "he who sleeps is less than an animal castrated the day before."

The archetype of Inversion is metaphor writ large; in the optimistic form which it assumes in our romantic dream narratives, it constitutes the supreme euphemization.[5] Nodier, Nerval, and Flaubert are saying that sleep is creativity; madness is insight; disgrace is triumph; and death is liberation. Lautréamont, on the contrary, affirms that purity is corruption, revolt is slavery, and God is evil. In the years immediately following the publication of *Maldoror*, Rimbaud completed the break with romanticism—to the extent that we have ever broken with it—by elevating Lautréamont's melodrama, at times, to an abstract and intellectual plane. He moves freely between word and world, frequently saying or implying at the conclusions of his poems that "this was an imaginative construct" (the refrain "elles n'existent pas" in "Barbare"), while elsewhere making the products and materials of writing into their own subject. "Voyelles" transforms written letters into an external decor; "Phrases" personifies the sentence as Muse. And the dizzy role-changing theatricality of the *Illuminations* strives to detach the enterprise of self-definition from the conceptualizing force of language, seen either as threat or as protector.[6] Such refusal of narrative coherence, such breaking of the metonymic chain, makes sustained literary works impossible; but in less radical forms, the de-euphemization of metaphor, the negative archetype of Inversion in the twentieth century, explains the enduring power of such fantasy literature as Yeats' "The Second Coming" and Eliot's "Wasteland."

ABBREVIATIONS

ACU	Carl Gustav Jung. *The Archetypes of the Collective Unconscious.* Vol. 9, part 1, of *CW.*
C	Charles Nodier. *Contes.* Edited by Pierre-Georges Castex. Paris: Garnier, 1961.
CW	Carl Gustav Jung. *Collected Works.* Edited by Herbert Read, Michael Fordham, and Gerhard Adler. 17 vols. New York: Pantheon Books, 1953–73.
CW2	Carl Gustav Jung. *Collected Works.* 2d ed. 17 vols. Princeton, N.J.: Princeton University Press, 1960–.
MAHS	Carl Gustav Jung, ed. *Man and His Symbols.* Garden City, N.Y.: Doubleday, 1964.
NAF	"Nouvelles Acquisitions Françaises." Manuscript repository at the Bibliothèque Nationale, Paris; includes four versions of Flaubert's *Tentation de saint Antoine.*
O	Gustave Flaubert. *Oeuvres.* Edited by Maurice Nadeau. 18 vols. Lausanne: Editions Rencontre, 1964–65.
O	Gérard de Nerval. *Oeuvres.* Edited by Albert Béguin and Jean Richer. 2 vols. Paris: Gallimard, 1952–56. (In Chapter 9 this abbreviation is used for the edition of Henri Lemaître.)
OC	Isidore Ducasse [Comte de Lautréamont]. *Oeuvres complètes.* Edited by Pierre-Olivier Walzer. Paris: Gallimard, 1970.
OC	Charles Nodier. *Oeuvres complètes.* 12 vols. Geneva: Slatkine Reprints, 1968.
PT	Carl Gustav Jung. *Psychological Types or the Psychology of Individuation.* London: Kegan Paul, 1946.
REV	Charles Nodier. *Rêveries.* Vol. 5 of his *Oeuvres.*
SDP	Carl Gustav Jung. *The Structure and Dynamics of the Psyche.* Vol. 8 of *CW.*
SE	Sigmund Freud. *The Standard Edition of the Complete Psychological Works of Sigmund Freud.* Edited by Lytton Strachey. 24 vols. London: Hogarth, 1953–74.

NOTES

Works cited in the Selected Bibliography or in the List of Abbreviations are given in shortened form throughout the notes.

Introduction

1. See Joseph I. Donohoe, "Ambivalence and Anger: The Human Center of the *Chanson de Roland*," *Romanic Review* 62 (December 1971): 251–61.

2. For a fine recent overview of such "preromantic" trends, see Paul Viallaneix, ed., *Le Préromantisme: Hypothèque ou hypothèse?* (Paris: Klincksieck, 1975).

3. Albert Béguin, *L'Ame romantique et le rêve* (Paris: Corti, 1963), p. 336. Bettina L. Knapp's recent book, *Dream and Image* (Troy, N.Y.: Whitston, 1977), surveys French dream literature from Descartes to Rimbaud from a strict Jungian archetypal perspective. Her study has the merit of combining an imposing knowledge of Western literature, and of the history of religion, with close readings of thirteen texts. I comment on this study in more detail in a forthcoming number of the *Romanic Review*.

4. At times, particularly in Nodier, there results a discontinuity of tone which will be apparent in the translations. Ordinary conversations, descriptions, and narration are written in a style much less elevated than that of the characters' and author's philosophical musings and reflections upon the spiritual order.

5. Michel Grimaud has recently defended this position in "La rhétorique du rêve: Swann et la psychanalyse," *Poétique* 33 (February 1978): 90–106. For contrary views, see H. J. Eysenck, *Uses and Abuses of Psychology* (Baltimore: Penguin, 1953), pp. 221–40 (an incisive attack on psychoanalysis as unscientific), and David Stafford-Clark, *What Freud Really Said* (New York: Schocken Books, 1966), p. 234: "The analysis of the dreams of real people makes it clear that only the free associations of the patient, and not the projections and interpretations of the analyst, can lead to a full understanding of the case. . . . [In literary criticism], one's own imagination inevitably fills in the gaps which genius always leaves in a character for that very purpose." In Chapter 1, I will argue that genius provides clues for the interpretation of gaps in the text surrounding them, thus providing something analogous to the latent content of dreams unearthed by analytic treatment.

Chapter 1

1. Helpful overviews of pre-Freudian theories concerning dreams are found in Rodolphe Louis Megroz, *The Dream World: A Survey of the History and Mystery of Dreams*

(New York: Dutton, 1939), pp. 1–80; Arthur James John Ratcliff, *The Nature of Dreams* (London: Nelson, 1939), pp. 81–89; and Max Serog, *New Light on Dreams: A New Approach to the Dream Problem* (Boston: House of Edinboro, 1953), pp. 25–37.

For the biblical and classical tradition on dreams, see John F. Priest, "Myth and Dream in Hebrew Scripture," and Amos N. Wilder, "Myth and Dream in Christian Scripture," both in Joseph Campbell, ed., *Myths, Dreams, and Religion* (New York: Dutton, 1970); Plato *The Republic* beginning of bk. 9; Aristotle, "On Dreams," in *Aristotle's Psychology*, ed. and trans. William Alexander Hamilton (London and New York: Sonnenschein and Macmillian, 1902), pp. 231–46; Cicero *De divinatione* 2:58–72; Artemidorus Daldianus, *The Interpretation of Dreams*, translated with commentary by Robert J. White (Park Ridge, N.J.: Noyes Press, 1975); and the Patristic writings in Morton T. Kelsey, ed. and comp., *Dreams: The Dark Speech of the Spirit; A Christian Interpretation* (New York: Doubleday, 1968), pp. 241–307.

The best two modern discussions of the dream as a physiological phenomenon are little known. They are Edward T. Adelson, ed., *Dreams in Contemporary Psychoanalysis* (New York: Society of Medical Psychoanalysts, 1963); and Roland Fischer, "A Cartography of the Ecstatic and Meditative States," *Science* 174 (November 26, 1971):897–904.

2. Phillip Wheelwright, *Metaphor and Reality* (Bloomington: Indiana University Press, 1962), pp. 78–91.

3. "On the Nature of Dreams," *SDP*, pp. 294–95. Like Jung, Nodier in his 1821 preface to *Smarra* identifies four coherent dramatic movements in dreams: "the author's subtlest device is to have embodied a fairly continuous tale, with introduction, complications, peripety, and denouement, in a series of bizarre dreams, where the transition between one and the other often hinges on a single word. Even here, however, he has merely conformed to the piquant whim of nature, which amuses itself by making us undergo, during the course of a single dream, interrupted several times by digressions, all the phases of a structured, complete, and more or less plausible adventure" (*C*, pp. 34–35).

4. Freud, "From the History of an Infantile Neurosis," *SE*, vol. 17, p. 97.

5. Freud, "The Ego and the Id," *SE*, vol. 19, p. 38.

6. See Calvin S. Hall, "Diagnosing Personality by the Analysis of Dreams," in *Dreams and Personality Dynamics*, ed. Manfred F. DeMartino (Springfield, Ill.: Charles C. Thomas, 1959), p. 205; and Robert R. Holt, "Freud's Mechanistic and Humanistic Images of Man," *Psychoanalysis and Contemporary Science: An Annual of Integrative and Interdisciplinary Studies* (New York: Macmillan, 1972), vol. 1, pp. 3–24.

Far too many literary critics still hold to the outdated mechanistic view of dream function. For example, Jean Decottignies defines the nightmare as "any kind of mental construct serving to gratify instinctual drives that are in conflict with reality and common sense" in "La Poétique du cauchemar en France à l'époque romantique," *L'Information littéraire* 24 (March-April 1972): 63.

7. Jan Frank, "Some Aspects of Lobotomy (Prefrontal Leucotomy) under Psychoanalytic Scrutiny," *Psychiatry* 13 (February 1950):35–42.

8. Graham F. Reed, *The Psychology of Anomalous Experience: A Cognitive Approach* (London: Hutchinson, 1972), p. 162.

9. Erik H. Erikson, *Identity and the Life Cycle: Selected Papers* (New York: International Universities Press, 1959), p. 149. This text is a greatly improved version of parts 1 and 3 of Erikson's *Childhood and Society*, (New York: Norton, 1950). Erikson later summed up his views on human development in his epilogue to *Young Man Luther* (New York: Norton, 1962), pp. 253–65. Lest we forget the id and the instincts, however, Erikson's warning is timely: "When men concentrate on an uncharted area of human existence, they aggrandize this area to become the universe, and they reify its center as the prime reality. . . . The 'id' was reified in psychoanalysis, and the instincts became the universe, in spite of the fact that Freud sovereignly referred to them as his 'mythology.' . . . Will we escape doing the same with the ego?" (*Childhood and Society*, p. 414).

10. Erik H. Erikson, "The Dream-Specimen of Psychoanalysis," *Journal of the American Psychoanalytical Association* 2 (1954):55.

11. See Alexander Grinstein, *On Sigmund Freud's Dreams* (Detroit: Wayne State University Press, 1968), which gathers together Freud's scattered remarks on his own dreams, and explains his personal and literary allusions. For brief comments on sublimation by Freud, see "Leonardo da Vinci and a Memory of His Childhood," *SE*, vol. 11, pp. 63–137, especially pp. 106, 122–23, 131; and "From the History of an Infantile Neurosis," *SE*, vol. 17, p. 114 (commonly referred to as "the Wolf-Man").

12. Erikson, *Identity and the Life Cycle*, p. 52.

13. For an example of the use of this concept in literary criticism, see Laurence M. Porter, "The Generativity Crisis of Gide's *Immoraliste*," *French Forum* 2 (January 1977):58–69.

14. One of Montaigne's additions to the revised edition of his *Essais* neatly illustrates the development of a sense of solidarity in the mature person. He had been discussing the reactions of "le vulgaire"—the common man—to death. He later wrote in: "et nous sommes tous du vulgaire."

15. Erikson, in "The Dream-Specimen of Psychoanalysis," pp. 54–55, says that the creative person, unlike others, must continually reassert his or her ego identity.

16. *Ibid.*, p. 17.

17. Freud, "On Dreams," *SE*, vol. 5, pp. 640–41.

18. Albert Sonnenfeld, "Elaboration secondaire du grimoire: Mallarmé et le poète-critique," *Romanic Review* 69 (1978):72–89.

19. Gérard Genette, "Vraisemblance et motivation," in *Figures II* (Paris: Editions du Seuil, 1969), p. 86n.

20. Freud, *Introductory Lectures on Psychoanalysis*, *SE*, vol. 15, p. 186.

21. Jung, "The Practical Use of Dream-Analysis," in *The Practice of Psychotherapy*, *CW*, vol. 17, p. 149.

22. Freud, "On the History of the Psychoanalytic Movement," *SE*, vol. 14, p. 36.

23. Walter J. Reis, "A Comparison of the Interpretation of Dream Series with and without Free Associations," in DeMartino, ed., *Dreams and Personality Dynamics*, pp. 211–25, esp. p. 224; Calvin S. Hall and R. E. Lind, *Dreams, Life, and Literature: A Study of Franz Kafka* (Chapel Hill: University of North Carolina Press, 1971); Calvin S. Hall, "The Dreams of Freud and Jung," *Psychology Today* (June 1968): 42–45, 64–65; Leopold Caligor and Rollo May, *Dreams and Symbols: Man's Unconscious Language* (New York: Basic Books, 1968); Jung, *Symbols of Transformation*, *CW*. See also Calvin S. Hall and R. L. Van de Castle, *The Content Analysis of Dreams* (New York: Appleton-Century-Crofts, 1966).

24. Alan P. Bell and Calvin S. Hall, *The Personality of a Child Molester: An Analysis of Dreams* (Chicago: Aldine-Atherton, 1971), pp. 2–4, 80, 94–96, 99, 121, et passim.

25. Charles Mauron, *Des Métaphores obsédantes au mythe personnel: Introduction à la psychocritique* (Paris: J. Corti, 1963); Claude Lévi-Strauss, "The Structural Study of Myth," in *Structural Anthropology* (New York: Basic Books, 1963), pp. 206–31.

26. Abraham H. Maslow, *Motivation and Personality*, 2d ed. (New York: Harper and Row, 1970), p. 231.

27. Jung, "The Psychology of the Unconscious Processes," in *Collected Papers on Analytical Psychology* (New York: Moffat Yard, 1917), p. 421. Compare his definition of "Subjective Plane" in *PT*, pp. 599–600. See also Serog, *New Light on Dreams*, p. 88, and Adelson, *Dreams in Contemporary Psychoanalysis*, p. 27, who dogmatically asserts that "every element of the dream refers to the dreamer himself or to some aspect of himself or his personality." Freud himself said that "dreams are completely egotistical" (*The Interpretation of Dreams*, *SE*, vol. 5, pp. 357–58). Lautréamont expressed a similar understanding of *Les Chants de Maldoror*, when, at the beginning of Chant VI, he referred to Chants I through V as the work's synthetic part and Chant VI as its analytic part.

28. Jung, "The Philosophical Tree," in *Alchemical Studies*, *CW*, vol. 13, pp. 347–48.

29. Erikson, "The Dream-Specimen of Psychoanalysis," p. 31. Freud rejects as "a meaningless and unjustifiable piece of speculation the notion that *all* figures that appear in a dream are to be regarded as fragmentations and representatives of the dreamer's own ego" ("Remarks on the Theory and Practice of Dream-Interpretation," *SE*, vol. 19, pp. 120–21).

30. *S/Z* (Paris: Seuil, 1970), pp. 183–84.
31. Charles Nodier, "De quelques phénomènes du sommeil," in *REV*, p. 169. Compare the congruent statement of Jacques Lacan: "It is through the *complex* that the images which inform the broadest units of behavior establish themselves in the economy of the psyche. The subject identifies himself with each of these images in turn, in order to perform, as a solitary actor, the drama of their conflicts" (*Écrits* [Paris: Seuil, 1966], p. 90).
32. Nerval, *O*, vol. 1, pp. 292 (*Sylvie*) and 363 (*Aurélia*).
33. Flaubert, *O*, vol. 12, p. 405 (letter to George Sand, July 1869).
34. *Ibid.*, p. 159 (letter to Taine, 1866).
35. Ducasse, *OC*, p. 131.
36. Freud, "A Short Account of Psychoanalysis," p. 209. For a recent defense of pluralism, see Frederick Crews, *Out of My System: Psychoanalysis, Ideology and Critical Method* (New York: Oxford University Press, 1975), p. xiv and chs. 1, 4, and 9. See also Morton Kaplan and Robert Kloss, *The Unspoken Motive: A Guide to Psychoanalytic Literary Criticism* (New York: Free Press, 1973). The best attempt so far to define the fantastic in literature is Tzvetan Todorov's *Introduction à la littérature fantastique* (Paris: Seuil, 1970). See also Barton Levi Saint-Armand's incisive review of Todorov in *Novel* 8 (Spring 1975):260–67, and my comments in the following chapter.
37. Edward Glover, *Freud or Jung?* (New York: W. W. Norton, 1950), p. 194.

Chapter 2

1. See Jacques Bousquet, *Les Thèmes du rêve dans la littérature romantique* (Paris: Didier, 1964), pp. 52–72. My preceding paragraph is also drawn from these pages.
2. See Léon Emery's excellent introduction to *Vision et pensée chez Victor Hugo* (Lyon: Audin, n.d.), pp. 1–8, and Ernst Kris, "The Contribution and Limitations of Psychoanalysis," in *Art and Psychoanalysis*, edited by William Phillips (New York: Criterion, 1957), p. 288.
3. Jean Rousset, *Forme et signification: essais sur les structures littéraires de Corneille à Claudel* (Paris: Corti, 1962), p. 88.
4. See Mary Elizabeth Storer, *Un Épisode littéraire de la fin du dix-septième siècle: La Mode des contes de fées* (Paris: Champion, 1928). For an opposing, rationalistic view, see Arthur J. Weitzman, "The Oriental Tale in the Eighteenth Century: A Reconsideration," *Studies in Voltaire and the Eighteenth Century* 58 (1967):1839–55. He claims that not until Beckford's *Vathek* can one discern a shift in aesthetic purpose—from the philosophical-satiric to the depiction of non-rational mental states—in the choice of the oriental tale as a genre.
5. Hamilton influenced Nodier. The long tooth of the sorceress Dentue in *Fleur d'Epine* appears to be the chief model for the same feature in Nodier's *Fée aux Miettes*, although the attribute is of course traditional in the crone figure of folktales. See Laurence M. Porter, "Hoffmannesque and Hamiltonian Sources of Nodier's *Fée aux Miettes*," *Romance Notes* 19 (1979), in press.
6. See André-M. Rousseau, "A la découverte d'Antoine Hamilton, conteur," *Études littéraires* 1 (1968):185–95.
7. Denis Diderot, *Oeuvres complètes*, ed. J. Assézat (Paris: Garnier, 1875–77), vol. 9, pp. 366–70.
8. *Encyclopédie*, vol. 14, p. 223. See also "Songe," vol. 15, p. 356, col. 2. Compare Voltaire, "Histoire de Siam": "The Imagination, finding itself alone [in dreams], parodies the drama Reason was performing during the day"; and "Lettre aux auteurs de la Gazette littéraire, 20 juin 1764," both in *Oeuvres complètes de Voltaire*, ed. Louis Moland (Paris: Garnier, 1877–85), vols. 32, part 2, p. 579, and 25, p. 193.
9. "Diderot and the Phenomenology of the Dream," *Diderot Studies* 8 (1966):218, 223, 244.

10. Marcel Raymond, *Jean-Jacques Rousseau: La quête de soi et la rêverie* (Paris: Corti, 1962), pp. 154, 214. See also *ibid.*, pp. 159–76, for a history of the concept of the *rêverie* in France.
11. Freud, "Five Lectures on Psychoanalysis," *SE*, vol. 11, p. 33. See also his "On the History of the Psycho-Analytic Movement," *SE*, vol. 14, p. 57; "Remarks on the Theory and Practice of Dream-Interpretation," *SE*, vol. 19, p. 117 ("within an analysis far more of the repressed is brought to light in connection with dreams than by any other method"); and Edward T. Adelson, "Facts and Theories of the Psychology of Dreams," in *Dreams in Contemporary Psychoanalysis*, ed. Edward T. Adelson (New York: Society of Medical Psychoanalysts, 1963).
12. "Mythological Themes in Creative Literature and Art," *Myths, Dreams, and Religion*, ed. Joseph Campbell (New York: E. P.Dutton, 1970), p. 140.
13. Charles Nodier, "De quelques phénomènes du sommeil," *REV*, pp. 160, 162; Gérard de Nerval, *Aurélia, O*, vol. 1, pp. 359, 412.
14. Diderot, letter to Sophie Volland, October 1760, in *Correspondance*, ed. Georges Roth (Paris: Editions de Minuit, 1955–70), vol. 3, p. 173.
15. Michel Foucault, *Madness and Civilization: A History of Insanity in the Age of Reason* (New York: Pantheon, 1965), p. 200. Lionel Trilling's essay "Freud and Literature" in his *The Liberal Imagination* (New York: Viking, 1950) also stresses Diderot's important role in anticipating depth psychology.
16. See Auguste Viatte, *Les Sources occultes du romantisme français*, 2 vols. (Paris: Champion, 1965), passim; Laurence M. Porter, "Charles Nodier and Pierre-Simon Ballanche," *Orbis litterarum* 27 (Fall 1972):229–36; and Laurence M. Porter, "Charles Nodier and Saint-Martin," *Romance Notes* 14 (Winter 1972):283–88.
17. Quoted in Jean Decottignies, *Prélude à Maldoror: Vers une poétique de la rupture en France, 1820–1870* (Paris: Colin, 1973), p.25.
18. Nodier, "De quelques phénomènes du sommeil," *REV*, p. 173.
19. In late eighteenth-century France, Mesmer's doctrine of animal magnetism led to a radical modification of the theory of the faculties and perceptions of the sleeper. The Marquis de Puységur conducted a famous series of experiments on Mesmerism in 1784. Mesmer's disciple Dr. Johann Koreff practiced magnetic medicine in Paris between 1823 and 1837 and visited Nodier at the Arsénal during this period; Hoffmann's *Le Magnétiseur* and Balzac's *Ursule Mirouet* also nourished the vogue. See Louis Figuier, "Le Magnétisme animal," *Histoire du merveilleux dans les temps modernes* (Paris, Hachette, 1860–74), vol. 3; Marietta Martin, *Un Aventurier intellectuel sous la restauration et la monarchie de juillet: Le docteur Koreff (1783–1851)* (Paris: Champion, 1925); and Robert Darnton, *Mesmerism and the Enlightenment in France* (Cambridge, Mass.: Harvard University Press, 1968). Our authors' dream narratives, however, make no clear reference to magnetism until Lautréamont describes Maldoror's magnetic influence upon his victims.
20. For an examination of the innovations of French romantic poetry in the perspective of genre history, see Laurence M. Porter, *The Renaissance of the Lyric in French Romanticism: Elegy, "Poëme," and Ode* (Lexington, Ky.: French Forum Monographs, 1978).
21. Reginald M. Hartland, *Walter Scott et le roman "frénétique": Contribution à l'étude de leur fortune en France* (Paris: Champion, 1928), p. 64.
22. See *Confessions of an English Opium-Eater* (London: Cresset Press, 1950), pp. 327–28.
23. The long chronological listings in the appendix to Hubert Matthey, *Essai sur le merveilleux dans la littérature française depuis 1800* (Paris: Payot, 1915), for example, mention only *Atala, René*, and *Les Martyrs* before Nodier's *Smarra*. A useful recent study which complements my book is Henriette Lucius' *La Littérature "visionnaire" en France du début du XVIe au début du XIXe siècle: Etude de sémantique et de littérature* (Bienne: Arts Graphiques Schuler, 1970). Dr. Lucius' essay is particularly rich for the period 1600 to 1750. She explores the changing meanings of the terms *voyant, vision*, and *visionnaire* and emphasizes the poet figure and the religious vision. She agrees that Nodier's *Smarra* inaugurates true dream literature in France (pp. 255–59). But she does not employ a psychological frame of

reference, and devotes only a page or two to the discussion of each literary work. She does not mention Diderot, the Gothic, and the fairy tale as important harbingers of the fantastic in romanticism.

Some modern critics still assert that authentic semblances of dream experience were developed only in the twentieth century. See Selma Fraiberg, "Kafka and the Dream," in Phillips, *Art and Psychoanalysis*, p. 27; and Lester G. Crocker, "L'Analyse des rêves au XVIIIe siècle," *Studies in Voltaire and the Eighteenth Century* 23 (1963):271–310: "Not until Kafka came along did literary dreams embody the distortions and incoherence of real dreams" (p. 309).

24. See Hartland, *Walter Scott*, pp. 96, 102; Alice M. Killen, *Le Roman terrifiant ou roman noir de Walpole à Anne Radcliffe et son influence sur la littérature française jusqu'en 1840* (Paris: Champion, 1924), p. 145. Marcelin Pleynet has appropriately stressed resemblances between the Gothic novel and Lautréamont in his *Lautréamont par lui-même* (Paris: Seuil, 1967), pp. 61–99, 145.

25. Masao Miyoshi, *The Divided Self: A Perspective on the Literature of the Victorians* (New York: New York University Press, 1969), pp. 7, 38. Besides the works already mentioned, other main sources for French romantic dream narratives were Shakespeare's *The Tempest* and *A Midsummer Night's Dream* (Nodier's Trilby resembles Ariel, and the five parts of *Smarra* each have an epigraph from *The Tempest); Tristram Shandy* and *Jacques le Fataliste;* the "Songe de Jean-Paul" as presented in *De l'Allemagne;* and Goethe's *Faust,* whose first part was translated by Nerval in 1828.

For a penetrating discussion of the love-death relationship and the Gothic in English and American literature, see Leslie A. Fiedler's *Love and Death in the American Novel* (New York: Stein and Day, 1966), pp. 56–57, 126–41.

26. Ross Chambers has published an excellent analysis, " '*Spirite*' de Théophile Gautier: Une lecture," *Archives des lettres modernes* 153 (1974).

27. James Hastings, ed., *Encyclopedia of Religion and Ethics*, 13 vols. (New York: Scribners, 1914–72), vol. 4, p. 581, s.v. "Demons and Spirits," a classic, richly informative article.

28. See Alfred de Vigny, *Le Journal d'un poète*, in *Oeuvres complètes*, ed. Fernand Baldensperger (Paris: Gallimard, 1948–50), vol. 2, p. 876, entry for 1823.

29. Arthur O. Lovejoy, *The Great Chain of Being: A Study of the History of an Idea* (Cambridge, Mass.: Harvard University Press, 1966; orig. pub. 1936), pp. 233–36, 255.

30. See *C*, pp. 309–10, 314.

31. "Le Diable rouge," *Almanach cabalistique*, in *O*, vol. 2, pp. 1215–19.

32. See Juan Cirlot, *A Dictionary of Symbols* (New York: Philosophical Library, 1962), s.v. "Inversion," and Gilbert Durand, *Les Structures anthropologiques de l'imaginaire: Introduction à l'archétypologie générale*, 3d ed. (Paris: Bordas, 1969), p. 317.

33. *O*, vol. 1, pp. 412–13.

34. As Flaubert reminded himself in a note from around 1849, "take care to respect *the logic of events*—they must be prepared. So *the visions* of part 2 [in *La Tentation de saint Antoine*] should derive (1) from Anthony's reflections, (2) from the [personified] Sins, (3) from Anthony's weaknesses and *transgressions*" (emphasis in original; see *NAF* MS. 23671, fol. 164). See also Flaubert's letter to George Sand, in which he explains that his greatest concern in composing the *Tentation* is to "succeed in finding a logical continuity . . . among the saint's various hallucinations" (*O*, vol. 12, p. 405).

35. "De quelques phénomènes du sommeil," *REV*, pp. 160–64.

36. See Ernest Jones, *On the Nightmare* (New York: Liveright, 1951), pp. 82–83, 99–111.

37. *Freud or Jung?* (New York: W. W. Norton, 1950), p. 184.

38. Countless variations on this basic pattern are possible: for example, the happy prison studied by Victor Brombert; the quest itself as fulfillment in Perse; the initial location which an ideal identity which one refuses to leave for involvement in an impure world in Villiers' *Axël*; the deliberate isolation of the better part of oneself from the world while the less worthy part is engaged in it; the steady constriction of one's identity in Balzac's *Le*

Père Goriot or in Boris Vian's *Les Bâtisseurs d'empire*; and the archetype of Withdrawal, Enlightenment, and Return which Joseph Campbell has characterized as the "monomyth" or "Urmyth" underlying all the rest.
  39. Joseph L. Henderson, "Ancient Myths and Modern Man," in Jung, *MAHS*, p. 128.
  40. Adelson, *Dreams in Contemporary Psychoanalysis*, p. 10.
  41. Jung, "On the Psychology and Pathology of So-Called Occult Phenomena" (1902), cited and helpfully clarified by Yolande Jacobi, *The Way of Individuation* (New York: Harcourt, Brace, and World, 1967), p. 12; see also pp. vii, 13–15, 24–28, 49, 96, 132–33. Jung first mentioned individuation explicitly in *PT* and presented his most detailed exposition of the concept in *Mysterium Conjunctionis: An Inquiry into the Separation and Synthesis of Psychic Opposites in Alchemy*, *CW*2, vol. 14, passim.
  42. See Jung, *ACU*, p. 187. For Jung's notion of complementarity (the unconscious harbors personality traits which complement ego consciousness but have been repressed by it), see *PT*, pp. 593–95. Erikson accepts this notion as valid for some patients: see his *Identity: Youth and Crisis* (New York: Norton, 1968), pp. 58–59. Karen Horney postulates a similar dynamic interaction of aggressive and compliant traits in the personality in *Neurosis and Human Growth*.
  43. See Laurence M. Porter, "The Devil as Double in Nineteenth-Century Literature: Goethe, Dostoevsky, and Flaubert," *Comparative Literature Studies* 15 (Fall 1978):316–35.
  44. See Bousquet, *Thèmes du rêve*, pp. 67–69.
  45. Adelson, *Dreams in Contemporary Psychoanalysis*, p. 266.
  46. See Charles Nodier, "*Blanche d'Evreux*, par Mme Périé Candeille," *La Quotidienne*, March 4, 1824, p. 2. See also his statement in *Discours prononcés dans la séance publique tenue à l'Académie française pour la réception de M. Ch. Nodier, le 26 décembre 1833* (Paris: Didot, 1834), p. 13; Pierre-Simon Ballanche, *Orphée: Oeuvres complètes* (Geneva: Slatkine Reprints, 1967; orig. publ. 1833), vol. 6, pp. 82 and 96.
  For para-religious tendencies in literature during the late eighteenth and early nineteenth centuries, see Albert Abraham Avni, *The Bible and Romanticism: The Old Testament in German and French Romantic Poetry* (The Hague: Mouton, 1969), and the review of that work by Laurence M. Porter in *Comparative Literature* 24 (Winter 1972):90–93; Gwendolyn Bays, *The Orphic Vision: Seer Poets from Novalis to Rimbaud* (Lincoln: University of Nebraska Press, 1964); Paul Bénichou, *Le Sacre de l'écrivain, 1750–1830: Essai sur l'avènement d'un pouvoir spirituel laïque dans la France moderne* (Paris: Corti, 1973); Léon Cellier, *L'Epopée humanitaire et les grands mythes romantiques* (Paris: SEDES, 1971); Brian Juden, *Traditions orphiques et tendances mystiques dans le romantisme français (1800–1855)* (Paris: Klincksieck, 1971); Hermine B. Riffaterre, *L'Orphisme dans la poésie romantique: Thèmes et style surnaturalistes* (Paris: Nizet, 1970); Walter A. Strauss, *Descent and Return* (Cambridge, Mass.: Harvard University Press, 1971); and Auguste Viatte, *Les Sources occultes du romantisme. Illuminisme—Théosophie, 1770–1820*, 2 vols. (Paris: Champion, 1965; orig. pub. 1928).

Chapter 3

  1. Brian Juden, *Traditions orphiques et tendances mystiques dans le romantisme français (1800–1855)* (Paris: Klincksieck, 1971), pp. 662–64.
  2. Jung, *PT*, p. 597.
  3. M.-L. von Franz, "The Process of Individuation," in Jung, *MAHS*, p. 191. See also Jung, *ACU*, p. 284.
  4. Jung, "The Practical Use of Dream-Analysis," in *The Practice of Psychotherapy*, *CW*, vol. 17, p. 153.

5. His rigid intolerance seems in part inspired by Scott's portrait of the monk Eustace in *The Monastery*, vol. 1, ch. 8.

6. The major characters' names in *Trilby* throw light on their personalities. Etymologically, Ronald means "strong ruler"; Daniel (Jeannie's husband's first name) means "God is my judge" (submission to authority); Jeannie, a form of John, means "God is gracious" and stresses charity and forgiveness. The coincidence that Trilby's first name is also John (p. 124) underlines his spiritual affinity to Jeannie.

7. See "The Psychological Foundations of Belief in Spirits," in Jung, *SDP*, pp. 301–18.

8. See Jung, *PT*, p. 599.

9. Jung, *ACU*, p. 197.

10. Jung, *PT*, pp. 70–71.

11. See Jung, *ACU*, p. 285; Jung, *Aion: Researches into the Phenomenology of the Self*, *CW2*, vol. 9, pt. 2, p. 9; and Anna Freud, *The Ego and the Mechanisms of Defence* (New York: International Universities Press, 1964: orig. pub. 1946), p. 87.

12. See, for example, Jean Chevalier et al., *Dictionnaire des symboles* (Paris: Editions Robert Laffont, 1969), p. 527; Juan E.Cirlot, *A Dictionary of Symbols* (New York: Philosophical Library, 1962), p. 34; and Gilbert Durand, *Les Structures anthropologiques de l'imaginaire: Introduction à l'archéotypologie générale*, 3d ed. (Paris: Bordas, 1969), pp. 238–46. Through the notion of *emboîtement* (nesting one thing inside another), Durand associates the dwarf with the fish and submersion, adding that "the symbolism of the fish seems to stress the inward-turning, intimist nature of swallowing," with its beneficent "capacity for preserving what has been swallowed indefinitely, and miraculously intact" (p. 245)—a perfect description of memories preserved in the unconscious or in the preconscious. Trilby often assumes the form of a fish.

13. As many critics have pointed out with regard to Nodier's humorous and satiric tales, he was clearly aware of the sexual meanings of such symbols as lizards, slippers, and horseback riding.

14. For a brief account of the relationship between Nodier's narrative art and his cosmological theories, see Laurence M. Porter, "The Narrative Art of Nodier's *Contes*: Diderot's Contribution to the Quest for Verisimilitude," *Romanic Review* 63 (December 1972):273–74. See also Pierre-Georges Castex, *Le Conte fantastique en France de Nodier à Maupassant* (Paris: Corti, 1951), p.35, where he describes the *conte fantastique* as a genre which preserves the possibility of either a rationalistic or a supernatural explanation for the marvelous events of the story: "Thus the author remains midway between the implausible fairy tale and pedestrian realism, or rather, his ingenuity reconciles two opposing forms of the fictional imagination."

15. Jung, *MAHS*, p. 103.

16. For "spiritual guide," Jung employs the Greek term "psychopomp." He defines it as "a mediator between the conscious and unconscious," which are to be united through the phenomenon of individuation, and as "a personification of the latter" (*Aion*, p. 16).

17. This theme of demonic urbanization is apparent in the legend of the storm-giant Arthur (*C*, pp. 128–29). No doubt the example of Scott's novels helped inspire Nodier, in *Trilby*, to depict one social order supplanting another.

18. See Jean Larat, *La Tradition et l'exotisme dans l'oeuvre de Charles Nodier* (Paris: Champion, 1923), pp. 410–13, and Josef Stadelmann, *Charles Nodier im Urteil seiner Zeitgenossen* (Munich: N.p., 1929), p. 10.

19. See Albert Joseph George, *Short Fiction in France, 1800–1850* (Syracuse, N.Y.: Syracuse University Press, 1964), p. 32. Nodier's appeal for a return to folk traditions as a basis for literary composition, in the passage quoted immediately above, comes from the preface to his *Légende de soeur Béatrix* (1837), the one *conte* by Nodier which, being listed in Stith Thompson's *Motif-Index of Folk Literature*, indisputably derives from oral tradition. Compare the important preface to Nodier's *La Fée aux Miettes* of 1832 (*C*, pp. 168–71).

Chapter 4

1. See Alfred Lombard, *Flaubert et saint Antoine* (Paris: Victor Attinger, 1934), pp. 17–18 (a fine study), and René Dumesnil and Don-L. Demorest, "Bibliographie de Gustave Flaubert," *Bulletin du bibliophile et du bibliothécaire* (1937), pp. 395–401, 452–60, 498–505, 549–55; (1938), pp. 25–32, 75–82, 134–42, 168–75, 311–17, and 404–14. Dumesnil's is the best of the many studies of the multiple manuscripts of Flaubert's *Tentation*. See especially the 1938 issue, pp. 27–29, 135–38, 315–17, and 408–13. For a recent overview see Laurence M. Porter, "A Fourth Version of Flaubert's *Tentation de saint Antoine* (1869)," *Nineteenth-Century French Studies* 4 (1975–76):53–66.

2. Gustave Flaubert, letter to Louise Colet, December 27, 1852, *O*, vol. 6, p. 392.

3. Concerning Flaubert's self-image as a saint, see Benjamin F. Bart, *Flaubert* (Syracuse, N.Y.: Syracuse University Press, 1967), p. 707; Harry Levin, "Flaubert: Portrait of the Artist as a Saint," *Kenyon Review* 10 (1948): 28–29; and René Jasinski's Flaubert chapter in his *A Travers le dix-neuvième siècle* (Paris: Nizet, 1975). Theodor Reik found "the deepest foundation of the artist's creations and his work habits" in "a bridge between infantile incest fantasies and the masochistic ascetic ideal." See Reik's "Die Psychogenese des Werkes" in his *Flaubert und seine "Versuchung des heiligen Antonius": Ein Beitrag zur Künstlerpsychologie* (Minden: J. C. C. Bruns, 1912), pp. 179–87.

4. See Bart, *Flaubert*, pp. 48–49, 666–67.

5. *Ibid.*, pp. 194–97, 230.

6. André Gide, *Journal, 1889–1939* (Paris: Gallimard, 1948), entry for April 9, 1908.

7. Letter to Jules Duplan, May 1857, *O*, vol. 9, p. 76. See also the famous letter of February 1, 1852, to Louise Colet, vol. 6, p. 225–26; pp. 210, 315; and the letters to Louis Bouilhet from June through October 1856, *O*, vol. 7, pp. 470–71, 489, 493, 498.

8. Letter to his mother, November 14, 1850, *O*, vol. 4, p. 496.

9. Flaubert, *Oeuvres complètes* (Paris: Louis Conard, 1910–54), vol. 17, p. 589. This volume contains the 1849 and 1856 versions of the *Tentation* as appendices to the 1874 text.

10. *O*, vol. 12, p. 159.

11. Letter to George Sand, *ibid.*, vol. 12, p. 405.

12. Flaubert, *La Tentation de saint Antoine*, ed. Edouard Maynial (Paris: Garnier, 1968), p. 245. In this chapter, page numbers in parentheses refer to this edition.

13. Two famous recent critics have created a distorted image of an excessively bookish Flaubert and saint. Michel Foucault exaggerates grossly by saying that all the saint's fantasies derive from the biblical passages he read, and that in the 1874 version evil has assumed an exclusively verbal form; see his "Un 'Fantastique' de bibliothèque," p. 15. Michel Butor quite misleadingly claims that there is no "day residue" specifically related to the temptations which assail Anthony; see "La Spirale des sept péchés," *Critique* 26 (May 1970):393.

14. NAF, 23671, fol. 107.

15. See Don-L. Demorest, *L'Expression figurée et symbolique dans l'oeuvre de Gustave Flaubert* (Geneva: Slatkine Reprints, 1967), pp. 323–24.

16. NAF, 23667, fols. 19, 44, 59.

17. Foucault discusses the nesting layers of the *Tentation* lucidly on pp. 16–26 of his article cited in note 13 above, although he exaggerates their complexity.

18. For an excellent evaluation of the historical accuracy of Flaubert's *Tentation*, see the *Oeuvres complètes*, vol. 17, pp. 655–65. Accounts of the saint's life are found in the *Catholic Encyclopedia* and in Hastings' *Encyclopaedia of Religion and Ethics*. The primary source is the saint's life by his disciple Athanasius.

19. See Jung, *PT*, p. 441, and *Aion*, p. 42; Freud, "Negation," *SE*, vol. 19, pp. 235, 239. "The devil is certainly nothing else than the personification of the repressed unconscious instinctual life," Freud claimed in "Character and Anal Eroticism," *SE*, vol. 9, p. 174, repeated in "Dreams in Folklore," *SE*, vol. 12, p. 188.

20. Paul Valéry, "La Tentation de (saint) Flaubert," *Variété V* (Paris: Gallimard, 1944), pp. 204–5. See also Jonathan Culler, *Flaubert: The Uses of Uncertainty* (Ithaca, N.Y.:

Cornell University Press, 1974), p. 181, who claims "The Saint has no psychology," and his pp. 136–37.

21. "Psychic growth . . . is in dreams frequently symbolized by the tree, whose slow, powerful, involuntary growth fulfills a definite pattern" (Jung, *MAHS*, p. 161).

22. Erik H. Erikson, *Identity and the Life Cycle*, pp. 99–100.

23. The 1856 version associated sexual feelings more directly with memories of the mother. Immediately after Anthony hallucinated her, he imagined the encounter of a shepherd and a whore with veiled face (the faceless woman is a common disguise for the mother in incestuously tinged fantasies). Then he had a vision of a group of frolicking, naked nymphs. Their multiplicity means that Anthony is defending himself against his sexual feelings by making their object diffuse. Finally he saw the Queen of Sheba. She is safely remote from Anthony's life because she is a legend from the past, yet her royal status suggests a maternal figure as viewed by the child.

24. There is an excellent treatment of this episode by André Chastel in his "L'Episode de la Reine de Saba dans la *Tentation de saint Antoine* de Flaubert," *Romanic Review* 40 (December 1949):261–67.

25. Jean Seznec, *Nouvelles études sur "La Tentation de saint Antoine"* (London: Warburg Institute, 1949), pp. 19–21, comments illuminatingly on this scene.

26. See Jung, *PT*, pp. 18–33, 70–75, for an overview of the Gnostic heresies which dominated the Alexandrian period; for a discussion of Tertullian and Origen; for speculations concerning how the Gnosis (like alchemy after it) anticipated depth psychology; and for comment on how Anthony's battles against demons, as reported by Athanasius, constituted an attempted repression of the personal unconscious.

27. For a definitive discussion see Benjamin F. Bart, "Psyche into Myth," pp. 317–42; and his *Flaubert*, pp. 670–75.

28. NAF, 23665, fol. 71A. In the psychosexual sphere, Anthony's recurrent visions of prostitutes like the Ennoia who accompanies Simon, and the latent homosexuality manifest in his effusions concerning Damis and Apollonius (Anthony says Apollonius charmed him more profoundly than the Queen of Sheba, and was worth all Hell put together as a temptation), derive from the fixation of libido on the mother, and its consequent diversion from ordinary heterosexual outlets. See Reik, *Flaubert*, pp. 182–83.

29. See Jean Seznec, *Les Sources de l'épisode des dieux dans "La Tentation de saint Antoine"* (Paris: Vrin, 1940), pp. 10–31.

30. Flaubert, letter to Mlle Leroyer de Chantepie, February 18, 1857, *O*, vol. 9, p. 203.

31. Letter to Mme Roger des Genettes, 1860, *O*, vol. 9, p. 246.

32. See F. J. Carmody, "Further Sources of *La Tentation de saint Antoine*," *Romanic Review* 49 (1958):291–92; and Victor Brombert, *The Novels of Flaubert: A Study of Themes and Techniques* (Princeton, N.J.: Princeton University Press, 1966), p. 200.

33. The historical Didymus was sixty years younger than Anthony, but Flaubert probably knew that "Didyme" was an appropriate name for Anthony's teacher because it was also a name for the apostle Doubting Thomas.

34. See Gilbert Durand, *Les Structures anthropologiques de l'imaginaire: Introduction à l'archéotypologie générale* (Paris: Bordas, 1969), p. 269; and Abraham H. Maslow, *Toward a Psychology of Being* (Princeton, N.J.: Van Nostrand, 1968), p. 29.

35. NAF, 23667, fol. 125; the deletion runs from the stichomythic exchange between Lust and Death to the apparition of the Sphinx.

36. Letter to Louise Colet, December 13, 1846, *O*, vol. 4, p. 229.

37. Durand, *Structures*, p. 360.

38. In his *Flaubert*, p. 184, Reik interprets this famous cry as deriving from "the wish to be free of all the tortures of conventionally bound sexuality, to be a natural form."

39. Letter to Mlle Leroyer de Chantepie, February 18, 1857, *O*, vol. 9, p. 203.

40. "That 'atheist' was, to my mind, the most religious of men, because he acknowledged only *God*," said Flaubert in November 1879 after having read Spinoza's *Ethics* for the third time (*O*, vol. 18, p. 515).

41. NAF, 23669, fol. 290/432; NAF, 23671, fol. 107.
42. Levin, "Flaubert," p. 43.
43. Jung, "Individual Dream Symbolism in Relation to Alchemy: A Study of the Unconscious Processes at Work in Dreams," in his *Psychology and Alchemy*, CW2, vol. 12, pp. 83–84. The early Christians sometimes identified the rising sun with Christ. The despairing Christ passage, inspired by Jean-Paul Richter and by Quinet's *Ahasvérus* is reproduced in the appendix of Louis Bertrand's *La 'première' "Tentation de saint Antoine" (1849–1856)* (Paris: Charpentier, 1908).
44. NAF, 23664, fol. 461.
45. NAF, 23667, fol. 46.
46. Letter to Louise Colet, May 27, 1853; *O*, vol. 6, p. 146. For a collection of similar statements with a lucid commentary, see Alison Fairlie, "Flaubert et la conscience du réel," *Essays in French Literature* 4 (1967):1–12, esp. pp. 2–3.

Chapter 5

1. *O*, vol. 1, p. 277. Further references to *Sylvie* come from this Pléiade edition.
2. See Karen Horney, *New Ways in Psychoanalysis* (New York: W. W. Norton, 1939), p. 283. This book offers an important review and critique of Freudian psychology by a longtime practitioner of it.
3. See Freud, "Notes on a Case of Obsessional Neurosis" (popularly known as the "Rat-Man" case), *SE*, vol. 10, pp. 232–33. This essay affords numerous insights into the personalities of Nerval's implied authors.
   Marcel Proust brilliantly discusses *Sylvie* as a "dream of a dream" and as a specious reality invaded by the dream, in his *Contre Sainte-Beuve* (Paris: Gallimard, 1971), pp. 233–42. For this reference I am indebted to Walter Kasell.
4. George Kurman's definition; see his "Ecphrasis in Epic Poetry." The classic example of ecphrasis is the description of the shield of Achilles in the *Iliad*.
5. See R. D. Laing, *The Self and Others: Further Studies in Sanity and Madness* (London: Tavistock, 1961), ch. 3, "Pretence and the Elusion of Experience," pp. 27–37, particularly p. 31.
6. In *Angélique* Nerval identifies this substrate as the "Sylvanectes," a tribal name close to "Sylvie." Both words evoke Druid tree worship.
7. Concerning the symbolic meanings of the round-dance, see Jung, "Transformation Symbolism in the Mass," in his *Psychology and Religion, East and West*, CW2, vol. 11, p. 276. The three other instances of the children's wedding motif in Nerval are listed and discussed in Pierre-Georges Castex, ed., *Sylvie* (Paris: SEDES, 1970), p. 154. Regarding the relationship between theater and religious experience in Nerval, see Dennis G. Sullivan, "The Function of the Theater in the Work of Nerval," *MLN* 80 (1965):610–17.
8. *Identity and the Life Cycle*, p. 164.
9. *Ibid.*, p. 89.
10. Freud observes: "It is highly probable that all complicated machinery and apparatus occurring in dreams stand for the genitals (as a rule, male ones). Also all weapons and tools." Moreover, hands in gloves, like feet in shoes, can symbolize the union of male and female genitals (*The Interpretation of Dreams*, *SE*, vol. 5, pp. 356, 359).
11. Rollo May, "Dreams and Symbols," pp. 1–128 in Leopold Caligor and Rollo May, *Dreams and Symbols: Man's Unconscious Language* (New York: Basic Books, 1968), p.43.
12. Stagnant water can indicate an unresolved psychic problem which has blocked the flow of life, according to Jung (*MAHS*, p. 199). In the last chapter of *Sylvie* "artificial ponds, hollowed out at enormous expense, futilely display their stagnant waters disdained by the swans" (p. 292).
13. See Freud, *The Psychopathology of Everyday Life*, *SE*, vol. 6, p. 266.

14. See Jung, *MAHS*, p. 153: in dreams "the volcano may refer to a significant memory trace, which leads back to a traumatic experience" (one unspecified in *Sylvie*).

15. Ernest G. Schachtel, *Metamorphosis: On the Development of Affect, Attention, Perception, and Memory* (New York: Basic Books, 1959), p.230.

16. For a perceptive discussion of the derivative nature of this last phase of the narrator's relationship with Sylvie, see Robert C. Carroll, "Gérard de Nerval: Prodigal Son of History," *Nineteenth-Century French Studies* 4 (Spring 1976):263–73.

17. See Jean Gaulmier, *Nerval et les filles du feu* (Paris: Nizet, 1956), p. 58.

18. This mood reflects the situation of the historical Nerval. See Castex, *Sylvie*, pp. 9, 15.

19. Freud observes: "Incapacity for meeting a *real* erotic demand is one of the most essential features of a neurosis. Neurotics are dominated by the opposition between reality and fantasy. If what they long for the most intensely in their fantasies is presented to them in reality, they none the less flee from it; and they abandon themselves to their fantasies the most readily when they need no longer fear to see them realized" ("Fragment of an Analysis of a Case of Hysteria," *SE*, vol. 7, p. 110).

Chapter 6

1. See Jung's "Dream Symbols of the Process of Individuation," esp. pp. 103–89; see also *Aion*, pp. 4–34, and specifically p. 11, n. 2.

2. Jung, *Symbols of Transformation*, CW2, vol. 5, pp. 213, 294.

3. Freud, *The Interpretation of Dreams*, SE, vols. 4–5, p. 338.

4. With a touch of Manichaeism, Nodier describes the colossal statue of Saint Charles Borromeo, which looms over the town and seems to oppose the powers of darkness. Its presence places the events concerning Lorenzo in 1697 or thereafter.

5. The Isola Bella, an arid reef, was transformed by Count Vitaliano Borromeo's magnificent chateau and garden, which he began to build in 1670.

6. "Phlégon" comes from the Greek *phlegein*, to burn, and fire is conventionally associated with love feelings in literature. Nodier also is indulging in a characteristic erudite joke here: the horse's name belongs to the classical author Phlegon of Tralles, a freedman in the reign of Hadrian, who compiled a collection of popular legends called *De rebus mirabilibus liber*. They include a tale of vampirism which Goethe reworked in his ballad *Die Braut von Korinth*.

7. Jung, "Dream Symbols of the Process of Individuation," p. 131.

8. Juan E. Cirlot, *A Dictionary of Symbols*, p. 349.

9. Alexandre Estignard, ed., *Correspondance inédite de Charles Nodier* (Paris: Pétiau, 1877), p. 279 (letter to Charles Weiss, November 6, 1838).

10. Cirlot, *Symbols*, pp. 313–14.

11. *Ibid.*, pp. 272–77.

12. Freud, *The Interpretation of Dreams*, p. 346.

13. "A large number of dreams, often accompanied by anxiety and having as their content such subjects as passing through narrow spaces or being in water, are based upon fantasies . . . of existence in the womb and of the act of birth" (*ibid.*, p. 399).

14. With regard to the hypothesis that the heavenly bodies in Polémon's vision reflect his self-concept, one should recall that Nodier elsewhere compared the life of our planet to "that of man considered as an individual" (*REV*, p. 248).

15. Nodier again whimsically designates these monsters in words pertaining to insects. "Psylles" are a species of insect as well as "snake charmers," and "morphoses" is a rare term for the metamorphoses which insects undergo during their development. See also the earlier use of "mantes" in *Smarra*.

16. Jung, *Symbols of Transformation*, p. 419.

17. "De quelques phénomènes du sommeil," *REV*, pp. 181–82.
18. *Nightmares and Human Conflict* (Boston: Little, Brown and Company, 1970), p. 66.
19. See D. Henriette Horchler, "Dream and Reality in the Works of Charles Nodier" (Ph.D. diss., University of Pennsylvania, 1968), pp. 74–78.
20. Jean Chevalier et al., *Dictionnaire des symboles*, pp. 220–21.
21. *Ibid.*, pp. 181–82.

Chapter 7

1. *OC*, Chant IV, stanza 8, p. 186. Roman numerals will designate chants and Arabic numerals stanzas (unnumbered prose segments) within a chant, thus: IV, 8.
2. Concerning pronoun shifting and double self-image in the *Chants*, see Julia Kristeva, *La Révolution du langage poétique* (Paris: Seuil, 1974), pp. 315–36. For a Jungian analysis which carefully distinguishes four "voices" in the *Chants*, see Klaus Winkelmann, *Lautréamont Impersonator.*
3. For two radically different interpretations of the *Poésies*, see the ardent Marxist-Surrealist interpretation by Georges Goldfayn and Gérard Legrand in their edition (Paris: Le Terrain Vague, 1960); and Oscar A. Haac's "Lautréamont's Conversion: The Structure and Meaning of the *Poésies*," *MLN* 65 (June 1950):369–75. Haac argues that revolt adopts the form of parody but retains its full force.
4. Since 1967, the main thrust of Lautréamont criticism has been to exalt the *Chants* and *Poésies* as pivotal, revolutionary documents in a parodic, self-conscious tradition. One must recall, however, that the self-referential, parodic tradition in prose fiction goes back at least as far as Cervantes. See Robin Rector Lydenberg, "Lautréamont and the Self-Conscious Tradition" (Ph.D. diss., Cornell University, 1973). For an introduction to the problem of discriminating among self-disclosure, objectivity, and parody in literature, see Allen Austin's "T. S. Eliot's Theory of Personal Expression," *PMLA* 81 (June 1966):301–7.
5. See Kristeva, *Langage poétique*, p. 192, and Marcelin Pleynet, *Lautréamont par lui-même* (Paris: Seuil, 1967), pp. 157–59.
6. Lucienne Rochon, "Lautréamont et le lecteur. Mythe—Mystagogie—Mystification," in Lucienne Rochon, ed., *Quatre lectures de Lautréamont* (Paris: Nizet, 1972), pp. 239, 246–48.
7. *Man's Search for Himself* (New York: New American Library, 1967), pp. 85–86.
8. For an excellent analysis of this situation, see Kristeva, *Langage poétique*, pp. 469–72. Pierre-Olivier Walzer, the editor of the *OC* (p. 1078), and Jacques Bousquet, in *Les Thèmes du rêve dans la littérature romantique* (Paris: Didier, 1964), p. 528, find no sadism in dream literature before 1870. However, plenty of sadism can be found in *Smarra*, not to mention *Aurélia* and the earlier versions of Flaubert's *Tentation de saint Antoine*—for instance, in the vision of Nebuchadnezzar throwing bones to the footless, handless captive kings crawling below his throne.
9. Freud, *The Interpretation of Dreams, SE*, vol. 5, p. 355.
10. See Hans Rudolf Linder, *Lautréamont: Sein Werk und sein Weltbild* (Basel: University of Basel, 1947), pp. 77–78.
11. See Jung, *The Development of Personality, CW*, vol. 17, p. 159.
12. See Miroslav Karaulac, "Le Problème du mal dans l'oeuvre de Lautréamont" (Ph.D. diss., University of Strasbourg, 1960), particularly pp. 28–37. A number of Karaulac's statements about the *Chants*, however, are inaccurate. See also Marcel Jean and Arpad Mezei, *Maldoror* (Paris: Editions du Pavois, 1947; reprinted by Nizet in 1959), particularly pp. 10–20; and Paul Zweig, *Lautréamont, ou les violences du Narcisse* (Paris: Minard, 1967), pp. 28–30.
13. Suzanne Bernard, *Le Poème en prose de Baudelaire jusqu'à nos jours* (Paris: Nizet, 1959), p. 230.

14. Peter W. Nesselroth, *Lautréamont's Imagery: A Stylistic Approach* (Geneva: Droz, 1969), p. 15.

15. Bernard points out Lautréamont's alternation of lyrical and sarcastic tone (which I would say corresponds to the alternation of geometry and chaos); see *Le Poème en prose*, pp. 240–43.

16. Ernest Jones, *On the Nightmare* (New York: Liveright, 1951), p. 261. He points out that in archetypal symbolism, the storm is naturally associated with danger at night and thus with the nightmare. The Babylonian and Hindu storm gods were also demons of the nightmare; and the Greek word for nightmare, *ephialtes*, still used by physicians in the nineteenth century, also meant "hurricane."

17. For an analysis of the way in which deliberate echoes of Lucretius in the *Chants* pay homage to a materialism which subverts the very possibility of the existence of a spiritual God, see Marcelin Pleynet, "Lautréamont politique," *Tel Quel* 45 (1971): 36–45. For the work's assaults on the institution of biological paternity and the family unit, see Kristeva, *Langage poétique*, pp. 464 – 65.

18. See Lucienne Rochon, *Quatre lectures de Lautréamont*, pp. 315–18.

19. Freud, *Introductory Lectures on Psychoanalysis, SE*, vol. 16, pp. 428–29.

20. Freud, "On Narcissism: An Introduction," *SE*, vol. 14, p. 96.

21. See Rochon's valuable article, "Le Professeur de rhétorique de Lautréamont: Gustave Hinstin," *Europe* 449 (September 1966):153–89, particularly pp. 182–85.

22. Freud, *Introductory Lectures on Psychoanalysis, SE*, vol. 16, p. 424.

23. Freud, *Totem and Taboo*, in *The Basic Writings of Sigmund Freud*, ed. A. A. Brill (New York: Modern Library, 1938), p. 879.

24. Erik H. Erikson, *Identity and the Life Cycle*, p. 131.

25. A helpful overview of cosmological systems, postulating both a higher God and a demiurge, is found in Denis Saurat's *Literature and Occult Tradition* (London: Bell, 1930); see particularly pp. 15–18, 150, 154.

26. Some critics claim that Maldoror is discontented here because he has been impotent. The text proves otherwise. The dog "se contenta . . . de violer à son tour la virginité de cette enfant délicate. De son ventre déchiré, le sang coule de nouveau le long de ses jambes" (the dog "satisfied himself . . . with ravishing in his turn that delicate child's virginity. Once again blood ran down her legs from her torn belly") (III, 2, p. 139) (Cf. V, 5, p. 204: "My sexual organs continually offer the sad spectacle of tumescence"). This never fulfilled desire is of course also a metaphor for spiritual dissatisfaction.

27. Cf. Von Franz in *MAHS*, p. 205n: "In dreams a mirror can symbolize the power of the unconscious to 'mirror' the individual objectively—giving him a view of himself that he may never have had before." Cf. also Jacques Lacan, "Le Stade du miroir comme formateur de la fonction du Je telle qu'elle nous est révélée dans l'expérience psychanalytique," *Écrits* (Paris: Seuil, 1966), pp. 93–100. Lacan argues that self-perception by means of a mirror reflection is an essential stage in the psychic maturation of human infants between six and eighteen months. For Maldoror to shatter the mirror which reflects him would constitute a regression to a stage preceding the elaboration of the image of an autonomous self.

28. See Gilbert Durand, *Les Structures anthropologiques de l'imaginaire*, p. 335, and Jung, *ACU*, p. 174. In dreams the hermaphrodite, says Jung, a "subduer of conflicts and a bringer of healing," mediates between conscious and unconscious.

29. A vision of "crenelations" is characteristic of the onset of a migraine attack, elsewhere suggested when Maldoror feels an iron bar smashing his head and when the narrator's forehead is split open by lightning (I, 8; II, 2). Such headaches are themselves symptoms of psychic repression.

30. Regarding the identification of Maldoror with the mother, see also Kristeva, *Langage poétique*, pp. 464–72.

31. Pp. 159, 160, 162–63, 166, etc. See Maurice Blanchot, *Lautréamont et Sade*, p. 287; Nesselroth, *Lautréamont's Imagery*, pp. 118–19; and Rochon, "Le Professeur de rhétorique

de Lautréamont," passim. The long, involved sentences are anticipated, *pace* Blanchot, in I, 11.

32. Lacan, *Écrits*, p. 507. I discuss the use of metaphor in Chant IV in Lacanian terms, at some length, in "Modernist Maldoror: The De-euphemization of Metaphor," *L'Esprit créateur* 18 (Winter 1978): 25–34.

33. By confusing the speakers in this passage, Zweig (*Lautréamont*, p. 63) inadvertently reorients the entire work. Linder's discussion (*Lautréamont*, passim) leaves the passage ambiguous.

34. Freud, *New Introductory Lectures on Psychoanalysis, SE*, vol. 22, p. 488. Compare Jung on the Terrible Mother as vampire in *Symbols of Transformation, CW2*, vol. 5, p. 370.

35. The name of this accomplice, the madman Aghone, fits into the scheme of Lautréamont's metaphors of chaos and geometry. Etymologically, "A-ghone" means "without angles, formless." This geometrical shapelessness corresponds to Aghone's moral unawareness: "since an event of his youth, he is no longer able to distinguish good from evil. Aghone is just the person he [Maldoror] needs" (VI, 7, p. 241).

36. The seventeenth-century Jesuit Nicolas Caussin complained that the Old Testament God, like an angry rhinoceros, had reduced the world to confusion. See Jung's discussion in *Transformation Symbolism in the Mass, CW2*, vol. 11, pp. 270–71. I cannot demonstrate that Lautréamont had read Caussin.

37. As Bousquet demonstrates at length in *Les Thèmes du rêve*, the urban setting in nineteenth-century literary dreams derives from earlier visions of Hell.

38. See Gaston Bachelard, *Lautréamont* (Paris: Corti, 1939), p. 83.

39. Concerning Chant VI, see also Claude Bouché, *Lautréamont: Du lieu commun à la parodie* (Paris:Larousse, 1974), p. 99.

40. Here I agree with Blanchot (*Lautréamont et Sade*, p. 367) and Linder (*Lautréamont*, pp. 48–52). The Hymn to the Ocean stanza (I, 9) is explicitly parodied in *Poésies II*, as Bouché points out (*Lautréamont*, pp. 162–63).

41. *Poésies I*, pp. 261, 262, 259, 263, 268.

42. For example, the hundreds of censored phrases in Flaubert's *Madame Bovary* constitute a perfect compendium of examples of "realism"—in the sense of acknowledging that one's physical body exists.

43. Kristeva points out (*Langage poétique*, pp. 343–58) that if one consults the editions of Pascal and Vauvenargues that Lautréamont actually used, his "corrections" of those *moralistes* in the *Poésies* are less extensive and less radical than commonly supposed. Bouché calls attention to many parodic elements throughout the *Chants* themselves, and summarizes his position well on p. 107 of his *Lautréamont*.

Chapter 8

1. *C*, pp. 179, 231, 263, 306, 296. See also pp. 185, 193, 246, 250, 318.

2. See Robert J. B. Maples, "Individuation in Nodier's *La Fée aux Miettes*," *Studies in Romanticism* 8 (Autumn 1968):47.

3. Jean Chevalier et al., *Dictionnaire des symboles*, p. 219.

4. See Jung, *Symbols of Transformation, CW2*, vol. 5, p. 534, n. 112.

5. See Jung, *ACU*, p. 199, and Claude Lévi-Strauss, "The Structural Study of Myth," *Structural Anthropology* (New York: Basic Books, 1963), p. 231, n. 6. The wrinkles lightly traced on the Fée's forehead as if by a sculptor's hand were inspired by Diderot's metaphor of the "ideal head" which is lightly marred for the sake of verisimilitude. See Laurence M. Porter, "The Narrative Art of Nodier's *Contes*," pp. 278–79, and "Hoffmannesque and Hamiltonian Sources of Nodier's *Fée aux Miettes*," *Romance Notes* 19 (1979): in press.

6. See pp. 179, 188ff., 194, 213, 220, 274–77, 312–13, 315, and 323. There are a dozen additional instances of significant anniversaries in Nodier's other *contes*.

7. In debt throughout his adult life, Nodier was repeatedly obliged to sell his cherished rare books and to compose advertising copy in order to augment his income. One therefore senses in Michel's renunciations of wealth a secondary meaning: the author's attempt vicariously to show that despite his financial difficulties, he is no failure. He does not desire what he does not have. For a thoroughgoing attempt to correlate the events of *La Fée aux Miettes* with events of Nodier's life, see Jules Vodoz, "*La Fée aux Miettes.*"

8. Jung, "The Symbolism of the Mandala," *Psychology and Alchemy*, CW2, vol. 12, p. 103.

9. See Freud, "A Special Type of Choice of Object Made by Men," *SE*, vol. 12, p. 174: "A man rescuing a woman from the water in a dream means that he makes her a mother . . . his own mother" (and in Jung's terms the *anima* is "anything that functions like a mother in our fantasy life").

10. See Emil A. Gutheil, *Handbook of Dream Analysis* (New York: Liveright, 1951), p. 59, and Freud, *Wit and Its Relation to the Unconscious*, in *The Basic Writings of Sigmund Freud* (New York: Modern Library, 1938), p. 733.

11. When Michel's uncle André wants to speak seriously with him, he says "we must talk reason in the captain's quarters" (p. 188).

12. Gilbert Durand, *Les Structures anthropologiques de l'imaginaire*, pp. 421–23.

13. Vodoz, "*La Fée aux Miettes,*" p. 265n.

14. Maples, "Individuation," p. 52.

15. See Freud, *New Introductory Lectures on Psychoanalysis, SE*, vol. 22, p. 490.

16. Vodoz, "*La Fée aux Miettes,*" p. 121, n. 2.

17. Maples, "Individuation," p. 55.

18. Concerning the manifold, changing legends connected with the mandrake, and Nodier's alteration of them, see Alfred G. Engstrom, "The Voices of Plants and Flowers and the Changing Cry of the Mandrake," in *Mediaeval Studies in Honor of Urban Tigner Holmes* (Chapel Hill: University of North Carolina Press, 1965), pp. 43–52. See also Durand, *Structures anthropologiques*, p. 341, n. 6, and Mircea Eliade, "La Mandragore et les mythes de la naissance miraculeuse," *Zalmoxis* 3 (1940–42):21ff.

19. The incident of the seizing of the button was probably inspired by Hamilton's *Zeneyda*, where an importunate widow treats the narrator the same way.

Chapter 9

1. Gérard de Nerval, *Oeuvres*, ed. Henri Lemaître, 2 vols. (Paris: Garnier, 1958), I. 753. Further references to *Aurélia* come from this volume, which offers excellent interpretive notes. Roman numerals refer to parts of *Aurélia*, Arabic numerals to chapters and pages.

2. See the interesting observations by Raymond Jean in his *La Poétique du désir* (Paris: Seuil, 1974), pp. 254–57.

3. See Ross Chambers, *Gérard de Nerval et la poétique du voyage* (Paris: Corti, 1969), pp. 373–76.

4. This conflict is stated quite clearly in the sonnet "Artémis" of *Les Chimères* (*O*, vol. 1, p. 702): "La sainte de l'abîme est plus sainte à mes yeux" ("The female saint of the abyss is holier in my eyes [than the saint of Heaven]").

5. Jung, *SDP*, pp. 36–37.

6. Jung, *ACU*, pp. 214–16.

7. Freud, "The Theme of the Three Caskets," *SE*, vol. 12, pp. 291–301, particularly p. 297.

8. Juan E. Cirlot, *Dictionary of Symbols*, p. 203.

9. Jean Chevalier, *Dictionnaire des symboles*, pp. 506, 517.

10. Jung, "The Symbolism of the Mandala," *Psychology and Alchemy*, *CW2*, vol. 12, p. 153.

11. Jung, "Dream-Symbols of the Process of Individuation," p. 137.

12. *Ibid.*, p. 173.

13. For a subtler, tripartite division of *Aurélia*, also presented in tabular form as "life-madness-art" superimposed on "revolt-expiation," see Chambers, *Gérard de Nerval*, p. 363.

14. Jung, *Aion*, pp. 12–13.

15. Stephen Shapiro, "The Dark Continent of Literature: Autobiography," *Comparative Literature Studies* 5 (December 1968):445. For a recent attempt to distinguish between the literary genres of autobiography and confessional novel (a distinction that Shapiro and most other critics fail to make), and a selected bibliography on the subject, see Laurence M. Porter, "Autobiography versus Confessional Novel," pp. 144–59.

For this second section of Chapter 9 only, I have placed large square brackets around editorial ellipses in quotations from *Aurélia* to distinguish them from authorial ellipses, which I interpret as clues to repression on the part of the narrator.

16. Shoshana Felman analyzes this interplay brilliantly in " 'Aurélia' ou 'le livre infaisable': De Foucault à Nerval." Her statement complements the present study well.

17. Marie-Jeanne Durry lists these self-accusations in her useful *Gérard de Nerval et le mythe*, p. 147. See also Jean Richer's edition of *Aurélia* (Paris: Minard, 1965), p. 73, where he remarks on the "vague feeling of guilt" which began to affect Nerval early in 1852.

18. Freud, "Mourning and Melancholia," *SE*, vol. 14, pp. 244, 248. See also *ibid.*, pp. 250–51; his *The Ego and the Id*, *SE*, vol. 19, pp. 49–53; also his "The Economic Problem of Masochism," *SE*, vol. 19, p. 170; and the *New Introductory Lectures on Psychoanalysis*, *SE*, vol. 22, p. 525.

19. Karen Horney, *New Ways in Psychoanalysis*, pp. 222–42.

20. Freud, "Notes on a Case of Obsessional Neurosis," *SE*, vol. 10, p. 239.

21. In this connection one should recall the historical Nerval's letter to his therapist, Doctor Blanche (November 27, 1853): "I was trying to do too much by defying death! It's in another life that [death] will restore the woman I love to me. Here I am not listening to the voice of a dream, but to the sacred promise of God" (cited by Durry, *Nerval*, p. 186, n. 2).

22. Concerning the love feelings of the historical Nerval, see Durry, *Nerval*, pp. 40–42.

23. Freud observes: "The megalomania is the direct result of a magnification of the ego due to the drawing-in of the libidinal object-cathexes—a secondary narcissicism which is a return to the original early infantile one" (*Introductory Lectures on Psychoanalysis*, *SE*, vol. 15, p. 424). Megalomaniacal fantasies seemed to be the most frequent subject of the historical Nerval's delusions. Ashamed, he suppressed the evidence of them when he could, as he suppressed the proof of his hostility in the story that he hid behind a tree at the asylum in Passy and tried to crush his therapist with a large stone. See Pierre Audiat, *L' "Aurélia" de Gérard de Nerval* (Paris: Champion, 1926), pp. 23, 24, n. 1.

24. For a clinical psychologist's view of delusions in real people, see Graham F. Reed, *The Psychology of Anomalous Experience* (London: Hutchinson, 1972), pp. 153–54.

25. See Carl Francis Keppler, *The Literature of the Second Self* (Tucson: University of Arizona Press, 1972); Robert Rogers, *The Double in Literature* (Detroit: Wayne State University Press, 1970); Otto Rank, *Beyond Psychology* (New York: Dover, 1958), pp. 62–101; Ralph Tymms, *Doubles in Literary Psychology* (Cambridge: Bowes and Bowes, 1949); Otto Rank, *The Double: A Psychoanalytic Study* (Chapel Hill: University of North Carolina Press, 1971; orig. pub. 1925). Best of these is Keppler's Jungian conclusion, pp. 189–210. Members of the MLA Seminar on the Double in Literature have compiled an extensive bibliography. Durry has some excellent remarks on the double in Nerval's life and works (*Nerval*, pp. 40–45, 96, 136–37). Susan Noakes discusses the relationship

between verb tenses and doubling in "Self-Reading and Temporal Irony in *Aurélia*," *Studies in Romanticism* 16 (Winter 1977):101–19.

26. See Freud, "Notes on a Case of Obsessional Neurosis," *SE*, vol. 10, p. 236.

27. See Jean Richer, ed., *Les Manuscrits d'"Aurélia" de Gérard de Nerval* (Paris: Les Belles Lettres, 1972), pl. 19, ll. 6–7.

28. Concerning the possible mother fixation of the historical Nerval, see Norma Rinsler, "Gérard de Nerval's Celestial City and the Chain of Souls," *Studies in Romanticism* 2 (1962–63):87–106; and Charles Mauron, *Des Métaphores obsédantes*, pp. 64–80, 148–56. Compare Theodore Lidz' *The Person: His Development throughout the Life Cycle* (New York: Basic Books, 1968), p. 354: "When an adolescent persists in pursuing an unrequited love, the romantic striving has a pathological character as if the boy or girl feels fated to repeat the frustrations of the oedipal situation."

29. Erik H. Erikson, *Identity: Youth and Crisis* (New York: Norton, 1968), p. 50.

30. Freud, "Leonardo da Vinci and a Memory of His Childhood," *SE*, vol. 11, p. 123.

31. See Freud, "Notes on a Case of Obsessional Neurosis," *SE*, vol. 10, pp. 175–76.

32. With regard to the hypothesis that the narrator's fantasies concerning a goddess derive from his frustrated desire for Aurélia, compare the manuscript from the Louvenjoul collection, reading "offenser la pudeur des divinités du songe" ("to offend the modesty of the dream goddesses"), cited in *O*, p. 753, n. 1.

33. "Their true significance lies in their being a representation of a conflict between two opposing impulses of approximately equal strength: and hitherto I have invariably found that this opposition has been one between love and hate" (Freud, "Notes on a Case of Obsessional Neurosis," *SE*, vol. 10, p. 192; cf. p. 239).

34. Compare the mystical ghost-dance religion among North American tribes toward the end of the nineteenth century. Realizing that they had been militarily overwhelmed by the white man, the Indians "attempted to hasten the end of the world by a massive and collective communion with the dead. . . . The dead invaded the earth, communicated with the living, and thus created a 'confusion' that announced the end of the current cosmic cycle" (Mircea Eliade, *Cosmos and History: The Myth of the Eternal Return* [New York: Harper and Row, 1959], p. 73).

35. Freud, "A Case of Paranoia," *SE*, vol. 12, pp. 70–71.

36. Needless to say, this episode also reflects the Orpheus myth, to which Nerval deliberately alludes. See Walter A. Strauss, *Descent and Return* (Cambridge, Mass.: Harvard University Press, 1971), pp. 50–80.

37. Audiat, *Nerval*, pp. 47–48.

38. Near the end of *Sylvie*, the narrator finally wins the actress Aurélie when his wealthy rival departs for Algeria to enlist in the *spahis*. The detail seems implausible since members of that military force were normally recruited only from among North African natives. So the peripety seems to correspond to a subjective rather than to an objective change: the African soldier returns because it is time for the tendencies he represents to be integrated into the narrator's conscious personality.

39. "Structuralism: The Anglo-American Adventure," *Yale French Studies* 36–37 (1966):160.

40. Lacan, *Écrits*, p. 249.

41. Strauss, *Descent and Return*, p. 57.

42. W.H. Auden, "The Virgin and the Dynamo," p. 258.

Conclusion

1. For a fuller discussion of the question of periodization, see Laurence M. Porter, "The Present Directions of French Romantic Studies, 1960–1975," *Nineteenth-Century French Studies* 6 (Fall-Winter 1977–78):3–6.

2. This view is lucidly presented in Léon Emery's preface to his *Vision et pensée chez Victor Hugo* (Lyon: Les Cahiers Libres, n.d.).

3. See Laurence M. Porter, "The Seductive Satan of Cazotte's *Le Diable amoureux*," *L'Esprit créateur* 18 (Summer 1978):3–12.

4. See Alfredo Zenoni, "Métaphore et métonymie dans la théorie de Lacan," *Cahiers internationaux du symbolisme* 31–32 (1976):187–98.

5. In narratological terms, the archetype of Inversion is a condensed minimal story, analogous to oxymoron, which is a condensed antithesis. A minimal story consists of three conjoined events, each taking place before the next begins. The first and third are stative; the third is the inverse of the first; the second event is active, and is the cause of the third ("he was unhappy, then he met a woman, then, as a result, he was happy"). See Gerald Prince, *A Grammar of Stories* (The Hague: Mouton, 1973), pp. 16–37. In Inversion the active causal event may be implied rather than stated, and it derives from a supernatural order whose rules transcend the logic of the material and demonic orders in which the other events of the story occur.

6. See Leo Bersani, *A Future for Astyanax: Character and Desire in Literature* (Boston: Little, Brown, 1976). I have discussed this question more fully in "Artistic Self-Consciousness in Rimbaud's Poetry."

SELECTED BIBLIOGRAPHY

A list of works consulted would include some nine hundred items, a list of works cited, about two hundred fifty. The list which follows omits many studies I greatly admire (Béguin and Castex on the dream and the fantastic, Poulet and Richer on Nerval, Sartre on Flaubert), and includes only those essays which at one point or another decisively reoriented my critical thinking. Reliable annotated bibliographies of Nerval and Nodier appear annually in "The Romantic Movement," the September supplement to *English Language Notes*. A combination of the annual bibliographies in Otto Klapp, *PMLA*, and René Rancoeur serves well for all our authors. I would suggest that the person approaching the psychological study of literature for the first time begin with Jung's *Man and His Symbols* and Erikson's *Identity and the Life Cycle*, then proceed to Freud's indispensable *Introductory Lectures* and *The Interpretation of Dreams*. Erikson's brilliant methodological statement, "The Dream-Specimen of Psychoanalysis," illustrates how psychiatrists approach non-literary dreams. The classic psychoanalytic interpretations of literary fantasy are Freud's study of Jensen's *Gradiva* and Jung's *Symbols of Transformation*.

Psychological Abstracts, published monthly, offers useful summaries of the world's literature in psychology and related disciplines, including the psychoanalytic interpretation of literature, in 850 journals. An intelligent critical bibliography of neo-Freudian literature by Michel Grimaud, "Recent Trends in Psychoanalysis: A Survey with Emphasis on Psychological Criticism in English Literature and Related Areas," appeared in *Sub-stance* 13 (1976):136–62.

The Dream in Psychoanalysis

Adelson, Edward T., ed. *Dreams in Contemporary Psychoanalysis*. New York: Society of Medical Psychoanalysts, 1963.

Erikson, Erik H. "The Dream-Specimen of Psychoanalysis," *Journal of the American Psychoanalytical Association* 2 (1954):5–55.

Freud, Sigmund. *The Interpretation of Dreams*. Vols. 4 and 5. "Remarks on the Theory and Practice of Dream-Interpretation." Vol. 19. In *The Standard Edition of the Complete*

Psychological Works of Sigmund Freud. Edited by Lytton Strachey. 24 vols. London: Hogarth, 1953–74.

Gutheil, Emil A. *Handbook of Dream Analysis*. New York: Liveright, 1951.

Jones, Ernest. *On the Nightmare*. New ed. New York: Liveright, 1951. Orig. pub. 1939.

Jung, Carl Gustav. *The Archetypes of the Collective Unconscious*. In *Collected Works*. Edited by Herbert Read, Michael Fordman, and Gerhard Adler. 17 vols. New York: Pantheon Books, 1953–73. Vol. 9, Part 1.

————. "Dream Symbols of the Process of Individuation." In *The Integration of the Personality*. London: Kegan Paul, 1948. See especially pp. 103–89.

————. *Man and His Symbols*. Garden City, N.Y.: Doubleday, 1964.

————. "The Practical Use of Dream-Analysis." In *The Practice of Psychotherapy. Collected Works*. Edited by Herbert Read, Michael Fordman, and Gerhard Adler. New York: Pantheon Books, 1953–73. Vol. 17.

Reis, Walter J. "A Comparison of the Interpretation of Dream Series with and without Free Associations." In *Dreams and Personality Dynamics*. Edited by Manfred F. DeMartino. Springfield, Ill.: Charles C. Thomas, 1959.

The Dream in Literature

Bousquet, Jacques. *Les Thèmes du rêve dans la littérature romantique*. Paris: Didier, 1964. See especially pp. 532–73 and 605–19.

Campbell, Joseph. *The Hero with a Thousand Faces*. 2d ed. Princeton, N.J.: Princeton University Press, 1968.

Chevalier, Jean, et al. *Dictionnaire des symboles*. Paris: Editions Robert Laffont, 1969.

Cirlot, Juan E. *A Dictionary of Symbols*. New York: Philosophical Library, 1962.

Durand, Gilbert. *Les Structures anthropologiques de l'imaginaire: Introduction à l'archéotypologie générale*. 3d ed. Paris: Bordas, 1969.

Hartman, Geoffrey. "Structuralism: The Anglo-American Adventure." *Yale French Studies* 36–37 (1966): 148–68.

Lovejoy, Arthur Oncken. *The Great Chain of Being: A Study of the History of an Idea*. Cambridge, Mass.: Harvard University Press, 1957.

Raymond, Marcel. *Jean-Jacques Rousseau: La Quête de soi et la rêverie*. Paris: Corti, 1962.

Rousseau, André M. "À la découverte d'Antoine Hamilton, conteur." *Etudes littéraires* 1 (1968): 185–95.

Todorov, Tzvetan. *Introduction à la littérature fantastique*. Paris: Seuil, 1970.

Vartanian, Aram. "Diderot and the Phenomenology of the Dream," *Diderot Studies* 8 (1966): 217–54.

Viatte, Auguste. *Les Sources occultes du romantisme français*. 2 vols. Paris: Champion, 1965; orig. pub. 1928.

Human Identity

Erikson, Erik H. *Identity and the Life Cycle: Selected Papers*. New York: International Universities Press, 1959.

Freud, Sigmund. "The Ego and the Id." *The Standard Edition of the Complete Psychological Works of Sigmund Freud*. Edited by Lytton Strachey. 24 vols. London: Hogarth, 1953–74. Vol. 19.

————. *Introductory Lectures on Psychoanalysis. The Standard Edition of the Complete Psychological Works of Sigmund Freud*. Edited by Lytton Strachey. 24 vols. London: Hogarth, 1953–74. Vol. 15.

————. "Leonardo da Vinci and a Memory of His Childhood." *The Standard Edition of the*

Complete Psychological Works of Sigmund Freud. Edited by Lytton Strachey. 24 vols. London: Hogarth, 1953–74. Vol. 11.

———. *New Introductory Lectures on Psychoanalysis. The Standard Edition of the Complete Psychological Works of Sigmund Freud.* Edited by Lytton Strachey. 24 vols. London: Hogarth, 1953–74. Vol. 22.

Glover, Edward. *Freud or Jung?* New York: Norton, 1950.

Horney, Karen. *Neurosis and Human Growth: The Struggle toward Self-Realization.* New York: Norton, 1950.

———. *New Ways in Psychoanalysis.* New York: Norton, 1939.

Jung, Carl Gustav. *Aion: Researches into the Phenomenology of the Self. Collected Works.* 2d ed. Princeton, N.J.: Princeton University Press, 1968. Vol. 9, part 2.

———. *Psychological Types or the Psychology of Individuation.* London: Kegan Paul. 1946.

Lacan, Jacques. *Écrits.* Paris: Seuil, 1966.

Laing, R. D. *The Self and Others: Further Studies in Sanity and Madness.* London: Tavistock, 1962.

Reed, Graham F. *The Psychology of Anomalous Experience: A Cognitive Approach.* London: Hutchinson, 1972.

Literature and Psychology

Austin, Allen. "T. S. Eliot's Theory of Personal Expression." *PMLA* 81 (June 1966): 301–7.

Barthes, Roland. *S/Z.* Paris: Seuil, 1970.

Booth, Wayne C. *The Rhetoric of Fiction.* Chicago: University of Chicago Press, 1961.

Faber, M. D. "The Suicide of Young Werther." *Psychoanalytic Review* 60 (1973):239–76.

Freud, Sigmund. *Delusions and Dreams in Jensen's "Gradiva." The Standard Edition of the Complete Psychological Works of Sigmund Freud.* Edited by Lytton Strachey. 24 vols. London: Hogarth, 1953–74. Vol. 11.

Jung, Carl Gustav. *Symbols of Transformation. Collected Works,* 2d ed. Princeton: Princeton University Press, 1968. Vol. 5.

Mauron, Charles. *Des métaphores obsédantes au mythe personnel: Introduction à la psychocritique.* Paris: Corti, 1963.

Porter, Laurence M. "Artistic Self-Consciousness in Rimbaud's Poetry." In *Pre-text/Text/ Context: Essays on Nineteenth-Century French Literature.* Edited by Robert L. Mitchell. Columbus, O.: Ohio State University Press, 1980.

———. "Autobiography versus Confessional Novel: Gide's *Immoraliste* and *Si le grain ne meurt.*" *Symposium* 30 (Summer 1976):144–59.

———. "The Devil as Double in Nineteenth-Century Literature: Goethe, Dostoevsky, and Flaubert." *Comparative Literature Studies* 15 (Fall 1978):316–35.

———. "The Generativity Crisis of Gide's *Immoraliste.*" *French Forum* 2 (January 1977): 58–69.

———. "Literary Structure and the Concept of Decadence: Huysmans, D'Annunzio, and Wilde." *Centennial Review* 22 (Spring 1978):188–200.

———. "The Seductive Satan of Cazotte's *Le Diable amoureux.*" *L'Ésprit créateur* 18 (Summer 1978):3–12.

———. "Syphilis as Muse in Thomas Mann's *Doctor Faustus.*" In *Medicine and Literature.* Edited by Enid Rhodes Peschel. New Haven, Conn.: Neale Watson Academic Publishing Co., 1979.

Flaubert

Flaubert, Gustave. *Oeuvres.* Edited by Maurice Nadeau. 18 vols. Lausanne: Editions Rencontre, 1964–65. (This work contains the correspondence.)

Selected Bibliography

————. *Oeuvres complètes*. Paris: Louis Conard, 1910–54. (Vol. 17 contains the 1849 and 1856 versions of *La Tentation de saint Antoine*.)

————. *La Tentation de saint Antoine*. Edited by Edouard Maynial. Paris: Garnier, 1968. (This is the 1874 version.)

————. "La Tentation de saint Antoine." "Nouvelles acquisitions françaises," 23664–71. Paris: Bibliothèque nationale.

Bart, Benjamin F. "Psyche into Myth: Humanity and Animality in Flaubert's *Saint-Julien*." *Kentucky Romance Quarterly* 20 (1973):317–42.

Foucault, Michel. "Un 'Fantastique' de bibliothèque." *Cahiers Renaud-Barrault* 59 (March 1967):2–33.

Reik, Theodor. *Flaubert und seine "Versuchung des heiligen Antonius": Ein Beitrag zur Künstler-psychologie*. Minden: J. C. C. Bruns, 1912.

Seznec, Jean. *Nouvelles études sur "La Tentation de saint Antoine."* London: Warburg Institute, 1949.

————. *Les Sources de l'épisode des dieux dans "La Tentation de saint Antoine."* Paris: Vrin, 1940.

Lautréamont

Ducasse, Isidore. *Oeuvres complètes*. Edited by Pierre-Olivier Walzer. Paris: Gallimard, 1970.

Blanchot, Maurice. *Lautréamont et Sade*. Paris: Les Editions de Minuit, 1963; orig. pub. 1949.

Kristeva, Julia. *La Révolution du langage poétique*. Paris: Seuil, 1974.

Pleynet, Marcelin. *Lautréamont par lui-même*. Paris: Seuil, 1967.

Rochon, Lucienne. "Le Professeur de rhétorique de Lautréamont: Gustave Hinstin." *Europe* 449 (September 1966):153–89.

Winkelmann, Klaus. *Lautréamont Impersonator: A Study in Poetic Autobiography*. Ottawa: Editions Naaman, 1974.

Nerval

Nerval, Gérard de. *Oeuvres*. Edited by Albert Béguin and Jean Richer. 2 vols. Paris: Gallimard, 1952–56.

————. *Oeuvres*. Edited by Henri Lemaître. 2 vols. Paris: Garnier, 1958.

Auden, W. H. "The Virgin and the Dynamo." In *Perspectives on Poetry*. Edited by James L. Calderwood and Harold E. Toliver. New York: Oxford University Press, 1968.

Durry, Marie-Jeanne. *Gérard de Nerval et le mythe*. Paris: Flammarion, 1956.

Felman, Shoshana. " 'Aurélia' ou 'le livre infaisable': De Foucault à Nerval." *Romantisme* 3 (1972):43–55.

Freud, Sigmund. "Mourning and Melancholia." *The Standard Edition of the Complete Psychological Works of Sigmund Freud*. Edited by Lytton Strachey. 24 vols. London: Hogarth, 1953–74. Vol. 14.

————. "Notes on a Case of Obsessional Neurosis." *The Standard Edition of the Complete Psychological Works of Sigmund Freud*. Edited by Lytton Strachey. 24 vols. London: Hogarth, 1953–74. Vol. 10.

Kurman, George. "Ecphrasis in Epic Poetry." *Comparative Literature* 26 (Winter 1974): 1–13.

Nodier

Nodier, Charles. *Contes.* Edited by Pierre-Georges Castex. Paris: Garnier, 1961.

———. "Piranèse, Contes psychologiques: À propos de la monomanie réflective." *Oeuvres.* 12 vols. Geneva: Slatkine Reprints, 1967. Vol. 11, pp. 167–204.

———. "De Quelques phénomènes du sommeil." *Rêveries. Oeuvres.* 12 vols. Geneva: Slatkine Reprints, 1967. Vol. 5, pp. 159–89.

Maples, Robert J. B. "Individuation in Nodier's *La Fée aux Miettes.*" *Studies in Romanticism* 8 (Autumn 1968):43–64.

Porter, Laurence M. "The Narrative Art of Nodier's *Contes*: Diderot's Contributions to the Quest for Verisimilitude." *Romanic Review* 63 (December 1972):272–83.

Vodoz, Jules. "*La Fée aux Miettes.*" *Essai sur le subconscient dans l'oeuvre de Charles Nodier.* Paris: Champion, 1925.

INDEX

*Laurence M. Porter is professor
of French and comparative literature at Michigan State University.
He received his undergraduate and graduate degrees from Harvard
University. He has published extensively in scholarly journals
here and abroad and is the author of*
The Renaissance of the Lyric in French Romanticism:
Elegy, "Poëme," and Ode.

*The manuscript was edited by Jean Owen.
The book was designed by Don Ross.
The typeface for the text is Janson, based on the original cuts
by Nicholas Kis about 1690; the display face is
DeVinne Ornamental, based on the original cuts by Gustav
Schroeder in 1894. The text is printed on Glatfelter's Writers Offset
text paper. The book is bound in Holliston Mills' Kingston
Natural Finish cloth over binder's boards.
Manufactured in the United States of America.*